"A thoughtful analysis of the traps th[...]
and a practical resource for making b[...]

Adam Grant
#1 *New York Times* bestselling author of *Hidden Potential* and
Think Again, and host of the podcast *Re:Thinking*

"A groundbreaking account of how the mind gets critical decisions
wrong and how to get them right. The author makes a compelling case
for the significance of tuning in to what matters in critical moments.
Convincingly argued, its core idea of psychological deaf spots merits a
lot more attention. Brimming with riveting and relevant stories for the
modern decision-maker, this game-changer leaves you wanting more –
and to do better."

Lord Sebastian Coe
President of World Athletics and Olympic gold medallist

"This is a sensational book. It has always struck me as highly likely that
despite – or more likely because of – the frequency and density with
which we are pummelled with information in the modern world, the
quality of human decision-making has mostly deteriorated, along with
our power to decode, interpret and prioritise what we see and hear. So
turn off your mobile phone and read this book instead."

Rory Sutherland
Vice chairman, Ogilvy

"If you want to decide like a pro and master the landscape of success,
this timely decision compass is for you. In golf, precision starts with
smart analysis and judgement as you reinterpret likely scenarios under
pressure and then apply proven strategies. Rooted in research, *Tune
In* should be standard reading in all classrooms and boardrooms as it
shows a winning template for high performers. Like all good books,
you'll return to it time and time again."

Paul McGinley
Professional golfer and 2014 European Ryder Cup captain

"A thought-provoking exploration of the challenges facing decision-makers in a modern world. This expert author tackles the complexities of judgment and unravels every-day traps faced in business and in sport. A must-read for anyone seeking to enhance their judgement and minimise human error."

Dr. Robert Cialdini
New York Times bestselling author of *Influence* and *Pre-Suasion*

"Some books leave you feeling smart. Others emboldened and ready to take on the world. The best books do both, and this is one of them. Written by a businesswoman who has not only been there, but most importantly done it, *Tune In* is chock full of insights that give you the 'What' and the 'How'. A book to be cherished."

Steve Martin
New York Times bestselling author of *Messengers* and *Yes! Secrets from the Science of Persuasion*

"One of the skills that most separates the strongest from the weakest of leaders is the ability to apply effective judgement. But with a plethora of opinions, an excess of data and sometimes an unconscious personal bias, decision-making can often feel like a random luck of the draw. This engaging, thought-provoking and influential book is a map for smarter decision-making, a great first time read but also an invaluable reference book that you will dip into again and again.

Nuala Walsh brings to life the reality of leadership and cleverly accelerates the reader's understanding of how to develop an innate understanding of human behaviour, making it your superpower. It's a relatable read that will help anyone in a leadership role. A rare combination of information and entertainment."

Debbie Hewitt MBE
Chair of The Football Association and chair of Visa Europe

"It is an honor to recommend *Tune In* – not just for me personally but because it contains information I believe in. In today's rushed world with rising technology, choices are made with greater information and speed. This book recognizes its positive and negative impact, urging greater consideration of psychological factors. For me, it adds to our ability to be self-aware.

Everyone makes decisions, from blue-collar workers to white-collar executives. The difference in my opinion is the number of people affected. A Dad buying a gift impacts his child. A police executive selecting weapons for effectiveness and safety affects an entire agency. In each case, decisions can be improved by understanding hidden factors. This book, written by someone who understands these factors, helps us prevent bad choices.

Sometimes, faced with inevitable mistakes, we console ourselves and others by recognizing effort over outcome. Every individual exposed to *Tune In* will become more aware of how mistakes cause hardship in our lives, comforted that they are now more prepared to not only make better decisions but to avoid mistakes. May the knowledge of the impact of our personal choice always contribute to a better world."

Jeffrey L. Rinek
Former FBI investigator and author of *In the Name of the Children*

"In *Tune In*, behavioral economist and business advisor Nuala Walsh takes us on an engaging journey of the mind and the scary ways it filters information. Our eyes and ears are constantly deceiving us, as Walsh so poignantly demonstrates again and again throughout this fantastic book. Convincingly argued, every leader – and aspiring leader – needs to understand not just their 'blind spots' but their 'deaf spots' to reinterpret what's really going on around them. If you want to improve people's lives and make better decisions, be sure to read *Tune In*."

Melina Palmer
CEO of The Brainy Business and award-winning author of
The Truth About Pricing

"Nuala Walsh teaches us valuable methods for applying critical thinking and behavioral science to improve our decision-making and avoid the catastrophic mistakes caused by tuning in to the wrong voices. An essential read."

Dr. Daniel Crosby
New York Times bestselling author of *The Laws of Wealth* and
The Behavioral Investor

"Powerful, pacy and provocative, this misjudgement masterclass will make you challenge how you think – and hear. Peppered with fascinating research, analysing the aspects of well-known historical events, *Tune In* prompts you to pause for thought and reconsider your understanding. It suggests how the modern leader could apply the psychology of human behaviour to prevent risk, protect reputation and add value to an organisation, regardless of industry. In my opinion, an essential book for today's leaders."

Tracey Davidson
Deputy CEO, Handelsbanken plc

"A book I would never want to have too far away from me! It's not only informative but really instructive and a valuable reference for any business."

Victoria Degtar
Global chief revenue officer, *TIME* magazine

"Anyone reading this practical book will love it. Not only is it highly relevant in today's tuned-out and polarised world, it gives decision-makers applicable ways to tune in to what really matters regardless of culture or profession. Accessible and insightful, it emphasises the neglected art of interpretation so that anyone can avoid decision deaf spots."

Allyson Stewart-Allen
CEO International Marketing Partners, and author of
Working with Americans

"At a time when tuning out has become all too common, *Tune In* reminds us that the key to success lies in our ability to recognize and avoid judgment traps. Whether you're a leader, an entrepreneur, a seeker of knowledge, or simply someone striving to minimize regret and maximize your impact, this powerful and persuasive book is your fast track to smarter judgment. The only book on decision-making you will ever need."

Dr. Dario Krpan
Assistant professor of behavioural science,
London School of Economics and Political Science

"This book engages the reader from the outset. Unpacking the understated complexity surrounding the decision-making process, the author expertly widens the lens to show the unintended impact of tuning out critical voices on our everyday lived experience, both professional and personal.

Written in an accessible, inclusive and authentic style, we're presented with a refreshing insight into groundbreaking behavioural change strategies that optimise our capacity and our capability to make more informed and confident decisions – irrespective of the context. Inspiring, witty and intellectually stimulating, this is a journey everyone should take!"

Dame Robina Shah DBE
Professor of psychosocial medicine and medical education

TUNE ᴵᴺ

TUNE
IN

How to make
smarter decisions
in a noisy world

NUALA WALSH

HARRIMAN HOUSE LTD
3 Viceroy Court
Bedford Road
Petersfield
Hampshire
GU32 3LJ
GREAT BRITAIN
Tel: +44 (0)1730 233870

Email: enquiries@harriman-house.com
Website: harriman.house

First published in 2024.

Paperback ISBN: 978-0-85719-995-9
eBook ISBN: 978-0-85719-996-6

British Library Cataloguing in Publication Data
A CIP catalogue record for this book can be obtained from the British Library.

*For Brian Gordon, an amazing husband
who is forever tuned in and in tune –
the smartest decision I ever made.*

CONTENTS

*"It is not important what is said,
what is important is what is heard."*

Jeffrey Fry

PREFACE

Despite popular opinion, the most underestimated risk facing modern society is not economic, political, technological or even climate risk. It's human decision risk, triggered by our tendency to tune out what really matters.

The cost? Persistent human errors and a collective downgrading of our decisions.

It's ironic. In a digitised world with countless platforms to express our voice, we hear less than ever. In a visual world saturated with curated images, we're seen but not necessarily heard.

It's not our fault, we're bombarded by an environment that operates against us. Overwhelmed by data, distraction and disinformation, we've too little time to pay attention to what truly matters.

You can't trust all you hear. Why? Because what you hear is rarely all there is.

Most people base decisions on who they see, not what they hear. Most people don't consider which voices they tune in to. Most people don't consciously filter the noise around them to decode the right signals when it matters.

We think we hear what matters, but history suggests otherwise. When you think you have the answers, you stop listening and start misjudging.

Today, we misjudge more than ever. But that can change.

In *Tune In: How to Make Smarter Decisions in a Noisy World*, I reveal why we consistently tune in to the wrong voices, failing to hear what really matters; and why we value what we see more than what we hear. Using decades of scientific evidence, I explain yesterday's mistakes in order to prevent those of tomorrow.

I offer decision-makers and problem-solvers a menu of easy-to-use techniques to master judgement in high-stakes situations. I highlight the most aggressive derailers that distort what we hear – or don't hear.

In short, I help you limit decision damage to get more decisions right than wrong. I help you avoid the crippling pain of regret and navigate the modern crisis of tone-deaf leadership.

Tune In is not about listening more or listening better. We already think we're exceptional listeners and decision-makers. While some of us are, most of us are not. In fact, most of us are binary, biased and bounded in our thinking. The well-intended still only hear at 25% efficiency levels. Even Ernest Hemingway asserts "Most people never listen."[1]

And there's no modern app that solves this mental malware.

Tune In is about judging situations more effectively by rebalancing what you see with what you hear and revaluing human explanation over rational explanation.

When you tune in, others feel heard. And only when others feel heard, do they hear you. This is the path to power, performance and prosperity.

While many people appreciate bias blind spots, few recognise the destructive power of deaf spots – until now. What sets *Tune In* apart is its focus on the dominant hearing-related biases that contaminate our daily decisions.

Who is this book for?

This book is for every individual who wants to maximise their decision impact and limit regret. It's for every ambitious ladder-climber striving to fast-track performance or side-track reputation error. And it's for the intellectually curious leader and learner, eager to advance their understanding of human behaviour and supplement their professional skillset.

While *Tune In* doesn't offer an instant fix, it does provide one guarantee: your impact, credibility and influence will be better off with this understanding than without.

Your decisions matter, more than you think.

In a hyperconnected global world, your decisions may feel small or even insignificant. Yet as a powerholder, each decision can change the direction of someone's life, whether you're hiring, firing, entertaining, negotiating, advising, preaching, teaching or issuing executive orders.

Tuning in is the first step to hearing what matters – and what others don't.

Today, too many employees, customers, environmentalists, citizens, teenagers and minorities feel their voices are not heard. It's why activism is rising, industries are striking, boards are failing, businesses are imploding, brands are distrusted, and the rate of scandals, scams and suicides is climbing.

Warning bells are not heard until the alarm bells sound.

As problem-solvers, we assume we operate with a full deck of cards. We don't. Most overlook the hidden ace: understanding human behaviour. Artificial intelligence can't solve everything. You need human intelligence.

Why did that happen? What did I miss? Why didn't I see it coming?

Understanding human behaviour empowers you to make sense of the seemingly senseless. For me, that's as essential as it is fascinating.

But if human error is rising across industries, so is opportunity.

With judgement at an all-time premium, Bloomberg ranks understanding behaviour among the hottest next-generation skills. More than any formal qualification, this psychological edge helps you to make judgements that change lives – yours and those around you.

In a noisy tone-deaf world, mishearing may not be your fault, but course correction is your choice. No one teaches you judgement. It's expected of those who hold power – and a differentiating skill to be mastered.

Mastering judgement begins with appreciating how today's decisions are shaped by context. I'll take you on a journey to become a more influential, respected and differentiated tuned-in *Decision Ninja*, equipped to pre-empt and prevent predictable errors, navigating an era where misjudgement is rising alongside opportunity.

Now, you can harness human insight as an undervalued superpower to live your best life and lead others to do the same.

What can you expect?

I think of this book in three ways:

- it's an insurance policy against *future* misjudgement;
- it's a behavioural x-ray that explains *past* misjudgement; and
- it's a real-time reputation and performance accelerator

Tune In is structured in three parts.

Part One sheds light on why we tune out and hear less than ever. I explore the nature, scale and cause of the misjudgement problem, explaining how a modern high-speed world affects not only who we hear but also how we decide. I highlight what I call the trilogy of error: psychological blind spots, deaf spots and dumb spots.

This lays the foundation for a pioneering framework introduced in **Part Two** where I pinpoint ten intangible factors that unconsciously bind and bias our perspectives: power, ego, risk, identity, memory, ethics, time, emotion, relationships and stories. The mnemonic 'PERIMETERS' summarises these factors.

I chose this word deliberately to reflect our innate tendency to think in a limited or bounded manner. Passively unmanaged, each factor becomes a potential bias-activating trap because each trap is a predictable source of misinformation.

Collectively, these traps contain a spectrum of 75+ psychological biases, fallacies and effects. But actively managed, each factor can be a rich source of influence, impact and advantage.

I draw on established theories by renowned scholars, esteemed psychologists and decorated scientists, illustrated with a reservoir of handpicked stories I hope you'll find as meaningful and moving as I do.

Showcasing the art of tuning in the right voices, you'll hear how a displaced fund manager built a $10 trillion Wall Street empire; an abused wife reinvented as a global rock'n'roll entertainer and an empathetic FBI investigator prompted multiple murder confessions. You'll also hear how a moon-landing astronaut preferred peer praise to presidential honours; a police officer saved an abducted child after 18 years; and a premier league footballer permanently changed government policy.

You'll hear how tuning out carries consequences: a CEO stripped of his knighthood; a $65bn fraud that cratered thousands of lives; the greatest miscarriage of justice in British history; widespread Russian Olympic collusion; Silicon Valley founders fired by their own board; and a couple that hid the most barbaric Nazi in history. That's in addition to persecuted journalists; de-licensed doctors; systemic sexual abuse; maritime disasters; roaming serial killers; and cheating academics.

Each trap warrants a dedicated chapter which you can read independently or revisit when facing a specific decision dilemma.

These judgement traps aren't exhaustive, the literature on

each could fill a library. Appreciating even one can reshape your mindset and retool your skillset. Bullet point chapter highlights are provided for convenience.

To counteract these traps, **Part Three** unveils an antidote – a menu of 18 science-based strategies that harness what I call 'decision friction.' These empirically validated strategies slow down judgement in real time, promote reason over reactance and prevent a predictable rush to misjudgement.

You'll meet your future self: a confident problem-solving Decision Ninja who skilfully upgrades their judgement capability and preserves both influence and power by selectively tuning in to the voices that matter and tuning out the rest.

The message is clear: when you tune in, you stand out rather than miss out, lose out or get left out.

I know that one book is not enough to neutralise decision risk, but I hope it's enough to stimulate you to tune in when the outcome matters.

Tune In is simply the start.

INTRODUCTION:
THE DEVIL IN DISGUISE

*"I am not a product of my circumstances; I am
a product of my decisions."*

Stephen Covey

O UR DECISIONS STEM from the company we keep, our character, external circumstances and context. The internal context of our mind is often underestimated. Even the most highly accomplished individuals can be blind to bias, deaf to decision traps and silent when it matters.

Ironically, even the greatest voice of all time can tune out the voices that really matter.

A LITTLE LESS CONVERSATION

Midway between Tennessee and Alabama nestles Tupelo, a working-class shanty town with a mostly black community. In 1935, a white boy was born in a 300-square-foot, two-room house on 306 Old Satillo Road. For $180, it was built without plumbing or electricity by his hard-working, church-going parents. As I stood within its tiny frame observing the outside WC, I couldn't help noting the irony that this entire house was smaller than the living room of a property the young man would later acquire for $102,500.

When he was 13, the family relocated to Memphis for a better life.

This shy mama's boy was an outsider in high school and occasionally bullied. After graduation, he drove trucks by day. By night, he embarked on a musical pilgrimage that would change his life.

Lacking formal training, he played guitar by ear and sang with a rare two-and-a-half-octave vocal range. Always experimenting, he fused gospel, pop, blues and country. Over time, his musical experiments would transcend racial boundaries, moulded by the singing style of the black community in which he was raised.

"I don't sound like nobody," he declared in 1957.

He didn't move like nobody either!

His shyness and inhibition evaporated on stage. Electric performances shocked like a supercharged bolt of lightning. His raw talent, smouldering looks and velvety Southern voice seduced audiences everywhere he went. He defied categorisation, "neither male nor female, black nor white, rock nor country."[1] Growling and grinding, swaggering his hips and quivering his lips, mothers feared this devil in disguise.

His artistic decisions paid off. In 1958, this homespun 19-year-old traded his trucks for Cadillacs and amassed his first million dollars, a far cry from his twin brother's burial in a pauper's grave.[2]

Over the next three decades, Elvis Aaron Presley inspired generations and disrupted the music industry forever. He became the greatest solo-selling artist of all time with 18 number one hits, unmatched by Michael Jackson, Madonna or Taylor Swift.[3]

The business changed, but this voice stood the test of time. BB King once said, "To me, they didn't make a mistake when they called him the King."

Author Peter Guralnick describes "a transcendent creature of his time. He was so potent… he sort of blew apart the boundaries of his own generation."

But a sense of invulnerability, exceptionalism and narrow perspective usually accompanies success. Ill-prepared for meteoric fame, Elvis blew apart something else: himself.[4]

The most important determinant of judgement is the context in which you decide – your internal mindset and external environment. In 1957, the same year 'Jailhouse Rock' was released, psychologist Herbert Simon introduced the idea of *bounded rationality*, noting that our perspective is unconsciously bounded by our experience, background, education and social circle. In other words, rational thought is limited by circumstances.

To understand others' decisions, you must understand their context.

I first visited Graceland in 1990 as a student with my now-husband. As I meandered through the musically adorned gates, I didn't fully appreciate the effect of context on decisions. That came decades later.

The company we keep and our social connections influence our personal and professional decisions. As astronaut Buzz Aldrin once wrote, "Show me your friends and I'll show you your future."

A cocooning inner circle, the "Memphis Mafia" indulged their leader's every impulsive whim, desperate to quell that famous hair-trigger temper. For 20 years, the on-call ingroup was rewarded with lavish gift-giving and a hedonistic lifestyle. "He was a very kind person. He'd do anything for you. But it was like he was on a roller coaster," tells Charlie Hodge. A compulsive-obsessive perfectionist, Elvis's pathological overspending bordered on irresponsibility. He probably signed more cheques than autographs!

It's not unusual for leaders to surround themselves with compliant enablers, groupies or grabbers. But it's perilous. The voice of truth is routinely silenced. After all, few bite the hand that feeds them.

When off-stage and off-camera, Elvis stayed within his private sanctuary, enjoying the safe perimeter of the Graceland gates. Sometimes spending weeks in a darkened bedroom, he shut out the world, shielded from reality. A self-imposed isolation fed his worst insecurities as he lived alone in his head. This cloistered bubble shrank his perspective further.

Whether you're at the top of your game or feeling disillusioned, depressed and depleted, it affects your decisions. Guralnick observes that Elvis "never fully came to terms with the burden of decision-making."

He didn't have to.

The superstar delegated his commercial and health decisions to trusted advisers, talismans and tailors. His untrained father became his accountant. He legitimised years of prescription usage, diet pills and comfort food to cope with workplace pressure, fear of failure and exhausting night-time performances.

Many people concede power to others, even when it's not in their best interests. For decades, he empowered an amateur agent to control his entire business. Initially lucrative, the cigar-munching 'Colonel' Parker negotiated multiple self-serving deals. His mother Gladys Presley distrusted the Colonel, saying, "He's the devil himself." A grateful Elvis saw things differently, telegramming how he loved him "like a father."[5]

After his army career in the 1960s, Elvis's serious acting goals went unfulfilled. Having completed 31 beach-and-bikini Hollywood films, he hankered for more substantial roles. "Those movies sure got me into a rut... the only thing worse than watchin' a bad movie is bein' in one."[6] But Hollywood paid three times more than music, and fans enjoyed his movies. Manager and client naively signed deals without reading scripts or insisting on quality clauses.

Who stops to think, challenge or probe when on a roll?

Peaks and troughs punctuate most careers. As formidable competitors emerged, like The Beatles, record sales dwindled. But a sensational 1968 television comeback marked a turning point. A *New York Times* rock critic wrote, "There's something magical about watching a man who has lost himself find his way home."[7]

The opportunity was short-lived. Despite owning five private jets, travel ambition slipped away. "I'd like to go to Europe… to Japan… I've never been out of the country except in service," he told a 1972 press conference.

This superstar failed to challenge the familiar voice that puppeteered his life. Despite exceptional power and privilege, the greatest voice of all time didn't use his voice strongly or frequently enough to be heard.

Why didn't he take control?

Ex-wife Priscilla suggests it was misguided loyalty and an "inability to stand up to the Colonel… to take responsibility for his own life." It's likely the ghost of poverty never left him. It's also easier to turn a deaf ear to inconvenient concerns than rock the boat, especially with a rising bank balance. The Faustian pact had long been sealed to bankroll a profligate lifestyle.

On the fast-track treadmill, reflection and reinterpretation are luxuries. Elvis admitted, "It's a fast life, I just can't slow down."[8] The high-octane stage performances mirrored his decision style.

Everyone curates their image. Over time, your trademark signature can become a weighty crown. "The image is one thing and the human being is another. It's very hard to live up to an image," Elvis lamented.[9] Priscilla explained, "His public wanted him to be perfect while the press mercilessly exaggerated his faults." In today's digital world, little has changed.

Like any customer-focused brand, the King was in tune with his audience. Addicted to their unconditional validation, fidelity and fatherhood couldn't compete. Double standards and serial philandering resulted, despite spirituality and nocturnal Bible-reading.

Facing divorce and insolvency, in 1973, his entire back catalogue of 650 recordings was sold in what was widely regarded among the worst deals in musical history. A gruelling tour followed, topping 168 events. The full-on, frantic cycle exacerbated his existing health conditions and a long-standing amphetamine addiction.

While the world clamoured to hear Elvis's voice, who did he hear?

Were there so many voices, he couldn't tune in to the right one?

Was his ego so dominant, he dismissed contrary views in *deaf ear syndrome*?

Despite the power to live his best life and ability to masterfully reinterpret songs, he didn't reinterpret red flags or heed the voice of advice when it mattered most.

His fawning entourage didn't hear his voice either. He wrote, "I feel so alone... I don't know who I can talk to anymore. Or turn to."[10]

One by one, the women in his life left him. They couldn't control him, and he couldn't control himself.

CEOs, celebrities, songwriters and high achievers often feel isolation. Feminist firebrand Sinéad O'Connor captures the loneliness of touring well. "There were a lot of people around me but no one could see me... and I couldn't see myself."[11]

Legendary tennis player John McEnroe understands too, "For most of your life as a tennis player, you're out there alone. For better or worse, it's just you – and that can be terrifying."[12]

From the top, the only way is down.

For Elvis, cracks penetrated that perfect celluloid image of slicked back hair and Cherokee cheekbones. "Just because you look good don't mean you feel good."[13] A sense of purpose eluded him, grasping at numerology and astronomy for answers.

By 1976, chronic depression had set in. "I'm sort of getting tired of being Elvis Presley," he told his producer.[14] Close friend Jerry Schilling observed, "He had a sadness, a loneliness. He was trying to fill a void that couldn't be filled."[15]

Overworked and overweight, he prioritised paying his 39-strong team. Why not course correct? He would say, "There are too many people who depend on me. I'm too obligated. I'm in too far to get out."

Like many powerholders, fear of anonymity, extreme cocooning and a dwindling bank balance can dwarf rational perspective. The lyrics, "We're caught in a trap, I can't walk out," were hauntingly prophetic.

A high-speed lifestyle peppered with both brilliant and misguided decisions finally took its toll on this once-in-a-generation talent.

With the last volt of supercharged energy stolen, in 1977, the world lost a legend.

The King was dead.

MOMENTS THAT MATTER

As I finalised this book, I found myself drawn to revisit Graceland after nearly four decades. I wanted to place the human decision-making journey, and perhaps even my own life, in context. As I re-entered the musically adorned gates, once again accompanied by my husband, I appreciated more fully the rapid passage of time, the value of legacy and the destabilising effect of context, character and company on our decisions.

I'm not a die-hard rock'n'roll superfan, but I felt unexplained regret at the premature loss of supreme talent and a voice that pervaded my childhood.

Perhaps it's also because over three decades in investment management, I witnessed superstar colleagues prematurely short-change their lives and self-sabotage their careers as they tuned in to the wrong voices and rushed to misjudgement.

Like many, I too sacrificed much on the altar of ambition to reach the C-suite in a male-dominated industry. As a serial

workaholic, my perspective started and stopped at the office door
– it was my Graceland.

I loved my job, accumulating enough airmiles to orbit the sun. I
had the privilege of money-can't-buy opportunities, interviewing
presidents and dining with moon-landing astronauts. I met
heroes and villains, Hollywood legends, royalty and Olympic
champions. I share some of these stories later.

But in my tunnel-visioned rush to acquire the next badge
or vanity title, I didn't always read the signals, decode subtle
messages or listen to the right voices when it mattered. At times,
I was 'tone-deaf' as an industry-feted leader once told me early
in my career when I wanted to do the right thing rather than the
convenient thing.

Today, out of the corporate rat race with the luxury of
reflection, as a behavioural scientist sitting on boards, lecturing
in universities and advising blue-chip companies, I appreciate
just how much selective *tuning in* is an underestimated source of
power – and *tuning out* is a universal judgement killer.

Whether you're a superstar, surgeon, parent or plumber, no one
wants to make decisions that harm the well-being of ourselves or
others. Yet we do.

No algorithm currently exists that prevents poor judgement.
It's a moral responsibility that starts with you. As Jerry Schilling
says, "Only Elvis could save Elvis."[16]

His short-circuited career could have concluded so
differently. In a frantic people-pleasing world, would you have
made better choices? Would you have asked questions and
questioned answers? Or tuned in to other voices? We want
to think so.

I stand in no moral judgement as we can't predict behaviour,
but we can predict bias.

8

In this book, I argue we unconsciously fall into similar power, emotion, ego, identity and relationship-based traps that squander opportunity and stop us living our best life. We're not superior in our own kingdom, regardless of age, title, talent, income or background.

We make similar mistakes. We underweight risk of excess and impulsivity, accepting information at face value. We pay homage to career over family, money over ethics, living for today not tomorrow.

We rely on what we see, not what we hear. We hear fake news, hate speech and flattery over the voice of truth, nuance and contradiction.

We encode misinformation rather than decode information.

We ignore the voices of conscience, wisdom and history. Instead, we tune in to our applauding crowd, inbox fans and short-term rewards.

Could tuning in to different voices and alternative interpretations have highlighted red flags? Perhaps. The truth is we can learn from history and science – and that is the purpose of this book.

Elvis's cautionary tale isn't unique. The factors that influence decisions contain judgement traps faced by all of us. Why? Because they're human traps that lead us astray.

I identify ten categories of misjudgement traps, each varying in intensity and impact.

Each of these traps may seem obvious or even familiar in a day-to-day setting, but just as they are familiar, they exert an unconscious effect on our decision-making process. That makes them potentially dangerous decision derailers.

Ask yourself how each of the following factors might influence your reasoning during high-stakes decision-making:

Power: your elevation of idols, authorities or experts.

Ego: your commitment to your own ideas above others.

Risk: your appetite for thrills and intolerance of doubt.

Identity: your craving to curate image and impress.

Memory: your ability to accurately recall data.

Ethics: your capacity to resist temptation or wrongdoing.

Time: your tendency to live in the past, present or future.

Emotion: your aptitude to regulate impulse and excess.

Relationships: your predisposition to follow the crowd.

Story: your readiness to accept stated narratives as fact.

If you're like most people, you'll recognise most of these. Each PERIMETERS trap is underpinned by multiple psychological blind spots, deaf spots and dumb spots that contribute to tuning out the signals that drive high-impact decisions and outcomes.

‖‖‖‖‖‖

Despite popular opinion, I believe the most underestimated risk facing this generation isn't economic, political, cyber or even climate risk. It's human decision risk and the ability to hear what really matters.

Your decisions matter a lot more than you think.

You're like the essential 12th juror in a court of law that shapes the direction of others' lives. Other people depend on you making the right call.

That crown carries a heavy weight of expectations about ascertaining what's right, fair, necessary or reasonable. Expectations exist whether you're a household name, umpire, doctor, referee, lawyer, trader, judge or parent.

As decision-makers, naturally you get many calls right, but your errors can be disproportionately damaging. A substantial body of research attributes disasters to human error. It accounts for 94% of road accidents, 88% of cyber-attacks and 80% of aviation accidents. [17,18] Even medical misdiagnosis is the fourth leading cause of death in the US.[19] Moreover, human error underpins cult followings, scams, scandals, miscarriages of justice, and much more.

Human error starts with tuning out the voices that matter: unheard customers, employees, voters, patients, mavericks or minorities. It's why business and governments are so distrusted. And why activism is rising, countries polarising, start-ups imploding and mergers failing.

Understanding why isn't an academic exercise or indulgent pastime. It's essential to business sustainability, economic livelihoods and leadership legacies.

Unfortunately, accountants or auditors don't factor human decision risk into spreadsheets, scenarios or systems. Its significance is overlooked until it's too late. There is no formula to calculate psychological risk, but the cost of ignoring it is incalculable. It warrants a far greater platform than it currently receives whether in business, sport, medicine, law or government.

Tuning out is a universal judgement killer. There's always a price to pay; that price is human error and a collective downgrading of our decisions.

You pay that price, and so do others.

Intellect, wealth, status and occupation provide little insulation from human error, whether it originates from mountain climbers, journalists, serial killers, students, venture capitalists, billionaires, therapists or rogue traders. Notwithstanding many good judgements of such professionals, their misjudgements are explored in this book. The same individual can be incredibly smart and incredibly stupid.

So why do we tune out and how can we prevent it?

Success lies in slowing down long enough to selectively hear the right voices. You don't want to hear every voice, the first voice, most senior voice or even the loudest voice, just the *right* voice for a given situation.

Despite the advances of artificial intelligence, there's no code for regret-free judgement. Some 80% of leaders admit their organisations don't excel at decision-making – and over half of all decisions are found to be ineffective anyway.[20] In a 10-year study, 45% of CEO candidates claimed responsibility for a decision disaster that either cost them a title or severely damaged a business.[21]

It's no wonder decision error costs the average Fortune 500 company an estimated $250m annually, as suggested by McKinsey. That's why honing judgement skills matters now more than ever.

In a noisy world, misjudgement is not entirely your fault, but better judgement is certainly your choice.

THE SOUNDTRACK OF YOUR LIFE

The million-dollar question is how to resolve the misjudgement puzzle. People crave a singular explanation, but there is none. Human behaviour isn't linear, it's complex with intertwined motivations and over 200 labels that explain 'tone-deafness.' Every day, we make an estimated 35,000 decisions, 95% unconsciously.

However, opportunity exists.

Humans are predictable, and what's predictable is preventable.

That's why I outline an antidote of 18 science-based solutions that boost interpretation ability and feed your 'sonic intelligence.' These include second-order thinking, probabilistic thinking, nudges, reframing, the Janus option and what I call 'decision friction.'

In this book, you'll learn how to fine-tune your interpretation and judgement skills to prevent crises before it's too late. With a diagnostic for every decision dilemma, you'll save time, filter misinformation quicker and architect decisions with higher impact.

It's my hope that more decision-makers, whether global leaders, policymakers, entrepreneurs, aspiring professionals and especially my own nieces and nephews, will appreciate how human understanding helps navigate this world regret-free.

The shy boy from Tupelo had a simple philosophy: "Truth is like the sun. You can shut it out for a while but it ain't going away." If he had slowed down long enough to reinterpret critical voices, his life might have turned out differently.

His story is our story. He paid a heavy price – you don't have to.

His story reflects the premium placed on smart judgement and the key themes in this book:

- the odds are stacked against good judgement in a high-speed, visual, data-driven, polarised and tuned-out world;
- understanding behaviour and separating what's logical from what's psychological can convert cognitive liabilities into assets; it makes the difference between being heard and unheard, between preserving power and losing power;
- by recognising deaf spots before drawing conclusions, you rebalance what you see with what you hear; it takes mere seconds of reasoning, reflection and reinterpretation.

Whether you want the corner office, a medal or a Mercedes, the smartest thing you can know is who to listen to – and who not to. If you don't, ask yourself, who else will suffer?

Tuning in can be a performance game-changer as well as a career differentiator, reputation accelerator and life enhancer.

I make it easier for you to hear the right voices and harder to hear the wrong voices. That way, it's more likely you'll hear others' voices – and others will hear you. Because you can't always trust the sources you hear, your insurance policy lies in reevaluating the messenger and confidently reinterpreting the message in real time.

This book shapes the story of every individual who wants to live their best life and enrich the lives of others. I truly believe you can, with a better understanding of human behaviour. There are few guarantees, but I offer one: you'll get a lot further with this behavioural insight than without.

Success, as you define it, hinges on *selectively* tuning in what really matters and tuning out the rest.

If discounting human risk will short-change your life, appreciating it can change your life.

It's time to tune in.

PART ONE

MISJUDGEMENT IN A NOISY WORLD

"Listen to the whispers and you won't have to hear the screams."

Cherokee Proverb

NOT EVERYTHING YOU hear is valuable, and not everything valuable is heard.

Decision-making doesn't exist in a vacuum. Our ability to tune in to the most relevant voice is dictated by our context. Despite the advances of the 21st century, our fast-paced, data-driven and highly visual world affects how we think, what we hear and, ultimately, what we decide.

While modern technology provides more platforms than ever to express our voice, the volume of conflicting, competing and contradictory voices dominates the airwaves. Despite increasing social pressure to hear the voices of customers, employees, stakeholders, voters and marginalised groups, that ability to tune in has been severely contaminated.

Countless channels broadcast messages 24/7. Notifications and newsfeeds bombard the mind, making it impossible to pause long enough to decode them and decide what serves us best. Instead, we judge events in a spinning ecosystem of digital noise, data overload and misinformation.

The result?

Most people hear less than ever before – and in turn, feel less heard.

Moreover, if you don't hear others, you've less chance of *your* message being heard.

To control our decision context, we must understand how

it's influenced by a tapestry of factors from culture to climate, character and the company we keep. I argue *context* combines with *cognition* to mould our interpretation, the essential step before judgement that dictates decision quality. This dictates our level of reward or regret, as summarised below.

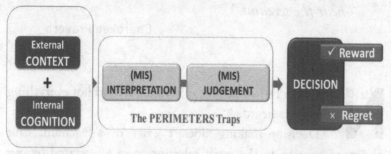

Busy decision-makers tend to neglect interpretation. It's not intentional. Yet as history shows, skipping interpretation can kill populations, platoons, passengers, prisoners, patients and products. You only have to think of genocidal atrocities or misinterpreted military instructions. Think of pilots mishearing air traffic controllers, doctors misdiagnosing unusual illnesses, organisations ignoring customer preferences or politicians dismissing citizen unrest.

This interaction of external context and internal cognition is the focus of the three chapters that follow in Part One.

Chapter 1 addresses how external sources of misinformation accelerate risk of misjudgement.

Chapter 2 explores how internal sources accelerate risk of misjudgement, namely the trilogy of error – psychological blind spots, deaf spots and dumb spots. I highlight *motivated reasoning* and *deaf ear syndrome* as key contributors.

In Chapter 3, I apply the *PERIMETERS Effect* to illustrate how context and cognition interact to shape bounded, biased and binary judgement. You'll find no shortage of business, legal, medical, technological, media and political blunders that demonstrate the prevalence of professional misjudgement.

Let's start with the external sources of information.

CHAPTER 1

MISHEARING, MISINFORMATION AND MISJUDGEMENT

"There is nothing more deceptive than an obvious fact."[1]

Arthur Conan Doyle

TUNING OUT EXPLAINS a lot. It tells us why the greatest artists and smartest professionals get duped. It explains why regulators miss Ponzi schemes and intelligence agencies miss terrorist warnings. It's the reason why boards continue to fail, mergers destroy value and start-ups implode. And it's why victims globally lose trillions of dollars to scammers, and organisations are defrauded by an eye-popping 5% of revenues every year.[2]

Tuning out is particularly egregious when holding power. Businesses, careers and nations get built on half-truths, innuendo and misconceptions.

Everyone wants to be heard. It's in our DNA. Poets write about it. Musicians croon about it. Beyoncé belts out, "Can You Hear Me?" Trailblazer Sinéad O'Connor once filled a hospital wall with the words, "I just want to be heard."[3]

As you yearn to be heard by customers, co-workers and stakeholders, they yearn to be heard by you. But in many cases, they're not.

In today's noisy world, many employees feel unheard – many *are* unheard. For instance, when Google, Disney, Amazon and other organisations ignored pleas for social justice, employees staged mass walkouts and strikes. Countless organisations were pilloried for tone-deaf return-to-work policies after the pandemic.

History shows how whistleblowers were ignored at organisations such as Enron, Theranos, Boeing, Volkswagen, and many more. Governance is under scrutiny, but fiduciary boards don't know what questions to ask when they don't listen to what's said – or not said. Reading between the lines is an underestimated skill in a noisy world.

Although listening is leadership 101, even customers feel unheard. Dwindling loyalty results. In recent years, McKinsey found customers are more willing to switch brands than ever.[4]

Generations of minorities have long felt unheard. Why? We tune out those who are different, dissenting or divergent. Instead, we gravitate towards familiar ingroups, further narrowing our worldview.

When policymakers disregard human rights concerns, protests, riots and social movements result. Think the Arab Spring or Free Tibet. The business world falls in line. Even Pepsi was forced to pull an ad with Kendall Jenner for 'tone-deaf' political insensitivity and trivialising Black Lives Matter.

In the daily dash to decide, we make snap judgements and jump to premature and false conclusions.

We interrupt other people's assertions rather than our own assumptions. A deafening context amplifies the risk of being deceived, distracted and deluded.

As psychologists say, "Genes load the gun, the environment pulls the trigger."

In this chapter, I describe the impact of external sources of misinformation on our decisions. In other words, where we decide (external context) influences how we decide (internal cognition). Amid so much noise, we can't hear ourselves think. Specifically, four factors subtly but substantively shape judgement, steering us to think in more binary and short-term ways:

1. A fast-paced, frantic lifestyle accelerates short-termism.
2. Data overload distracts and overwhelms the mind.
3. Visual stimuli increase what we see and reduce what we hear.
4. Polarised systems and structures embed binary perspectives.

This is illustrated in the schematic below.

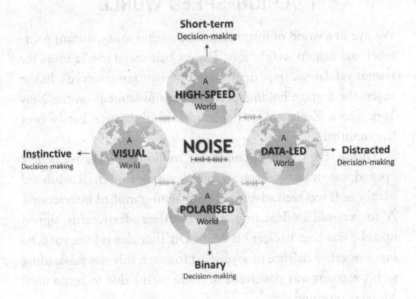

These factors diminish the time, attention and patience available to reinterpret the most important information and conversations.

As a result, we mishear what's said or, alternatively, infer what's not said. We misinterpret what we think was said rather than reinterpret what was actually said.

This accelerates a rush to misjudgement and predictable human error.

Boards, leaders, regulators, parents and policymakers don't misjudge on purpose. Mishearing makes it hard to know who and what to pay attention to. But it costs financially, reputationally and even socially. Author Dan Pink's one million online followers ranked "not listening" as the #1 most irritating trait in others.

Let's explore how a fast-paced world might shrink our willingness and ability to tune in.

1. A HIGH-SPEED WORLD

We live in a world of instant meals, instant money, instant pain-relief and instant weight loss. Tweets bait social media users for instant validation. Impatient investors want faster returns. In the 1940s, the average holding period of an investment on the New York Stock Exchange was seven years. Today, it's barely over five months.

During the Covid-19 pandemic, millions of ordinary people opened day-trading accounts on the easy-to-join Robinhood platform. It was well advertised with semi-gamified interactions. A 20-year-old student from Illinois, Alexander Kearns, signed up as he was keen to clear his debts. On Thursday 11 June 2020, he saw a negative balance of $730,165. However, this was misleading as his account was positive. The trade wasn't due to settle until Monday morning.

Unfamiliar with investment trade processing mechanics, Alex made the worst possible rush to misjudgement and committed suicide the following morning. He left a note, asking: "How was a 20-year-old with no income able to get assigned almost a million dollars' worth of leverage?"[5] Inexperienced with sophisticated instruments, he admitted he had "no clue."[6]

Misunderstanding the context and under pressure, he misinterpreted the data. His perimeter view dangerously narrowed.

Today's fast-paced ecosystem amplifies the probability of making fast-paced decisions. It's ironic. We pay professionals a lot of money to make considered decisions yet applaud prompt replies and reward rapid solutions.

Organisation systems and structures unconsciously contribute to a 24/7, fast-moving culture and perceived decision urgency. Employees are force-fed a diet of speed as high-octane industries demand a conveyor belt of quick wins. Lawyers, consultants and therapists bill fees by the minute rather than the hour or the day. Athletes secure medals within hundredths of seconds. Even fighter pilots win aerial battles under 40 seconds.[7]

Business books declare that winners adapt faster than losers. Employees race to the top. And those with stamina are rewarded. No wonder executives aim to "retire by 50," "be first to market" or "double sales within a year."

A 10-year study of 17,000 C-suite executives found quick decisions are even considered more important to success than good decisions.[8] Those who decided "earlier, faster, and with greater conviction" were 12 times more likely to become high-performing CEOs.

Tick tock, tick tock. "Think Fast, Think FedEx." The message is pervasive. Ferrari is "Faster than Fast." Verizon is "Moving at the speed of life." BlackBerry claimed "Anything worth doing is worth doing faster." Even Presley's tagline was "Taking care of business in a flash."

These messages subliminally reinforce a speedy decision context, encouraging us to live life in the fast lane. By contrast, Mae West's mantra was "Anything worth doing is worth doing slowly."

Deciding fast, deciding slow

How did you make your last big decision? Did you decide quickly and instinctively? Or did you conclude slowly and reflectively, possibly with a pros and cons list or algorithmic model?

Nobel Prize-winner Daniel Kahneman explains how people access two cognitive systems.[9] The fast, auto-pilot mode is System-1 and the slower, more deliberative mode is System-2. When people reason, they unconsciously lean towards one or the other.

For example, when you make coffee, play sport or travel to work, you use instinctive System-1. When you make high-stakes, expensive or capital-intensive decisions, you use System-2. Both are error-prone. System-1 instinct can lead you disproportionately astray. Think hot-blooded affairs, inappropriate comments or hair-trigger tempers! Despite well-considered System-2 reflection, miscarriages of justice and misconduct result. Think Enron's fraudulent accounts or the Central Park Five travesty. Misjudgement results.

It's important to note three things about how we decide:

1. We're emotional before we're rational. The trick is to regulate impulses long enough to reason.
2. Decision-making will always be context-, culture- and values-specific.
3. One mode of thinking isn't better than the other. While instinct may help you pick paint (*I like blue*) or even habit (*I always pick blue*), it's less effective when choosing a house (*I like it but can't afford it*).

The problem occurs when problem-solvers jump to conclusions rather than reflect. In one study, 80 psychologists performed clinical evaluations of patients within a mere five minutes rather than undertaking a more considered evaluation.[10] I take longer making coffee! While sometimes expertise explains instant diagnoses, often quick decisions are the product of a high-speed world and a short-term mindset.

It's now or never

How often do you accept data from people without validating or interpreting its contents? Most of us do. In a short-term world, we overly trust the message and the messenger.

In a *Harvard Business Review* article, Duke professor Dorie Clark compares a study where 97% of leaders claimed to value long-term, strategic problem-solving, yet in another study, 96% admit not having the time to develop strategy as they're too busy firefighting. It's a common dilemma.

Long-term forward thinkers and problem-solvers are rewarded by their organisations – they're four times more likely to be identified as high-potential. Moreover, they're six times more likely to be seen as effective leaders.

While long-term thinking is critical to decisions around strategy, relationships, investment, education and even animal conservation, the culture of now is the new currency which is accelerating short-term thinking. It means long-termism is less practiced in modern society.

Do you speed read and speed date? Do you skim headlines and just take the gist? Everything from communications to books, movies, social media chats and investment horizons is shortening.

While few want to plough through a one-million-word Proustian tome, pithy sentences lose essential richness. Modern communication has become reductionist, peppered with 280-character soundbites, slogans and summaries.

Even Hollywood scenes are shrinking. Modern screenwriters

draft snappier scripts than in the 1970s.[11] Netflix releases micro-serials in digestible chunks. And we gratefully binge-watch! It satiates an impulsive content craving.

The length of the average best-seller has reduced. In 2021, 38% of books exceeded 400 pages, a third less than the previous decade.[12] Shorter books now stay two weeks longer on the best-seller list. What's more, time-constrained readers can access summaries in the Blinkist app.

Over time, companies pay the price of these faster, short-term choices in terms of survival rates. In 1958, the average lifespan of an S&P 500 company was 61 years. Today, it's 18 years. McKinsey estimates 75% of the current S&P 500 will be non-existent by 2027.

Of course, reflection is no guarantee you'll neutralise bias, but overwhelming evidence concludes that critical reasoning leads to smarter decisions.

The requisite focus is harder in a distracting, digital and data-rich world – a key factor that affects our cognition.

2. A DATA-LED WORLD

Trevor Birdsall, a 32-year-old from Bradford, England, joked that his shy friend was terrorising women across the north of the country. Except it was no joke. When they cruised red-light districts, his friend disappeared for long periods, later boasting he had hit prostitutes and hadn't paid. Birdsall didn't know whether to believe him or not. His suspicions grew as stories of the Yorkshire Ripper flooded the media. "It crossed my mind there might be a connection."[13]

Eventually, he tipped off police. By then, over 30,000 statements, 250,000 names and millions of car number plates had been manually collected. Side-tracked by data, police missed Birdsall's warning despite his friend being listed as a "triple area sighting" and interviewed nine times over five years.[14]

More women were killed despite Birdsall's call. Captured at a random vehicle check point, his friend Peter Sutcliffe confessed to 13 murders. The Yorkshire Ripper blamed the voice of God.

Sometimes the right voices aren't heard in time. The 1981 Byford Report into the case concluded, "the backlog of unprocessed information failed to connect vital pieces of related information."[15]

An unintended result of the modern information tsunami is an overloaded, distracted and inattentive mind. We tune out.

Data and the overloaded mind

Being overloaded is the new normal. Microsoft find that 68% of employees don't have enough uninterrupted time, and 64% say they don't have enough time to do their job.[16]

It's not surprising. Contemporary workers are information-rich yet constantly interrupted by pings, rings and dings. Every 12 minutes, six billion people swipe smartphones. According to Carnegie Mellon, unexpected interruptions lower task performance by 20%.[17] We can't hear ourselves think.

We're drowning in data, pumped and dumped on us all day long. Data volume has multiplied by a factor of 32 in a decade, all of it competing for our attention. Yet we scroll, skim and seek even more data. Retailers ram your inboxes. LinkedIn enthusiasts invite you to subscribe to hundreds of newsletters. Colleagues send 100-page snapshots!

Our brains can't cope. Our ability to distil what matters shrinks rather than expands. As Nate Silver writes, "Distinguishing the signal from the noise requires both scientific knowledge and self-knowledge."[18]

It's too hard to decipher signals and spot coincidences, contradictions or inconsistencies. Instead, we nod politely and take what's said at face value. Open-source AI tools and the popularisation of ChatGPT means even more misinformation is taken at face value, leading to misinformation masquerading as fact.

Accepting information at face value can create the delusion of information value.

In this vortex, it's reasonable to think more data means better decisions. But too much data can fool us into imagining patterns where there are none.

University of Oregon professor Paul Slovic found that people exposed to 88 variables were no more accurate in their predictions than those exposed to five variables.[19] With more data, confidence rather than accuracy tends to increase.[20] Like money, more data doesn't make you happier, smarter or more accurate. More is only comforting, like that second tub of Häagen-Dazs. In reality, a third can make you ill!

Predictive technology doesn't help either! Grammarly, Chat GPT and Gmail write our letters, complete our sentences and auto-fill forms. Apps suggest what films to watch, what restaurants to visit and even whom to marry.

Why think for ourselves? When too much or too little data constrains our ability to reason, our cognition is affected and decisions become boundedly rational. And when the mind is bounded in this way, we're vulnerable to the PERIMETERS Effect – in other words, any of the ten factors will unconsciously limit our rational thought.

Data and the distracted mind

If you're overloaded with data, it's impossible to concentrate and make good decisions. Some regurgitate the first thought that springs to mind, whether it's inaccurate, inappropriate or intimidating. FTX founder Sam Bankman-Fried surely did.

When the cryptocurrency exchange collapsed, System-1

panic set in. He informed the media he was "too swamped with work and too distracted by other projects to pay attention to the risks welling up in the trading firm." He confessed, "I didn't have enough brain cycles left to understand everything going on." He later told the court he aimed for just 60,000 unread emails at a time – and frequently failed.

Distraction dampened rational thinking, triggering deaf spots that removed the voice of reason.

Distraction carries a spectrum of decision consequentiality. For example, how distracted are you on your birthday? Do you make better or worse decisions? Analysis of 47,489 surgeons who conducted 980,876 emergency procedures found patients significantly more likely to die on surgeons' birthdays.[21]

No one is immune.

The BBC reported actor Alec Baldwin was distracted on his mobile phone during *Rust* movie training, specifically while trainers were instructing actors never to point a prop gun.[22] Baldwin later misfired a prop gun, accidentally killing a camerawoman.

At the 89th Oscars, accounting firm PwC handed presenters the wrong envelope for the Best Picture winner. Embarrassing! They blamed "human error." *Vanity Fair* suggests an employee was distracted, tweeting celebrity pictures moments before. It was cringeworthy, but no lives were lost.

In this fast-paced world, no wonder concentration is shrinking. It's not just you. The Centre for Attention Studies at King's College London found 49% of adults feel attention is shortening.[23] At work, we think about going for a run. When on a run, we think about work. We can't relax or focus. As Herbert Simon suggested, a wealth of information creates a poverty of attention.

Social media users now spend even less time curating comments on hot topics. Danish physicist and expert on network attention Sune Lehmann analysed the top 50 Twitter trends. In 2013, the average conversation circulated for 17.5 hours. By 2016, it had dropped to 11.9 hours.[24] Today it's probably less. Hot topics cool quicker as the mind tunes in to the next source of novelty.

As Nobel Prize-winning author André Gide says, "Everything's already been said but since no one was listening, we have to start again."

Data and the inattentive mind

Informatics professor at University of California Gloria Mark found people shifted attention every three minutes, regardless of age or occupation.[25] By 2021, the average screen time had dropped over a decade from 74 seconds to 47 seconds.[26]

You're probably thinking, "That's not much." However, when workplace details matter, every second of hesitation makes a material difference. Consider a capital-intensive project that still haunts NASA engineers.

In 1998, the $125m Mars Climate Orbiter was launched with great fanfare to collect atmospheric composition data. This was ground-breaking technology. After ten months of travel, the Orbiter suddenly disintegrated into the atmosphere. Communication fell silent between ground control and the spacecraft.

What happened? Perplexed technicians couldn't understand. It boiled down to human error.

The contracted Lockheed Martin engineers who built the spacecraft had used imperial units of measurement in the software while the Jet Propulsion Lab used the metric system to figure out the vehicle's location in space. Because Lockheed engineers failed to convert their measurements into metrics, the data error compounded as systems couldn't communicate with each other. Attention to a minor but material detail that might have only taken seconds to sort was lost in the magnitude and pressure of a high-stakes project.

Author and journalist Johann Hari argues that inattention is rising, almost approaching a social crisis.[27] He cites several contributing macro-factors such as life-draining algorithms, social media platforms, poor diet, pollution, stress and sleep deprivation. For instance, the National Sleep Foundation cites the average amount of sleep has dropped by 20% over the last century. Being in a zombie state affects vulnerability to human error. Standard protocols and processes aren't followed. Important inputs get missed whether product labels, safety instructions or fine print.

Sleep-deprived professionals risk not noticing information that's missing in a legal contract, glitzy advert, court case or sales pitch. They may grasp snapshot data rather than historic data or wrongly equate true motives with stated motives. In a frenzied or overwhelmed state, reliance on handy heuristics also rises. But heuristics are inherently biased.

We simplify life by relying on what and whom we see. Why? Judgement is hard and we prefer easy. As a result, what you see is what you get, especially in today's visual world.

3. A VISUAL WORLD

On the morning of 12 January 2007, a young violinist played Bach's Chaconne in a Washington DC subway. For 43 minutes, 1,097 government employees passed. Only seven commuters stopped to listen to the baseball cap-wearing violinist. He earned a mere $32.17, observing:

> I'm surprised at the number of people who don't pay attention at all, as if I'm invisible. Because, you know what? I'm makin' a lot of noise!

Only one woman recognised world-renowned Joshua Bell. Just days before, he had played his 1713 $3.5m Stradivarius violin in Boston's Symphony Hall for hundreds of dollars a ticket.[28]

People assume different meanings in different contexts. Author of the *Hidden Brain* podcast Shankar Vedantam suggests, "Your mind is different, your ears are different, and the music you hear is different."[29]

The physical context changes what and how you hear, even when you're committed to listening, whether it's to a client's woes or a child's wishes.

We rely on what we see more than what we hear, but what you hear is never all there is.

Thousands of images on smartphones, television, TikTok and Instagram overstimulate our brains. While this serves and satisfies us, the problem is we assume that what we see is much more reliable than what we hear.

For instance, brands assume online reviews dominate word-of-mouth influence because digital disproportionately dominates our lives. Yet research finds chatrooms, blogs and viral videos only account for 7% of word-of-mouth influence.[30] Why? Social media comments about brands constitute visual rather than aural feedback. We forget about the weight of face-to-face discussions. If Amazon disappoints or delights us, we instantly tell others before we type.

We also trust what we see and form perceptions that become flawed decision inputs. Remember how frumpy Susan Boyle's cavernous voice surprised X-Factor viewers and judges? It's why millions of TV viewers enjoy witnessing this instinctive bias being overcome on *The Voice*. It's why some companies use blind CVs and orchestras hold blind auditions.

While we think we evaluate strategies, situations and strangers fairly, experience suggests otherwise.

Who doesn't prejudge candidates, neighbours or Instagram

profiles? Who doesn't size up strangers before engaging in conversation? Who doesn't flick past slides in meetings before hearing the presenter? We choose movies based on thumbnails and judge books by their covers.

Imagine you're handed a photo of three smiling people. A man has his arm draped around a younger woman's waist. As an older woman looks on, it seems like any other party, except it isn't. The man is Prince Andrew. The woman is socialite Ghislaine Maxwell, found guilty of trafficking the underage girl. A photo is static, but its interpretation changes with context and time.

Interpretation is the difference between seeing a party photo, a photoshopped snap or evidence in a criminal trial.

Seeing is believing

Even professionals instantly believe what they see despite expertise.[31] At age 82, Dutch art critic and 1660s Johannes Vermeer scholar Abraham Bredius responded so emotionally to seeing the *Christ at Emmaus* painting, he failed to spot it was a forgery. It had been replicated by Hans Van Meegeren and sold for millions.

Critics failed to ask the obvious question. Why were so many of Vermeer's rare works on the market within a short period? The forgery was later discovered in the office of Hitler's vice chancellor, Hermann Göring.

Over-reliance on visual data is pervasive. Some claim to witness UFO sightings and paranormal events. Religious devotees swear they see statues of the Virgin Mary weep. Preoccupied analysts summarise pie-charts and graphs with a single glance. *Daily Mirror* editor Piers Morgan was duped by fake pictures of British soldiers abusing Iraqi prisoners. Blinded by the need for headlines and vulnerable to half-truths, he likely saw what he wanted.

Under pressure, we tend to trust the image we see rather than interpret the words we hear.

We also misjudge based on demeanour. The guilty tend to look shifty, right? Sometimes they look unremorseful.

What if the 12th juror thought the same? Many do. And innocent people pay the price.

Albert Mehrabian's '7–38–55 rule' states 55% of communication impact comes from visual body language while intonation accounts for 38%, and words 7%. Put another way, people only recall 7% of what you say but 93% of how you say it.

One implication of visual dominance and low interpretation is stereotyping. Based on a study of 222,838 Lyft drivers, black drivers in Florida are 24–33% more likely to be stopped by police than white drivers, even when all drivers travel at the same speed. Moreover, black drivers are likely to pay 23–34% more in fines.[32] Florida doesn't have a fast-driving black population. It has a discrimination problem.

It's not just Florida, it's global. Justice is neither blind nor fair.

People instinctively over-index on their senses, particularly sight over sound. New York University psychologist Emily Balcetis asked students which sensory faculty they would prefer not to lose.

Which would you choose?

Over 70% elected to keep their sight. In other words, 70% were willing to sacrifice their hearing, smell or taste.

As Florida drivers, Joshua Bell, Piers Morgan and Abraham Bredius exemplify, first impressions are biased snapshots – and are often wrong.

Love at first sight

We fall for what we see. So why do images and first impressions dominate interpretation? The answer lies in three fields: physics, neuroscience and education.

Firstly, take physics. You see lightning before hearing thunder. Fans see a goal scored before hearing the crowd roar. Alec Baldwin would have seen a flash before hearing that fatal gunshot. At 340 metres per second, sound travels slower than light which travels at 300 million metres per second.

Secondly, consider neuroscience. There's only so much data our brains can process but people still crave the false security it offers. "It is perhaps a pity that my eyes have seen more than my brain is able to assimilate or evaluate," laments Apollo 11 astronaut Michael Collins.[33] Our brains process images faster than words.[34] MIT neuroscientists estimate that image-processing takes 13 milliseconds, faster than you can read this sentence.[35]

Thirdly, education plays a role. In the 1920s, psychologists proposed three types of learning: visual, auditory and kinaesthetic. The majority of people learn through visual images and pictures, some learn by listening while a tiny minority learn from hands-on activities.

Despite listening being a critical skill to sustain the average livelihood and business, it's a crater-sized curriculum gap. So too is understanding of human behaviour. As Elon Musk tweeted, cognitive biases "should be taught to all at a young age."

School programmes emphasise reading books rather than reading behaviour. Teachers emphasise listening to conversations rather than interpreting motivations. Teachers reward students who echo their views and memorise text rather than thinking independently. So children learn others' tunes rather than create their own.

Leaders emphasise listening to customers, shareholders and the market, then tune out disagreeable comments, irritating naysayers and inconvenient regulators, not to mention discordant or criticising voices.

We tune in to voices with which we feel in tune. We tune out voices with which we feel out of tune.

We can learn much about hard-core listening from musicians. Consider Japanese educator Shinichi Suzuki, who taught music through intense listening rather than traditional sheet reading. Since the 1950s, thousands of violinists have learned the Suzuki method of small steps, repetition, interpretation and memorisation.

At seven, Mozart could name a musical note on hearing it. Listening was his judgement superpower. It can be yours.

Despite our ability to make sound judgements through careful listening and reinterpretation, visual dominance leads us to tune out important information and contributes to psychological deaf spots.

Another external factor that misdirects our judgement is the modern polarised world reflected in fractured politics, religion and even sport. It triggers us to think in polarised and binary ways.

4. A POLARISED WORLD: THEM 'N' US

An ancient parable tells how a farmer lost his horse. The neighbours commiserated, "That's too bad." And the farmer replied, "Is it good or bad? It's hard to say."

A few days later, the horse returned with seven other horses. Delighted neighbours said: "That's great!" But the farmer just shrugged, commenting, "Is it good or bad? It's hard to say."

The next day, the farmer's son rode one of the new horses but fell and broke his leg. Neighbours sympathised, "That's hard luck." Again, the farmer just shrugged.

A week later, army officers knocked on village doors to draft young men. Seeing the son's broken leg, they moved on. Neighbours gasped, "How lucky is your son!" And the farmer replied, "Is it good or bad? It's hard to say."

We think in polarised ways.

In September 2022, the relatively unknown Liz Truss succeeded Boris Johnson as British prime minister. Two days later, Queen Elizabeth II passed. Leapfrogged into the global spotlight, Truss acquired an audience of billions. Her inaugural speech reflected a commitment to growth, "I will take action… I am determined to deliver."[36] And therein lay the problem.

Within a week, Truss revealed a budget rebuked as an economic flop. With Thatcherite conviction, Truss rammed home an aggressive policy, ignoring the appeals of the International Monetary Fund. To ministers, she appeared "invincible."[37] With polarised thinking, she refused to hear the voice of common sense. This policy crashed the mortgage market, sank sterling and forced a £65bn Bank of England bailout.

This rush to communicate and failure to secure party buy-in were expensive rookie errors. Truss lost perspective about her mandate to lead 67 million citizens. Several biases contributed. The *Financial Times* called her binary mantra "Go big or go home."[38] In effect, the public sent her home. She lasted 44 days in office.

The great divide: binary judgements

Like the farmer, we reduce choices to 'either/or' conditions. Is a policy good or bad, right or wrong, positive or negative? Will I visit Rome or Paris on holidays? Choices are narrowly, if wrongly, positioned as win or lose.

Binary classifications are embedded in tiered systems and structures. Marketeers segment customers into Gen X, Y or Z personas. Colleagues are sporty or academic, introverts or extroverts, high or low potential. Markets are regulated or unregulated, labour is skilled or unskilled. Even milk is low-fat or full-fat.

Shakespeare's Hamlet said, "There is nothing either good or bad but thinking makes it so." This dichotomised thinking negates nuance. Not everything fits into a neat box as preferences are fluid.

While one-dimensional classifications make sense, if our world is punctuated with oversimplified categories, segments or choices, it prohibits lateral thinking. For example, rigid categories in the popular five-point employee performance rating system can deter lazy managers from considering 360° feedback. What about extenuating circumstances? Talent gets overlooked, stripping firms of its intellectual capital.

Sometimes polarisation is strategically used to boost organisational or social compliance. For instance, after 9/11, George W. Bush wanted to bind the country against a common enemy. He announced, "You're either with us or you're with the terrorists." It's a *false dichotomy*. A binary mindset creates the impression of all-or-nothing situations. A binary mindset shrinks perspective.

The world isn't two-dimensional. Fixed mindsets fuel dangerous religious, sporting or political division. The problem compounds with a "take it or leave it" attitude. Liz Truss convincingly demonstrated how perspective gets annihilated with goal-focused rigidity and an unwillingness to reflect or course correct.

Reluctance to reflect

In the King's College London attention study, 47% of respondents claimed 'deep thinking' had become a thing of the past.[39] It's understandable. Thinking is exhausting. It's why most people prefer the immediacy of quick decisions over the intensity of deliberation.

"Thinking is to humans as swimming is to cats; they can do it but they'd prefer not to," said Daniel Kahneman.[40] He's not wrong.

Reluctance is understandable in a noisy world as physical and mental capacities deplete. It's the *fatigue effect*. Ironically, we like being active and busy.

Beware of extremes! One study found 64% of male participants preferred to self-administer a mild electric shock than stay idle for 15 minutes.[41] One outlier administered 190 shocks.

Even in football, goalkeepers dive to save penalties. It's our *action bias*. We want to do stuff.

Apparently, inaction reduces happiness. Dr Matthew

Killingsworth and Harvard's Professor Dan Gilbert used a smartphone to test self-reported happiness. In a paper of the same name, they determined that "a wandering mind is an unhappy mind."[42]

The judgement challenge is that when we're active, we're not listening, reinterpreting what we hear or asking "What's missing?"

Even when we are listening, tests show we only hear at 25% efficiency.[43] That's a 75% gap.

Why does this happen when we genuinely want to hear others? Again, neuroscience provides an answer. Our brains process data four times quicker than the fastest talker. It's hard to keep up.

On balance, a visual, data-overloaded and distracting world leads us to think in narrower ways than we should – scrolling, skimming or summarising at speed. As a result, we hear less of what matters.

But we can tune in.

When you ask a question, how long do you wait before jumping in? Teachers typically wait less than a second. Some even less if they're impatient!

Educator Mary Budd Rowe explored whether longer pauses would improve children's response quality. It turns out a three-second pause generated between three and seven times more reflection. What's more, it generated a greater willingness to listen and apply critical thinking.[44]

The lesson? Every second of interpretation counts.

In the 1970s, Alvin Toffler's *Future Shock* predicted the human defence mechanism would be to "simplify the world in a way that confirmed our biases." He was right. To understand the world, we simplify complex matters and generalise from small samples.

A range of psychological mind bugs act as judgement killers and stop you from hearing the voice of rationality. To counter the trilogy of error, we must filter what matters. That's the focus of the following chapter.

ıılıı|ıılı **THE DECISION NINJA** ıılıı|ıılı

WHAT TO REMEMBER

- Being smart is not about who or what you know, it's about how you think.
- Context shapes how we judge situations, strangers and strategies. Modern life doesn't help us hear what really matters. It provides excuses to tune out.
- Context combines with cognition to make us think, hear and act in binary, biased and bounded ways.
- Four inter-related factors amplify risk of misjudgement:
  1. A fast-paced world. Speed is not only accelerating short-term thinking but shredding and shrinking attention.
  2. A data-deluged world. With too many voices and distractions, it's hard to detect the signal from the noise.
  3. A polarised world. People judge with a binary lens. The world is nuanced, not one- or two-dimensional. The most intelligent interpretation is in 3D.
  4. A visual world. We rely on what we see not what we hear. Neuroscience, physics, education and digitisation explain why.
- Humans dislike constant reflection, preferring handy shortcuts. Every extra second of reflection counters decision risk.
- Algorithms are no substitute for human judgement which is now at an all-time premium.
- Society demands we hear all voices. In a remote-controlled high-speed world, all voices are not equal in every situation either.
- The trick is to hear selectively the voices that matter and filter the useful from the useless.

CHAPTER 2

JUDGEMENT KILLERS: BLIND SPOTS, DEAF SPOTS AND DUMB SPOTS

"Of all the ways of defining man, the worst is the one which makes him out to be a rational animal."

Anatole France

IN GREEK MYTHOLOGY, when Cassandra rejected the God Apollo, he cursed her gift of prophecy by ensuring she was disbelieved when telling the truth. At times, we're all like Cassandra, screaming into a void where no one is listening.

Leaders at Rampart Investment Management told a financial specialist to replicate the stellar results generated on the 17th floor of New York's Lipstick Building. It was 1999. Within five minutes Harry Markopolos knew Bernie Madoff's numbers were illogical and discovered the biggest Ponzi scheme in history. He claims it took just under four hours to mathematically prove fraud.[1]

Interpretation was in his DNA. According to his mother, he used to tell teachers that he had the right answers, but they had the wrong questions.

In *No-one Would Listen*, Markopolos tells how he flagged

suspicions about these phantom returns to the Securities and Exchange Commission (SEC). He was ignored for nine years. He also informed the *Wall Street Journal* but the story was deprioritised and defanged. It later described him as "a little bit nuts."[2]

When Madoff allegedly managed $6bn in assets, "three times more than any known hedge fund," the market's lack of response was a glaring signal something wasn't right. Wall Street's well-remunerated investors replaced the voice of common sense with the voice of greed. They rationalised these Houdini results as "perfect market timing."

Markopolos told the *Guardian* newspaper, "The risk-return ratios had never been seen in human recorded history."[3] For Madoff's strategy to be real, he would have had to have had more options on the Chicago Board Options Exchange than existed.

Based on 14 years of data, Markopolos compiled 29 red flags to substantiate his case. In 2005, he sent a 21-page memo to the SEC in Boston called 'The World's Largest Hedge Fund is a Fraud.' Boston passed it to New York. In 2007, the SEC interviewed Madoff and his primary hedge fund investor, Fairfield Greenwich Group but "found no evidence of fraud." The regulator believed the voice of an industry titan over a self-professed nerdy geek.

Nobody heard what mattered when it mattered.

A year later, the $65bn Ponzi scheme collapsed. Millions of investors lost their life savings. Markopolos told his story to the US House of Representatives in 2009.[4] This time, his voice was heard.

Was tuning out caused by context, cognition or a combination?

The previous chapter reveals how external context derails judgement. This chapter explores how internal mindset can compromise judgement. Any scandal you read about or decision dilemma you face can be traced to a suite of biases which either accelerate or decelerate a rush to misjudgement.

You've likely heard of bias blind spots but perhaps are less familiar with deaf spots or even dumb spots. In 1969, to help therapists interpret behaviour and improve decision-making, psychoanalyst Rudolf Ekstein recommended integrating observations from what therapists saw and heard with what patients said. He categorised these as follows:[5]

- blind spots (inability to see a problem)
- deaf spots (inability to hear accurately)
- dumb spots (inability to speak wisely)

Each of these psychological phenomena cause us to misjudge what we see, hear and say.

I call this the *trilogy of error*, illustrated below.

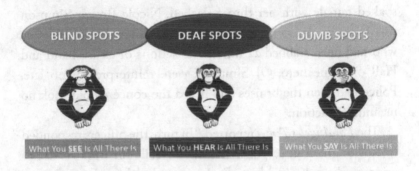

This trilogy is a potential source of misinformation that affects how we think. It reminds me of the 16th century Japanese maxim "See no evil, hear no evil and speak no evil." Rather than adhering to a one-dimensional or two-dimensional view, Ekstein's 3D perspective is central to sound judgement.

In this chapter, I explore the nature of this trilogy and illustrate how deaf spots lead to a reservoir of material errors, from wrongful convictions to CV inflation, scams, cheating, missed FBI warnings and pilot error.

The message is simple. What you see is not all there is, what you hear is not all there is, and what you say is not all there is.

Like the SEC, the smartest leaders and powerholders are subject to blind spots, seeing only what they want. Let's start there.

BLIND SPOTS: WHAT YOU *SEE* IS NOT ALL THERE IS

A stunning 34-year-old model in Brentwood told police, family and friends that she feared her ex-husband's violent rages. On New Year's Day in 1989, she made a frantic 911 call to the Los Angeles Police Department. When officers arrived, she was in the garden dressed in sweatpants and bra crying, "He's going to kill me!"[6] Against protocol, officers didn't arrest her husband.

Five years later, on 12 June 1994, officers discovered a blood-soaked female with her throat slashed. Nicole Brown Simpson was lying in the same garden beside a waiter, Ron Goldman, who had been stabbed 22 times. The actions of ex-husband and Hall of Fame hero, OJ Simpson, were reinterpreted too late. Police had seen the bruises and heard the concerns but took no meaningful action.

The *Los Angeles Times* reported, "In turn, the officers responded to Rockingham in response to Nicole's calls for help 7–8 times prior to the 1989 incident. Each time, the defendant was not arrested and no report was taken."[7] A history of fraternising, back-scratching and celebrity-worshipping existed within the police force. Officers heard but didn't hear, bounded by Simpson's celebrity aura.

Blind spots aren't new. The American Psychological Association defines them as "a lack of insight or awareness about a specific area of behaviour or personality." Because recognising feelings or motives can be painful, blind spots defend "against recognition of repressed impulses or memories."[8]

In my work with the Innocence Project, I've been privileged and humbled to meet wrongfully convicted exonerees. In 2001, Termaine Hicks stumbled across a woman who had been raped in an alley. When reaching for his phone to dial for help, Pennsylvania police arrived. They shot him in the back three times, assuming he was retrieving a gun. The victim didn't pinpoint Hicks as the rapist, but officers did, guilty of binary thinking.

Unlike their attitude towards wealthy Simpson, did officers associate an ordinary man of colour with crime? Did they rush to premature judgement and think Hicks guilty or worry they had just shot an unarmed black man?

Hicks spent 19 long, wasted years in prison.[9] After a legal battle, he was exonerated. I heard him speak about the day he learned of a successful appeal. It was utterly moving.

Somebody heard me. It was like a message in a bottle to someone stranded on an island.

Speaking with poise not poison about his exoneration, "You don't know how to relax after you've been fighting so long." When binary thinking is taken to extremes, polarisation can spark hate crimes and discrimination. We'll return to this later.

Psychologist Emily Pronin suggests that understanding bias helps explain behaviour.[10] We interpret situations based on personality and beliefs but also based on culture, context and companions.

Nobel prize-winning economist Richard Thaler points to the concept of "supposedly irrelevant factors."[11] He argues irrational factors like social norms, mood, weather or framing influence behaviour. For example, you may critique others' work more harshly because you're hungry or not save for a rainy day because it's sunny. These influences seem irrelevant but they're not.

Some people are bias-deniers. You might be too? In fact, 90% of people think they're less susceptible to bias than the average person.[12] And 71% of forensic scientists feel the same.[13]

Former Chairman of KPMG UK Bill Michael told employees there was "no such thing as unconscious bias." The idea was "complete and utter crap." He was later fired for telling pandemic-stressed staff to "stop moaning."[14] I guess it's easier to point to a disrupted supply-chain or digital process than a disrupted mental state. It's also easier to self-delude.

Despite decades of evidence validating the existence of biases, those same biases prevent people from noticing or accepting them. It's the *paradox of bias*. How can you curtail what you don't notice?

There's no algorithm or app for ensuring unbiased judgement. If there were, the lucky developer's share price would rock the stock market!

Being smart or senior is no guarantee you'll tune in to the voices that matter, interpret data accurately or avoid sources of inattentional blindness. However, doing so might just save your career.

Inattentional blindness

In a stimuli-saturated world where attention is limited, the propensity to stereotype and be side-tracked is enormous. The irony is we're too busy to notice what's useful or important, so we stick to what we know and take it as truth.

Kahneman coins this 'what-you-*see*-is-all-there-is' or WYSIATI.[15] In other words, you think your view is accurate, but it's narrowly limited to what you know which is based on what you perceive or experience. It's consistent with Simon's idea of bounded rationality.

If you pay maximum attention to what's in front of you, you miss additional details. It's like seeing Graceland but not the pink Cadillac in the driveway. It's like seeing the tree but not the forest. It's a form of *inattentional blindness* caused by over-focus on a detail. I first learned about this on an Executive course with an unforgettable experiment by Harvard's Dan Simons and Chris Chabris.

You might want to try it first at www.invisiblegorilla.com. There's one chance in this test.

The class was shown a video of two teams passing a basketball – one wore black t-shirts, the other white t-shirts. Our task was to count the basketball passes by the team wearing white. No skill was required, just observation. I counted six – the number was apparently irrelevant.

I was so busy counting I didn't spot a student dressed in a black gorilla suit walk between the players and thump its chest for nine seconds. Seriously!

The lecturer asked what we had seen online. Most said nothing. What gorilla? The cynics (me!) needed a video replay. There it was.[16] The experiment exemplifies what we miss when over-concentrating.

I've since noticed this in simple ways, like playing Connect Four with my husband during lockdown. The sole purpose of the game is to form four coloured lines, red or blue. Fixating on your blue line strategy stops you from spotting your opponent's red line moving towards victory. The loser's excuse!

This inattentional blindness is evident in more than just games.

During World War II, the British press covered the exploits of RAF test pilot John "Cats Eyes" Cunningham who displayed an exceptional track record of destroying enemy aircraft at night. Media splashed pictures of him wearing sunglasses indoors and regaled tales of obsessive carrot-eating to explain his gifted nocturnal vision. It was a deliberate distraction. Cunningham's aircraft was carrying new airborne interception radar. The Germans never suspected, believing what they saw.

Building on Kahneman's concept, I suggest 'what-you-*hear*-is-NOT-all-there-is.' This emphasises deaf spots rather than blind spots. We're confident based on what we think we hear. Deaf spots cause us to tune out valuable data points, motives, cues, trends, labels and signals.

These psychological deaf spots "spoil our ability to observe and comprehend what stands contrary to our convictions," according to HR expert Paul Kaponya.[17]

In other words, there's always another interpretation.

DEAF SPOTS: WHAT YOU *HEAR* IS NOT ALL THERE IS

A Bing Crosby study captures the concept of 'what-you-*hear*-is-NOT-all-there-is' well.[18] Dutch researchers told participants that a recording of white noise contained segments of the classic song 'White Christmas,' and to press a button when they heard it. The recording contained no such music. Yet a third of those listening pressed the button each time.

Why? They expected to hear it. Susceptibility to mild hallucinations is common under stress, symptomatic of a modern noisy world.

What we hear is not always reality. And we can't always trust what we hear. Yet we do.

Sometimes the truth is within earshot and unheard. Chris Tarrant, veteran host of the *Who Wants to Be a Millionaire* quiz show, sat next to intense contestant Major Charles Ingram. After 15 questions, Ingram won the £1m jackpot. Instead of being super happy and popping champagne corks, he was overheard having a massive row backstage with his wife. A suspicious production team later analysed the audio tapes. Ingram had cheated. His wife and another contestant coughed when hearing the right answer.

Like I missed the gorilla, Tarrant missed what was literally within earshot.

Inattentional deafness

A first cousin of inattentional blindness is *inattentional deafness*.[19] While academics have linked inattentional deafness to high workload, the principle is broader. You don't hear something because your attention is fixed. A University College London report suggests our visual focus renders us 'deaf' because sound and vision share limited neural resources.[20] For example, you mightn't hear the phone ring if you're reading. Or Ryanair's last call if you're duty-free shopping.

This overfocus is dangerous if you're a surgeon oblivious to beeping monitors or a distracted bus driver unaware of wailing sirens or horns.

In a visual world, fire alarms, cries for help, microwave pings and barking dogs fade into the background. It's why TV producers blast adverts at higher decibels than normal to jolt the viewer and capture their attention.

Inattentional deafness is closely related to psychological deaf spots and insensitivity to listening.

Sometimes, we tune out deliberately. We switch off braggers and bores, complainers and critics, those who shout, threaten or lecture us. We tune out bad news, dull speakers, safety demonstrations, conflicting advice, nagging partners and whining customers.

But tuning in selectively and strategically is in our best interests. The bragger can alert you to a hot trend, the boring speaker may have a cure for cancer. Even a whining customer can destroy your reputation on social media.

Behaving against our best interests isn't new. Over 2,500 years before iPads, iPhones or iRobots, Plato referred to our poor self-control as "akrasia."[21] The trick is to listen selectively and strategically to the right voices.

·ıll|ı·|ııl|ı·|ıl|ı·

Inattentional deafness carries criminal, corporate and commercial consequences. In the 1970s, two inventors, a Belgian Count and his Italian associate, approached executives at Elf Aquitaine, the state-owned French petroleum firm. They claimed a revolutionary way to detect oil beneath the ocean. Without proprietary crude oil supply, Elf was under massive commercial pressure. Banning scientists from meetings for patent protection reasons, the innovators demonstrated aircraft that would 'sniff' oil from the ground, eliminating a capital-intensive extraction process.

Contracts were signed. Over four years, the government invested nearly $200m in this top-secret project.[22]

But it was a hoax.

Tests failed and no oil was ever located. Elf Aquitaine leaders likely anticipated the glory of strategic rescue and resurgent profitability rather than applying the sensible sniff test.

Few of us challenge ready-made solutions when uncertain or under pressure, consistent with the PERIMETERS Effect. It's easier to accept convenient answers.

Misjudgement happens subliminally. Common hearing-related biases prompt us to tune in or out of voices, from conscience to the crowd, from scammers to idols.

Several biases accelerate deaf ear syndrome, especially when fuelled by emotion. For instance, we hear what we hope is true (wishful hearing); deny what we find unpalatable (ostrich effect); and accept or reject messages based on feelings about the messenger (messenger effect). We'll discuss these more in Chapter 11.

Two pervasive biases that always accelerate deaf spots and are worth exploring are *default to truth* and *confirmation bias.*

DEFAULT TO TRUTH: BELIEVING WHAT YOU HEAR

Sometimes the most obvious remarks are taken at face value.

If your partner says, "It's not working out," is this a warning or a relationship death knell? How often do you reinterpret someone consistently staying late at the office? Are they disorganised, brown-nosing, ambitious, being unfaithful or avoiding going home? If your boss suggests "getting to know your direct reports," are they being diligent, digging into your performance or calculating your exit? Is the neighbour who never speaks to you odd, introverted or in a witness protection programme?

Hidden motives are rampant in business and what you hear is rarely all there is.

Alternative interpretations matter. Reinterpreting seemingly innocuous statements is just smart and streetwise, but neglected.

So why do we default to believing others? Is it apathy, ignorance or convenience?

Tim Levine researched deception for two decades and explains our instinct to suppress doubt or anomalies as *truth-default theory.* He argues that we're truth-biased and fail to imagine the worst-case scenarios. It's why jurors struggle to convict parents of killing their own children. It's why intimate-partner murders are reduced to 'crimes of passion' rather than premeditated intent. The thought is inconceivable. It's what academics term the 'domestic discount.'

Assuming wholesale honesty makes us vulnerable to deception and deaf spots, whether fake CVs, contrived illness or research based on falsified data. Even decorated professors experience deaf spots.

A 2012 study concluded that signing official forms at the top rather than the bottom improved honesty by 10.25%. Like pledges, it primed the signer's honour code and claimed to reduce likelihood to cheat.

This insight was based on several studies, one using car insurance data. Written by five luminaries from Harvard and Duke University, it was academic nirvana and a sexy marketing finding. Governments and organisations applied this widely cited insight.

In 2020, independent researchers concluded this popularised finding didn't replicate due to a randomisation failure – an embarrassing dilemma.

What to do? The 2012 authors disagreed about whether to recall the article or not. One author, Professor Max Bazerman, wanted a recall but was outvoted. In his book *Complicit*, he tells how he queried the car insurance data, and although he heard ambiguous answers, he defaulted to truth and moved on.

In August 2021, a sensational blog proved the car insurance data was doctored. Ironically, a paper testing the effect of honesty was fraudulent.

Fingers pointed at the car study lead, Duke professor and author about dishonesty Dan Ariely, who had once written, "We cheat up to the level that allows us to retain our self-image as reasonably honest individuals."[23] He denies any wrongdoing.

Bazerman blames himself.

I suspected the data was problematic and shared my suspicions with my co-authors. I took their answers at face value and believed them when I should have continued to demand better answers.

Bazerman shouldn't feel bad. Don't we accept things at face value every day? Analysis of 206 studies with 24,483 judges indicates people spot deception just over half of the time.

Ironically, within a year, another 2012 author was accused of data falsification and removed from her distinguished post. Despite the pressures of the publish-or-perish academic environment, second-order questioning is an essential default for robust and replicable research.

The reality is that most humans are poor lie-detectors. Ask many a betrayed partner!

What you hear is never all there is

Bernie Madoff says if regulators had contacted counterparties, they "would've seen it."[24] He was shocked nobody questioned his judgement. Not getting caught was "amazing to me... it never entered the SEC's mind that it was a Ponzi scheme."

Spin doctors spin. Employees brown-nose. Ladder-climbers exaggerate. Psychics believe they commune with the dead. The problem is smart people tend to trust more than most. That makes them more vulnerable to scams, identity theft and immoral persuasion.

Do you spot lies? Are you too trusting? Or always falling for April fools' jokes?

Naturally, deception is more likely in a noisy world if you're too exhausted to tune in and decode data.

It's easy to tune in to someone we like, respect or find funny. It's harder to spot a placatory boss, predatory paedophile, deceptive date or smooth-talking candidate.

For instance, even head-hunters struggle to decode candidates' answers. Part of this is explained by the *halo effect*. *Fortune Magazine* uncovered multiple high-powered CEOs with embellished CVs.[25] Billionaire David Geffen justified fabricating his UCLA graduation to get a mailroom role in talent agency William Morris. "It's an idiotic thing that you have to be a college graduate to be an agent... Did I have a problem with lying to get the job? None whatsoever."

It's not just academics, head-hunters and voters who are gullible. PR executive and Prince Edward's then fiancé, the Duchess of Edinburgh, was embroiled in a *News of the World* sting with a fake Saudi prince. Recorded bad-mouthing politicians, criticising tax policies and potentially exploiting royal connections, this entrapment forced her resignation and "much regret" for her "own misjudgement."[26] What you hear is not all there is.

Moreover, trusting doctors get fooled by what they see and hear. Consider caretakers with Munchausen syndrome by proxy who fake the illnesses of those in their charge. Lisa Hayden Johnson's son wasn't sick. Yet she fabricated stories and TV appearances, even earning him a Children of Courage Award from former British prime minister Tony Blair.

What you hear is rarely all there is. If patterns appear suspicious, they usually are. Even when patterns don't appear suspicious, they might be!

Without being perpetually paranoid, every second of interpretation counts, especially from those we trust or admire.

·ıl|ı·|ıı|ı·|ıl|ı·

Secret Service analysis reveals that in 31 out of 37 cases, school shooters share their plans with at least one person in advance.[27] Even highly trained professionals miss signals. Concerned citizens tipped off the FBI about Nicholas Cruz's violent behaviour yet they failed to investigate. Seventeen deaths followed in Florida's Parkland massacre on Valentine's Day in 2018.

In other cases, romantic partners are pre-warned. Take Washington-based 15-year-old Jaylen Fryberg who shot four classmates in the head over lunch. He had previously sent photos and messages to his ex-girlfriend. "Just please talk me out of this and the guns in my hand."

Ghosted, he replied, "Ok, well don't bother coming to my funeral."

Fryberg continued the next day, "I set the date. Hopefully you regret not talking to me… You have no idea what I'm talking about. But you will… Bang bang I'm dead."[28] He then shot himself.

We don't believe extreme claims will materialise in truth-default theory.

In the stress-filled workplace, it's easy to miss cues. A construction boss instructed two employees to dig trenches under his Chicago house. Sounds reasonable. Or does it? The workers prepared the site and spread lime to avoid a rancid smell.

For what? They never asked. The boss never explained.

In this crawlspace, serial killer John Wayne Gacy had buried 29 bodies. Gacy remarked, "If they didn't know what was down there, they were stupid."[29] The employees accepted instructions at face value, even after Gacy gifted them their missing colleague's car. They were *inattentionally deaf*.

There's hope for the easily deceived. Police officers and investigators trained in deception detection manage to reach 60–80% efficacy.[30] Instead of second-guessing or pursuing suspicions, we must consciously stop seeking supporting data to confirm our views. This leads to the mother of all biases: confirmation bias.

CONFIRMATION BIAS: VALIDATING WHAT YOU HEAR

Novelist Michael Peterson was accused of killing his wife Kathleen in 2001. She was discovered with gruesome scalp injuries at the bottom of the stairs in their North Carolina home. Peterson believed "trying to convince others of my innocence is a waste of time."[31] He was right, referring to confirmation bias. This justified him taking the Alford Plea which acknowledges overwhelming evidence but maintains innocence.

So what is confirmation bias?

Like first impressions, first conclusions take root. An idea enters your mind and happily lodges. As cognitive misers, we don't want to think too much, so we filter subsequent information to justify those beliefs, whether about politics, competitors, sport, markets or candidates. It helps that we retrieve supporting arguments more easily than opposing arguments.

Any change of position is unlikely. Who wants to look weak, stupid or wrong? Not us. Consequently, projects overrun, markets crash, competitors crater and bad chairs oversee boards. In extreme cases, war results, whether between Ukraine and Russia or in the Middle East.

This psychological glitch is prevalent not just in war rooms but operating rooms, boardrooms, newsrooms, chatrooms, classrooms and courtrooms.

In one study, 89% of jurors claimed to discuss facts in-depth, respect fellow jurors and listen acutely to evidence. Yet in separate research, only 24% of jurors changed their minds during trials which can last weeks or months.[32] That's a lot of evidence. Yet 76% of jurors stick to their intuition, unaware of the power of early opinion formation on subsequent information processing.

Might this explain short jury deliberation times? For instance, it took Peterson's jury four days to reach a verdict whereas it took the OJ Simpson jury just four hours. If you're interested, the Guinness World Record is one minute to acquit a New Zealand cannabis grower!

Of course, it could be argued that jurors discuss details in depth, listen to evidence and still maintain their original position. However, it's more likely confirmation bias is at play and jurors unconsciously use courtroom evidence to confirm their guilt or innocence hypothesis rather than weighing data objectively on its merit. People are no more capable of suspending judgement indefinitely than they are of suspending balls in the air.

Consider the case of 18-year-old British babysitter Louise Woodward.

Rationalising what you hear

Woodward was charged with the second-degree murder of eight-month-old Matthew Eappen. Her lawyer, Innocence Project founder and former OJ Simpson attorney Barry Scheck, pursued a defence strategy of guilty or not guilty. In effect, that strategy removed the manslaughter option.

During a sensationalist trial in Massachusetts, Woodward appeared as a vilified Brit who giggled inappropriately on the stand. Her casual demeanour didn't help jury objectivity.

Dr Patrick Barnes testified that Eappen's death resulted from the 'classic model' of shaken baby syndrome rather than from previous injuries. Human rights lawyer Clive Stafford Smith disputed the theory. "It's based on a 1972 hypothesis... by British neurologist Norman Guthkelch... with no factual basis."[33] Neverthless, Woodward was sentenced to 15 years.

Woodward was later declared innocent. On appeal, Judge Hiller Zobel interpreted the facts with a fresh ear. She heard something others didn't: "The circumstances in which the defendant acted were characterised by confusion, inexperience, frustration, immaturity and some anger, but not malice."

Zobel reduced the verdict to involuntary manslaughter. Barnes later regretted his mental rigidity, admitting "Because we were biased by the triad representing shaken baby syndrome, we would not believe the (other) story."

This case echoes the 2007 kangaroo court of Seattle student Amanda Knox. When an Italian jury convicted her of 21-year-old Meredith Kercher's murder in Perugia, conviction was based on circumstantial evidence, furtive romantic exchanges and stories of sexual depravity. There was little jury consideration of inference, innuendo or inconsistent argument, just an abundance of overconfidence, stereotyping and the illusion of truth.

We're obsessed by what we haven't got but not by what we don't know.

If we don't update beliefs with new evidence, ingrained reasoning goes unchecked. You accept what prosecutors, preachers, neighbours or bosses tell you, especially when it's convenient and what you want to hear. This is a problem at scale when it contaminates organisational decision-making.

The stubborn organisational mind

Confirmation bias is rife at every level. Scientists and academics select research to prove their hypotheses right rather than prove them wrong – or even find out what might be wrong. It's a default mindset. High-ranking executives are often deeply intransigent in their views. You might know a few! I certainly do.

Consider Marissa Mayer, former CEO of Yahoo. Yahoo acquired 53 technology-based entities over her 2012–2017 tenure. And 52 failed.

When should your conviction be reconsidered?

Yahoo's misjudgement dates back to 1998 when they rejected buying Google for $1bn. Imagine! In 2002, Yahoo offered $3bn but Google demanded $5bn.

Four years later, Yahoo tendered $1bn for Facebook. An insulted Mark Zuckerberg terminated discussions when Yahoo lowered the price. In 2008, Microsoft offered $44.6bn to buy Yahoo, but were refused. In 2017 as Mayer moved on, Yahoo was sold to Verizon for ten times less at a mere $4.5bn.[34]

When we hear evidence that confirms our mental model, why bend beliefs? If you think a partner is unfaithful, every furtive gesture confirms it. If you think property prices will rise, why prepare for a crash? The internet provides ample evidence to support every opinion. Smart people also find compelling reasons quicker.

In 1993, Tony Blair believed evidence about Iraqi weapons of mass destruction, and stood shoulder-to-shoulder with the US in the "hardest, most momentous, most agonising" decision of his life.

Responding to Iraqi war inquiry criticisms, he said, "I express more sorrow, regret and apology than you can ever believe."[35] However, in the next breath, he justified this as "not the wrong decision."

Conspiracy theorists, Holocaust deniers and propagandists exhibit extreme confirmation bias.

In another example, radio host Alex Jones announced the 2012 Sandy Hook school shooting massacre was a hoax, despite its 26 victims. Technology helped spread misinformation as YouTube recommended his InfoWars website videos 15 billion times.[36] Vilification continued for a decade as parents were branded "crisis actors" and their children's graves desecrated.

Jones was ordered to pay $1bn compensation.[37] He blamed his mental "psychosis" yet professed "I'm done saying I'm sorry."

There's an audience for every 'crazy' story. It's a stark reminder that you can't trust all you hear.

˙ı||ı˙|ıı|ı˙|ıı|ı˙

A useful tip is that listening influences up to 40% of performance.[38] If you're known as a good listener, you're generally ranked as a good leader. In the 1957 classic book *Are You Listening?* Ralph Nicholls estimated 40% of the average person's job relates to listening, up to 80% for senior leaders.

Tuning in dictates our salary yet we tune out. Why?

Confirmation bias and default to truth are deaf spots that keep us tone-deaf in a zone of misinformation, preventing any change of mind. No one is immune – bankers or builders, baristas or bartenders, milliners or millionaires.

Try noticing this prevalence with your family or colleagues. You'll be surprised.

These blind spots and deaf spots don't work in isolation on our judgement but rather in a trilogy of error. The third phenomenon is the psychological dumb spot. In other words, if people choose to self-silence, you can't hear their voices. This renders both the messenger and the recipient subject to misinformation and lacking the big picture – discussed next.

DUMB SPOTS: WHAT YOU *SAY* IS NOT ALL THERE IS

A 15th century English proverb pervaded my childhood: "Children should be seen and not heard." While it wasn't something my four sisters or I ever subscribed to, such a saying would be unheard of in today's activist era of self-expression. But these lay the groundwork for psychological deaf spots, the inability or unwillingness to speak out, as described by Ekstein.

You can lose your voice anywhere – workplace, pub, club, gym or confessional.

A religious affair

Thousands of innocent children abused by Catholic priests self-silenced or were silenced and intimidated by authority figures. For those unaffected, it's hard to understand how parents didn't spot warning signs or why victims didn't speak out until years later.

But context is everything.

For decades in Catholic Ireland, priests were not just symbolic figures but semi-deities. Religious orders ran primary schools, hospices, boarding schools and nursing homes. The parish priest was placed on an apostolic pedestal – a revered, God-infused figure of humanity. Influencing government policy, the Church forbade abortion, divorce, gay marriage and contraception. At this time, it was a sin for a single woman to be at a dance after midnight. And women were seen as God's procreation vessels. That explains my granny's 12 sisters!

A parish priest's home visit was interpreted as a royal visit. The best cutlery was polished, the house sparkled and sanitised, the Cadbury's chocolate fingers served on doily-decorated plates. Mothers donned their best dresses as children sat angelically. The vow of poverty meant Father Joe lived frugally until offered "a little something" by his adoring parishioners – and it wasn't always Jameson whiskey!

The vow of celibacy forbids sexual activity which is why, in 1992, Irish parishioners were shocked when Bishop Eamonn Casey fathered a child. This indiscretion was the tip of the iceberg. Over time, stories of archbishop cover-ups circulated as hundreds of adults revealed childhood abuse. I met one teenage girl who was abused by five priests and paid 8,000 euro to "get herself some therapy." She used it to buy a Morris Minor car for her children instead.

A culture of conformity became ingrained. Voices were repressed as a deaf ear was turned to the truth. Even Vatican novitiates were advised to "hear a lot, see everything and say nothing."[39] Extensive bystanding was normalised as protected priests were transferred across parishes in misguided loyalty. Regardless, loyal Catholics still attended 9 o'clock Sunday mass.

Yet this was like putting a lid on a boiling kettle.

Some public figures used their position to agitate change. In 1992, singer-songwriter Sinéad O'Connor ripped up a picture of Pope John Paul II, frustrated at the denial of Catholic abuse. Conservative Ireland wasn't ready to hear the truth. Vilified, threatened and ridiculed for sacrilege, today she would have been feted for courage and fortitude. Fellow musicians said, "She was harassed simply for being herself."[40]

Wanting to be heard, she has been. It's a pity that sometimes, we're heard more in death than in life. Within days of her death, *Billboard* reports her music streaming rose 2,885%.

The sound of silence

People stay silent in various ways. Take the cowardly practice of ghosting candidates, colleagues or dates. Ignoring emails or calls is not only unprofessional but often backfires on the ghost.

Dumb spots proliferate where employees maintain silence or conceal misconduct.

In my whistleblowing research, following exposure to a hypothetical bullying scenario, 91% of outraged employees announced their intention to speak up. Minutes later, only 9% clicked a whistleblowing website for instructions.[41]

I identified dozens of complex situational, dispositional, cultural and organisational reasons why employees stay silent, even though it harms many others. It essentially boils down to fear of retribution, low confidence in remedy and desire to avoid censure. Moreover, we react allergically to threatened ego or position.

Radioactive challengers can suffer "dire consequences to careers and lives."[42] Whistleblowers are labelled disloyal, disgruntled and dangerous. An Australian study found that 82% of whistleblowers experienced excessive harassment, 60% lost their jobs, 17% lost their homes and 10% attempted suicide.[43]

Brands profess to want misconduct reported. Do they? Enron's Sherron Watkins expected gratitude for revealing "cultural rot," only to find herself progressively demoted and ostracised.

You can't believe all you hear.

When we witness wrongdoing, do we assume others will intervene? Many do. It's called the *bystander effect*. Penn State University football coach Jerry Sandusky was convicted of 45 counts of abuse with ten boys, excluding his adopted son. When officials learned he was abusing boys, they covered it up. Among others, Penn State President Graham Spanier failed to report wrongdoing. Did he diffuse responsibility or make a self-preserving decision? He lamented, "I deeply regret that I didn't intervene far more carefully."[44]

This misjudgement ruined lives and cost Penn State $60m.

Screaming into a void

Nineteenth-century US statesman Frederick Douglass once cited, "To suppress free speech is a double wrong. It violates the rights of the hearer as well as those of the speaker."[45]

Outspoken citizens in communist countries face severe penalties. In 2020, Ren Zhiqiang criticised President Xi Jinping's pandemic leadership, referring to him as "a bare-naked clown insisting on acting as emperor." Brave! Or foolish? Zhiqiang's voice reverberated across China's 9,562,910 km² landmass. Following allegations of bribery and party violations, he was sentenced to 18 years in prison, labelled "disloyal and dishonest" for "vilifying the image of the party and country."[46]

A year later, former tennis doubles World No.1 Peng Shuai underestimated the effect of her inflammatory 1,600-word Weibo post that accused retired vice-premier Zhang Gaoli of sexual assault. Immediately censored, she disappeared.

The tennis industry used its voice to make a statement. International calls for her safety led to withdrawal of the "misunderstanding." Consistent with the International Tennis Federation support, the Women's Tennis Association suspended tournaments in China. Similarly, the US boycotted the 2022 Beijing Olympics. Predictably, Shuai announced her retirement.

It's not just communist countries that repress voice. In the Middle East, despite claims of gender equality, several females from Dubai's royal family have attempted escape, according to the *New Yorker*.[47]

In Britain, Coutts private bank decided to close the account of an outspoken politician whose views were deemed "not compatible" and "pandered to racists." Veteran CEO Alison Rose lost her job and forfeited £7.6m in compensation as a result.

People who tune in build reputations, people who tune out destroy them.

Those who don't speak up are equally complicit in preserving injustice or corrupt leadership.

Inconvenient voices

Speaking up doesn't guarantee being heard, as Markopolos and various whistleblowers in the military, aviation, tobacco and chemical industries learned. Too often, organisations exhibit tone-deafness. Some increasingly use non-disclosure agreements as a silencing tool. Why? The truth is inconvenient and expensive.

In 2011, Boeing faced intense competition from the fuel-efficient Airbus A320neo. In response, they redesigned their Max-737 engine, leading to a software solution that operated under specific conditions, albeit without a fail-safe. Boeing concluded this revision didn't warrant pilot notification or expensive supplemental training. Nevertheless, employees were concerned about test failures, factory conditions and labour shortages.[48]

Concerned employee Ed Pierson warned Boeing leadership and the Federal Aviation Authority (FAA) about the operating environment, "once before the Lion Air crash and again, before the Ethiopian Airlines crash." On one occasion, an FAA employee heard "13 engineers, a project pilot and four managers" express doubts that the new design was fit for purpose. Warnings were ignored as the FAA certified the engine. *Inattentional deafness* and refusal to compromise led to the loss of 346 passenger and crew lives.

You might reasonably ask: is tone-deafness a gender or personality issue? Personality influences whose voice is heard first – usually the extrovert's. But personality doesn't dictate who speaks up. My experimental research confirmed no significant personality differences in likelihood to whistleblow. Similarly with gender, men were no more likely to speak up than women.

These examples represent a tiny fraction of the damage incurred from tuning in to the wrong voices. That said, silence is a strategic tool that can be used for good.

THE CONTAGION OF VOICE

The Dalai Lama believes that "silence is sometimes the best answer." Silence is indeed considered a virtue in some circles. For instance, Buddhist and Trappist monks take obligatory vows of silence. Worshippers fall silent for spiritual prayer. Citizens take a one-minute silence to mark respect. Since 1996, US students have held a Day of Silence to showcase LGBTQ+ voices. And after non-stop Zoom calls or noisy children, most parents yearn for the sound of silence!

In a noisy world, silence allows people to pause and tune in creatively. Beethoven wrote his ninth symphony while deaf, without hearing any notes or interruption from others. Ozan Varol writes:

> The less he could hear, the more original he became. When he became deaf, he couldn't hear the musical fashions of his time so he wasn't influenced by them. With the soundtrack of other musicians tuned out, he fully tuned in.[49]

In business, the savvy salesperson, recruiter or negotiator leverages silence strategically. They know it affords time for candidates or buyers to process offers.

Uncomfortable silence also makes you reveal more than you want. I know a savvy Head of HR who excelled at this. Similarly, Apple's Tim Cook deliberately uses long pauses. Amazon's Jeff Bezos adopts "silent starts" in meetings allowing teams concentration time to study reports.

Voice is contagious and can work for or against you. Within 24 hours of actress Alyssa Milano asking her Twitter and Facebook followers to indicate their exposure to sexual assault or harassment, 45% of US Facebook users registered #MeToo. When Harvey Weinstein's sexual harassment scandal broke, 80 women spoke up.[50] Following the investigation into British DJ and paedophile Sir Jimmy Savile, Metropolitan Police reported that 500 women came forward.[51] Similar effects were seen with actor Bill Cosby, rapper R. Kelly, Fox anchor Bill O'Reilly, USA Gymnastics doctor Larry Nassar, and so on.

Contagion can be misguided too. Over six years, actor Kevin Spacey faced allegations of nine counts of sexual assault. Both UK and US courts found him not guilty. He cried at the verdict. His story reminds me of the false accusations against Cliff Richard for historic sex crimes. This premature rush to judgement also featured in the cancellation and condemnation of Russell Brand long before legal conclusions about wrongdoing were ever ascertained.

Too many people suffer from a public crush to condemn and trial by media.

·ıı|ı·|ıı|ı·|ıı|ı·

Using your voice to challenge the crowd can pay off. The English Football Association (FA) embarked on the £789m Wembley

Stadium in early 2000. With competition for resources, the 330-acre site at Burton-upon-Trent came under threat. The board proposed mothballing the project to its 120 council members. Although council has no formal vote on investment decisions, when two members passionately argued to preserve this site, the board reconsidered.

It's not easy. When you change your mind, you sacrifice the dopamine hit of being right. That hurts your pride. At a cost of £105m, today The FA owns one of the biggest football centres in Europe, St George's Park. Contagion is a springboard for business as much as social justice.

It's never too late to be recognised either. Two decades after their voices saved a national icon, FA chair Debbie Hewitt MBE publicly acknowledged these individuals at a council meeting, presenting them with framed images of the institution they saved – a welcome human leadership touch.

Tuning in to the right voices can counteract psychological blind, deaf and dumb spots. The next chapter shows how internal and external misinformation sources fuse in the PERIMETERS Effect.

ılı|ı·|ı **THE DECISION NINJA** ılı|ı·|ı·
WHAT TO REMEMBER

- You can't trust all you hear. The trilogy of error makes us psychologically blind, deaf and dumb to what's said, implied or meant.
- The *paradox of bias* prevents us from recognising bias if we don't believe it exists.
- What you *see* is not all there is. Blind spots overemphasise what we see, literally and figuratively. The biggest error is not pausing to decode information.
- What you *hear* is not all there is. Deaf spots amplify the tendency to mishear, tune out or not hear. Several biases amplify narrow thinking and inattentional deafness, i.e.:
  1. Default to truth. Poor at detecting deception, we dismiss what seems impossible, reject worst-case scenarios and think the best of others. We can't imagine what's beyond our experience.
  2. Confirmation bias. When we validate what we think we know rather than discover what we don't, we validate falsehood.
- What you *say* is not all there is. Dumb spots occur when we self-silence as others can't hear our voice. Speaking up doesn't guarantee being heard. Too many Cassandras scream into a void.
- Fear drives sustained silence in organisations and regimes lacking psychological safety.
- Commercial and social power exists in leveraging the contagion of voice. Be a voice of change not an echo. To be heard, first tune in and hear others.
- Good judgement means listening selectively and rebalancing what is seen with what is heard.

CHAPTER 3

YOU CAN'T TRUST ALL YOU HEAR

"Those who were seen dancing were thought to be insane by those who could not hear the music."

Friedrich Nietzsche

A N OMINOUS SIGN hung over the door next to a man's body in the People's Temple of Jonestown, Guyana. It read: "Those who don't remember the past are condemned to repeat it." It was 18 November 1978, a day the world would never forget.

Why did hundreds of Americans abandon their families, migrate to a tropical rainforest and follow a stranger to their death? Why did they turn a deaf ear to Reverend Jim Jones's Messiah complex? Why did they not spot the rhetorical similarities to genocidal dictators, from whom Jones had learned so much?

What was it about the situation, their personalities and mindsets that made each believe in the same utopian dream? What made 304 mothers poison their children with a cyanide-laced grape cordial on instruction from 'Father'?

Attracted by the equality movement, hippie Stanford attorney

Tim Stoen volunteered his services to Jones's church. A social justice radical in an era of anti-Vietnam war protests, he soon converted to the Temple's ideology. Over a decade, Stoen became Jones's trusted aide.

Gradually, Stoen grew disillusioned with the Temple's cult-like propaganda and human rights abuse, leading him to defect. He left behind his six-year-old son, having signed a paternity affidavit naming Jones as the father. Consumed with regret about a "terrible decision," all attempts to gain custody failed.

Stoen and some Jonestowners' relatives took their concerns public. They warned the San Francisco Supreme Court, disclosing the "paranoid megalomania," the beatings, death threats, dedication demands and staged attacks to sustain compliance. Their warnings fell on deaf ears, except for those of one man.

Congressman Leo Ryan was persuaded to visit the compound. At first, everything seemed normal. Members even laid on a concert. But secretly, some begged for help, including 15-year-old Thom Bogue.[1] Bogue hated compound life and didn't initially appreciate the implications of the 'White Nights' suicide dress rehearsals. As he re-evaluated the rhetoric, his escape plans intensified.

During Ryan's visit, Jones was infuriated, feeling his control crumbling. Accompanied by 16 defectors, Ryan left for the airstrip but was brutally executed along with four NBC crew. While boarding the plane, Bogue heard shots and fled to the jungle. Hours later, 909 Americans committed mass revolutionary suicide in a display of unbridled loyalty to Jones's voice.

As the mass suicide mobilised, some Jonestowners hid. Others accepted their fate. One woman in the inner circle, Christine Miller, was heard pleading to save the children.[2] She was silenced by Jones's grandiosity, "Without me, life has no meaning." Making his case, "I'm the best friend you'll ever have."

Bitterness dominated Jones's final moments. "Tim Stoen will have no one else to hate." He refused to save his son. "He's no different to me than any of these children here." Then he issued the fatal instruction, "Bring the vat with the Green C [cyanide] so adults can begin."

How did this happen? We dislike not knowing why people make certain decisions, especially those that stretch beyond our perimeter worldview or frame of reference. And when we don't know, we speculate. Jones's appeals to his flock to die with dignity and without fear were redundant. His terrified followers were heard screaming hysterically on tapes that were later recovered.

Jonestowners' misjudgement can be attributed to context combined with cognition and peer effects.

What we decide is based on where we are, who we're with and the voices in our heads. This determines the bandwidth and boundaries of our perspective.

·ıllı·|ııl|·|ıll|·

Jones exploited a range of common biases to generate this level of supreme control. According to Stanford psychology professor Philip Zimbardo, "the CIA would have to acknowledge that Jones succeeded where their MK-Ultra program failed in the ultimate control of the human mind."[3] Followers accepted what they heard. And the crowd provided the social proof and reinforcement necessary to validate their decisions.

They didn't hear what mattered when it mattered most.

Reflecting on this, you may sit in your courtroom of private opinion thinking, "I wouldn't have done that." You may think you're more like reformed Stoen than didactic Jones or his followers. You may think this is just another group of lost souls.

Yet you've more in common than you may think. We all do. How often do you choose the wrong voice or not change your mind?

Tim Stoen tuned in to his voice of conscience when it mattered. Having initially encoded propaganda, he later decoded the conflicting messages despite the high stakes involved. Years of beliefs were shattered as he reinterpreted the dictates of his leader and a complicit crowd, including himself.

In the previous chapter, I explained how the trilogy of error stops us from hearing what matters. The cult of Jonestown exemplifies how we overweight admired messengers, don't hear hidden agendas and self-silence when challenge proves uncomfortable.

In this chapter, I illustrate how each PERIMETERS trap triggers biases that narrow our perspective. I introduce the concepts of motivated reasoning and *deaf ear syndrome*, championing the art of reinterpretation. Why? Because what you hear is only part of the picture. And few events, conversations, claims, tragedies, scandals or stories ever have singular explanations.

To illustrate, it's worth exploring how the PERIMETERS Effect played out in Jonestown.

THE PERIMETERS EFFECT

We can't always trust what we hear. Our judgement is a composite of internal and external factors. When uncertain, under pressure or intense scrutiny, several unconscious factors activate the tendency to think narrowly and limit what is really heard, namely **P**ower, **E**go, **R**isk, **I**dentity, **M**emory, **E**thics, **T**ime, **E**motion, **R**elationships and **S**tories – the PERIMETERS traps.

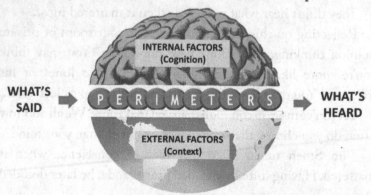

Several traps play out in most everyday situations. When these limit your perspective and derail your best judgement, that's the PERIMETERS Effect. Let's explore each in Jonestown.

If you're like most others, you've probably been seduced by the magnetism of those with Power, gravitas and authority. Jonestown followers enthusiastically conceded their independent voices to serve Jones. In turn, this adoring flock fuelled his self-belief and oversized Ego. A narcissist who listened only to himself, Jones positioned himself as a protective prophet, boasting about his courage, mercy and love. "I want you to be what I am and something greater."

Equally, followers were overconfident in their pursuit of the right path. Few perceived major Risk in relocating their families to the Guyana jungle. Likely swayed by the ideal of a perfect world, they neglected the probability of a suboptimal outcome, let alone a disastrous one.

Like any group membership, being a Jonestowner imbued a sense of Identity, shared community and purpose. The socially adrift embraced inclusion at a temple that rewarded its flock spiritually. And its flock reciprocated financially – at least 30 devotees signed over their house deeds!

The dominant desire for belonging overshadowed rational evaluation. An ingroup formed. Anyone caught attempting to escape was humiliated. One mother publicly called for her son's execution, such was Jones's devout following.

Over time, members forgot life outside the compound. The Memory of sunny beaches and palm trees faded. Alienation and isolation were reinforced by repeated rantings about interfering outsiders. One member was recorded saying, "I want to take my so-called dad and sister, and stab them to death with a pair of scissors, and run 'em piece by piece through the garbage disposal."

Jones's slick hair, attractive looks and magnetic style captivated followers. His son Stephan explains, "A guy like my dad found out what you wanted to see and showed it to you." This exploited a human vulnerability.

We rely on what we see, not what we hear. Is your judgement influenced by who or what you see? We know it is.

The Temple's message of social change would have justified any members' lingering Ethical concerns about propaganda or ill-treatment. It's likely Jones morally disengaged with reality, believing his beneficence licensed his ultimate plan.

The Timing of this community formation is interesting. At the time, people sought personal change, responding intuitively to the message and the messenger. We hear what we need when we need it, after all. Following reports of sexual and physical abuse, the US government tuned out then commenced investigations – too late.

The 1970s anti-Vietnam movement sparked Emotion, namely anger at the government and fear of a repressive Jim Crow South. The predominantly black congregation wished for a better future, tuning in to the voice of this evangelical preacher. They didn't predict their own demise.

Bonded Relationships cemented community cohesion. Groupthink limited challenge as the voice of the crowd motivated individuals to comply with the rhetoric, follow orders and ingest cyanide. Validating social psychologist Robert Cialdini's well-established theory of social proof, in hindsight, herding was predictable. Their belief was so entrenched that no other truth would be tolerated.

Stephan recounts, "On some level, we all wanted to belong."

Like a Broadway stage actor, Jones was an impressive orator who articulated compelling Stories, persuading captive followers of his superior reasoning. His staged miracle healings framed this narrative perfectly.

As this mass cult demonstrates, each PERIMETERS trap is independently powerful. No single trap was responsible for this tragedy but each triggered associated delusions, fallacies and biases in both leaders and followers. Any combination can generate a *force multiplier effect*, affecting individual and collective judgement.

Multiple biases occur in any one situation, complicating identification of each and exacerbating consequences at scale.

Again, context matters. Members could have reinterpreted their situation, but the Guyanese jungle became a physical and mental perimeter. This echoes the insular context at Graceland or indeed, in any workplace. Would this tragedy have happened if the People's temple had stayed in San Francisco and not relocated to Guyana? The isolated jungle compound provided the contextual glue to reinforce conformity. It was a perfect storm – and a judgement hell. Of course, cult suicides happen near large cities too, as Heaven's Gate demonstrated outside San Diego in 1997. It's the psychological and physical isolation of the community that reinforces behaviour – and the power of its social norms

Another key factor to consider, motivated hearing, contributes to lack of rational judgement.

MOTIVATED TO MISHEAR

People hear what they want in *motivated reasoning*. It's true of any believers of pre-packaged propaganda pumped out by organisations, governments, fundamentalists, religions or far-right radical groups. This psychological term can just as easily be called *motivated hearing*.

Consider a 1979 study of attitudes to capital punishment. Groups with opposing views about the death penalty read two fabricated reports, one supporting the death penalty as an efficient deterrent and the other rejecting it. Both groups assessed the report's credibility.

Which group do you think moved position?

In fact, neither did. Attitudes polarised and both groups emerged with more entrenched opinions than ever.[4]

The data always tells you the story you want to hear. "If you torture the data long enough, it will confess to anything," according to economist Ronald Coase.[5]

Israeli psychologist Ziva Kunda argues that we draw self-serving conclusions because we believe our views are more plausible than anyone else's.[6] Kunda showed two groups an article that explained how caffeine could increase the risk of breast cysts. Most thought this credible, except for one group – the heavy coffee drinkers. No surprise! The coffee drinkers were motivated to mishear the truth.

In some cases, wanting to be fooled is foolish.

We filter information to justify whatever belief we hold, whether it's about market forecasts, political elections, family planning or strategy selection. Just as we do with confirmation bias, we're motivated to mentally retrieve supporting arguments more than opposing arguments. It's why executives often replicate rather than reinvent strategic decisions. People fear appearing weak, stupid or wrong.

People tune out incrementally, just as the SEC leadership in Boston and New York tuned out Markopolos's repeated warnings about Madoff for nine years, with just one employee who tried to help. It's no different to ignoring red flags about an illicit affair, children taking drugs or a boss scheming a restructure.

If you neglect active data interpretation as a habit, your mental perimeters shrink decision by decision over time, and you don't notice.

Like the parable of the boiling frog, when the water heats slowly, the frog doesn't feel itself being boiled alive. If you go through life oblivious to psychological deaf spots, you risk being like that boiling frog – misjudging, miscalibrating and missing signals that deplete your influence.

Psychologist Annie Duke rightly believes "two things determine how your life will turn out: luck and the quality of your decisions."

The first is uncontrollable; the second is an underestimated source of advantage and relies on the ability to hear what matters.

That requires intelligent interpretation.

DEAF EAR SYNDROME

When organisations tune out reported, perceived or actual flaws, researchers term this *deaf ear syndrome*.[7] Nowhere is this more evident than with deal-hunting private equity firms and venture capitalists who scour the market for the next Mark Cuban or Richard Branson. In 2010, some were convinced it was WeWork's co-founder Adam Neumann, an entrepreneurial dyslexic who lived in 13 different homes by the age of 22.

According to the *Wall Street Journal*, modest Neumann boasted about his intention to become the prime minister of Israel, the "president of the world," and the first trillionaire. Behind his vision to build the first physical social network was a culture of tequila parties, drug taking and inappropriate conduct. "We are here in order to change the world... Nothing less than that interests me."[8]

His star twinkled, named as one of *TIME*'s most influential people in 2018. By 2019, Neumann boasted a staggering 528 office locations in 29 countries. WeWork aggressively undercut competitors, reportedly losing $219,000 an hour during expansion. Rules were bizarre. His wife was a vegan, so overworked employees were banned from expensing meals with meat.[9] No wonder turnover was dizzying.

In shoddy governance, the WeWork board approved hundreds

of millions in investments, decisions for which they were well rewarded by this house of cards. Neumann used funds rather eclectically and invested in unrelated ventures such as wave-pools and gyms. Venture capitalists misinterpreted his cheerleading style for strategic substance.

A former investor told reporters, "Basically, we chose wilful ignorance and greed over admitting this was obviously batshit crazy."[10]

Pre-IPO, Morgan Stanley valued WeWork at $96bn. JPMorgan estimated $102bn. Eventually, investors saw through the Spielberg smoke and mirrors. The IPO was pulled, triggering a lawsuit for an "overhyped strategy and misrepresented accounts." Ultimately, investors, employees and suppliers paid the price.

When it mattered most, investors dismissed warnings and accepted Neumann's wild exaggerations and Rumpelstiltskin promises. *New Yorker* reporter Charles Duhigg was told, "All the bankers saw was a big payday, and so they told Adam whatever he wanted to hear."[11]

One investor that haemorrhaged was Japanese billionaire and SoftBank founder Masayoshi Son. Arriving late to a WeWork pitch in 2016, he invested $4.4bn after a 12-minute tour of the premises.[12] Being charmed by the bon viveur culminated in an estimated $23bn loss from further investments.[13]

Reuters describes how Son later admitted poor judgement. "Son says he overestimated Neumann's good side, turned a blind eye to things like corporate governance, and that he should have known better."[14] SoftBank compounded this error by pouring $100m into another soon-to-be failure, FTX. However, Son's track record also reflects a stunning $20m bet on Jack Ma's Alibaba. "I don't look for companies, I look for founders."[15] Similar to most investors, venture capitalists have mixed fortunes.

They also pride themselves on intuitively sniffing out talent.

Like Bredius's fake Vermeer, wishful thinking partly accounted for WeWork's failure and SoftBank's chequered judgement. It blended with professional misinterpretation and motivated hearing.

These examples illustrate the Decision Ninja's need for more conscious information interpretation, especially in high-stakes situations.

IT AIN'T NECESSARILY SO: THE ART OF INTERPRETATION

During a botched armed robbery, British police apprehended an 18-year-old illiterate teenager. They ordered his accomplice to hand over a gun. The teenager shouted to his friend, "Let him have it."

Did he mean, "Hand over the gun" or "Open fire"? It wasn't obvious.

The friend fired and killed an officer.

The teenager was charged with incitement. It was 1953 and Derek Bentley was the last man hanged in Britain. Having rushed to misjudgement, it took 45 years for the courts to grant Bentley a posthumous pardon.

Interpretation is the difference between hearing an instruction of peace and an incitement to violence.

We think people know what we mean. When did someone last insult you? Do you take offence, sulk or ghost the offender only to discover that wasn't what they meant or wasn't even directed at you? How many bruises and brawls are based on misinterpretation? I've found that there's often more offence taken than given. Our ears deceive us. Our minds hear what's unintended. We catastrophise comments or misconstrue tone of voice, fuelled by the paranoia of persecution.

Sometimes no decoding is necessary, like when Jones urged, "We're not letting them take our life, we're laying down our life."

But it's sensible in a noisy modern world during high-stakes situations and emotion-driven moments.

Consider a court of law where judicial verbal instruction to a jury is assumed to be clear. Analysis by UCL's Professor Cheryl Thomas revealed that while the majority of jurors thought they understood the judge's instructions, only 31% could recall the two core questions. This improved to 47% when written, suggesting jurors understand more what they see rather than what they hear.

Being an accurate 12th juror isn't easy.

In any context, passive hearing and active listening aren't the same as interpretation. Of course, we want to believe the overpromising politician, backslapping colleague, worshipping priest or silver-tongued salesperson. But in high-stakes cases, reappraisal and reinterpretation are essential steps that come after listening and before judgement:

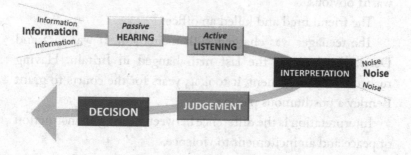

As the great Russian composer Igor Stravinsky once declared, "To listen is an effort, and just to hear is no merit. A duck also hears."

Interpretation matters.

President Ronald Reagan urged a "Trust but verify" approach to Russian nuclear disarmament. Without being perpetually paranoid, I think a "Distrust and verify" approach may be more appropriate.

Interpretation is a small step in theory but a giant leap in practice.

This is where second-order thinking comes in – thinking beyond what we think we know to dimensions we don't usually think about. That requires repeatedly asking questions like "And then what?" to drill down to second- and third-order consequences. You'll find new ideas quickly emerge.

It's a real skill to manage constant interference from a noisy world and overcome a capacity-constrained mind. It's also a real differentiator.

Interpretation is emotion-based. Every uncomfortable situation can be reframed positively or negatively to sell you something or make you feel better. Take a top source of anxiety – public speaking. By reframing nerves as excitement that boosts your performance, various scientists show how this can reduce anxiety. University of Rochester psychologist Jamie Jamieson suggests, "The aim is to change your interpretation of anxiety rather than suppress it."[16] We return to reframing later when exploring curated narratives.

It's important to anticipate the impact of our actions. But first-order thinking isn't enough. With second-order thinking, you consider not just the immediate consequences but the knock-on effects and collateral damage.

As Iranian writer Kamand Kojouri advises, "Don't be fooled by the words. Listen to the tune behind them."

Many professions do this well. Artists perfect the ability to tune in and reinterpret arrangements, hearing fresh tunes in old melodies. For instance, 352 of Bob Dylan's 357 songs have been covered. Every day, journalists, detectives, intelligence agents, analysts and therapists thoughtfully reinterpret information in newsrooms, police departments, war rooms and consultation offices. It's their day job.

Some research finds women are particularly adept at finding nuance before reaching conclusions. Equally, other research will argue that women are prone to a desire to be liked and may be less clinical. However, the world is not so binary and easily bifurcated.

Regardless of gender or profession, accurate interpretations and evaluations are contaminated by factors such as cultural nuance and language.

LOST IN TRANSLATION: DECODING NUANCE

Two people can hear the same scream, pitch, phrase or conversation but interpret it differently based on context, source and perimeter worldview.

Compare "Get on the floor" as instructed by a DJ, firefighter or bank robber. Compare "I want you" as expressed by a boss, a lover or a commander. Does its meaning change in Turkey, Tallahassee or Tibet? Communication is tough in any circumstance but when harried, overwhelmed or distracted, you can't trust what you think you hear. Context matters.

Language evolves which makes interpretation and translation more difficult. For example, the word 'shellshock' was coined in World War I by psychologist Charles Myers to describe what's now termed post-traumatic stress disorder.[17] Over 650 new words were added to the Oxford dictionary in 2022 including 'Jedi,' 'nomophobia' and 'easy-breezy.'[18] The online word of 2023 was 'Rizz' for charisma. Can you interpret these?

Moreover, interpretation is individual-specific. Even the word 'perimeter' might evoke variance. To a NASA astronaut, it may conjure up images of the distance from Earth. To a maths teacher, it's the surrounding area of a two-dimensional shape. For most of us, it's likely a boundary wall or dividing structure.

Michael Collins's application to the space programme depicts the individual nature of interpretation. He recounts being shown Rorschach inkblots, a psychological test often used with applicants. He was asked what he saw on a blank eight-by-ten sheet of white paper. "Well, of course, that's 11 polar bears fornicating in a snowbank." The examiner had a humour bypass, and Collins failed the test.

A year later, he reapplied. This time he announced, "I see my mother and my father, and my father is slightly larger and more authoritarian but not much more than my mother." He passed.

Language pronunciation is also a judgement killer. When artificial intelligence apps couldn't interpret user questions about Korean car manufacturer Hyundai, the company took out ads to clarify the pronunciation of its name.

Was it "Hyun-day" as pronounced in the US, "Hi-un-die" in Europe or "Hoon-dai" in South Africa?[19] Humorous sketches varied from an app interpreting Hyundai as a "Hawaiian Tie" shop, a "Highland Eye" pub and a High'n'Dye salon.

Interpretation remains a challenge in any language. Beyond pronunciation, add intonation, nuance, innuendo, muttering, stammering and euphemisms to make it even harder. Of course, interpreting drunk chatter is another skill entirely. Best to discount most of what you hear!

᎐ᏝᎥᏝᎥᏝᎥᏝᎥᏝᎮ

Cultural nuance affects interpretation accuracy. As explained in *Working with Americans*, international business expert Allyson Stewart-Allen observes the importance of cross-cultural interpretation.[20] While Americans typically adopt simple, explicit fact-based reasoning, such as, "We're at war," the Brits adopt complex implicit reasoning like "Emotions are escalating."

You only know what's left out or missing in a conversation if you understand the culture. "Cultural misinterpretation is one of the greatest scourges in business or in battle. Sometimes it's accidental and sometimes deliberate." She's not wrong.

Of course, misinterpretation occurs within cultures too. Responding to Pearl Harbour's 1941 attack and other post-World

War II events, England and the US demanded unconditional surrender by Japan in the 1945 Potsdam proposal.

During his reply speech, the Japanese prime minister rejected the proposal using the specific word "*mokusatsu*." Although historians later lobbied for a more constructive explanation, this was widely interpreted as "ignore" or "treat with silent contempt." Shortly after, President Harry Truman dropped atomic bombs on Hiroshima and Nagasaki, killing 200,000 citizens.[21] Only then did Japan surrender, ending the Pacific War.

If interpreting translation is one challenge, interpreting subtext is quite another.

DON'T TRUST WHAT YOU HEAR

Encoding rather than decoding explicit information is a common leadership liability. Why? Because critical information lies in subtext and nuance, like contractual fine print. Researchers argue as follows:

> Bias thrives wherever there is the possibility of interpreting information in different ways… people tend to reach self-serving conclusions whenever ambiguity surrounds a piece of evidence.[22]

Was this the case with the main al-Qaeda architect of 9/11?

According to the Combatant Status Review Tribunal, Pakistani fundamentalist Khalid Sheikh Mohammed's computer contained hijacker images and details, chat transcripts, soldier lists, letters from Osama bin Laden and threats to Arab embassies. The CIA interrogated Mohammed for four years at Guantanamo Bay using sleep deprivation, rectal rehydration and 183 waterboards.[23]

Mohammed confessed to 31 crimes committed over 20 years,

including the 1993 World Trade Center bombing, the beheading of American reporter Daniel Pearl and targeted bombings of NATO's European headquarters, nuclear plants, the New York Stock Exchange and Heathrow airport. He admitted the planned assassinations of Bill Clinton, Jimmy Carter and Pope John Paul II.

That's a long list!

CIA officials told *ABC News* he "lasted the longest under waterboarding, two and a half minutes, before beginning to talk."[24]

Finally, he broke. Or did he?

Would you believe an ego-depleted soldier who withstood four years of intense interrogation? The *New York Times* suggests it's not clear how many of this enemy combatant's expansive claims are legitimate. Moreover, he wouldn't speak under oath as it contravened his religious beliefs.[25] Even the Army Training Manual warns that excess torture "can induce the source to say whatever he thinks the interrogator wants to hear." What you hear isn't all that's meant or true.

It reminds me of the controversial Reid technique that encourages false confessions by relying on truth-distortion, suggestion, witness isolation and intimidation. Interrogators speak for about 90% of the time, breaking down the individual. Think of the Central Park Five jogger rape case where all recanted their coerced confessions. Or Gerardo Cabanillas who was promised probation and falsely confessed to rape only to spend 28 years in prison until the Innocence Project exonerated him, based on DNA evidence.

You can't trust all you hear.

Questions must be reinterpreted with an inquisitive mind. In PR training, the interviewee is always taught to avoid 'gotcha' questions such as "When did you last beat your wife?" Any version of "I don't," "never" or "what wife" becomes a tabloid headline.

One solution is to reverse-engineer and reason from first

principles, stripping out assumptions to separate underlying ideas or facts.

Why? Under pressure and even when not, people misinterpret accurate information rather than pausing to reinterpret misinformation.

Misinterpretation potential results not just from nuanced language but from organisation structures.

Silos and echo chambers

Everywhere I've worked, competitive silos have existed across regions and functions despite management rhetoric of 'one firm'. Sales, marketing and IT departments battle for scarce promotions, budgets and kudos. Battles get ugly!

By design, structures embed echo chambers and polarise how we think. Silos mean perspectives go unheard as great ideas get consigned to the graveyard. Ingroup thinking forms. This not only conceals commercial risks but, unmanaged, can crush innovation and limit knowledge-sharing. Modern remote working and Zoom-mania perpetuates ingroups, making it harder to hear outgroups.

Message manipulation starts at the top. A head of HR once told me that rules change at board level. Cocooning CEOs conceal skeletons, typically stage-managing information relayed to analysts, shareholders and directors. Concealing bear-traps, executives merely cite "small problems." AI can help. It's why analysts and investment managers, like Dutch firm Robeco, use algorithms to decode audio transcripts of earnings calls. Hesitations, microtremors, fillers and word choice point to what is not said.[26]

Despite their fiduciary responsibility, so-called 'country club' boards don't challenge enough. And 300-page board reports don't help!

With too many examples to mention, you only need to recall the well-documented governance failures like Volkswagen's $14.7bn false emissions claims, WorldCom's accounting irregularities, RJ Reynolds' minimisation of nicotine addiction or DuPont's dumping of 7,100 tons of chemical waste.

In *Disaster in the Boardroom*, Professor Randall Peterson and Gerry Brown suggest six patterns of governance failures: conforming, subordinated, imbalanced, bystander, bureaucratic and distended boards.[27] In each type, multiple boards heard what they want and believed stories presented by self-serving and self-preserving power hunters.

Of course, some opportunists take advantage of silos to hear what others don't. Traders thrive on price distortions and leverage market anomalies. It's their job to detect silos and capitalise upon them. They hear what others don't.

OPPORTUNITY: HEAR WHAT OTHERS DON'T

Intelligence agencies have a mission to protect national security. That's exactly what FBI special agent Kenneth Williams did when he spotted suspicious activity in an Arizona flight school. A number of Arab pilots wanted to learn how to take off but not to land. While Williams reinterpreted the situation, tone-deaf officials ignored the red flags in the pre-9/11 'Phoenix Memo.'

Sometimes, we answer too many questions and question too few answers.

Similarly, US investor Michael Burry predicted the collapse of the mortgage-backed securities market. It's a well-documented story. Just as the FBI ignored Williams's warning and the SEC tuned out Madoff's inconsistencies, rating agencies didn't listen to quirky Burry. As not classically attractive, did agencies focus on what they saw rather than what they heard? Tuned out and complicit in a circle of deceit, agencies protected their self-interest. Ironically, Burry made millions as banks lost millions.

Smart decision-makers take time out to tune in and be in tune with reality.

If interpretation is a skill, honing it is time well invested. From an organisational perspective, understanding how to interpret behaviour could save billions in consultant fees. Organisations spend a staggering $160bn globally on consultants every year. That expenditure could fund a lot of schools, roads, hospitals, bridges, food assistance and housing allowances for those in need!

It's not just analytics that defines good judgement, but the decision process used. Consultants Dan Lovallo and Olivier Sibony assessed 1,048 leadership decisions over five years. What mattered most to revenue and market share was the decision process rather than factual analysis – by a factor of six.

Part of this process is intelligent and intentional interpretation.

Poor interpretation and sloppy decisions lead to numerous ill-effects from unwieldy workarounds to expensive recalls, economic loss and reputation damage.[28] Employees tend to bear the brunt as WeWork, Boeing and many others learned. In November 2023, WeWork filed for Chapter 11 bankruptcy. In a vicious cycle, misinterpretation cripples balance sheets. For example, faulty accelerators cost Toyota $1bn. A fire-catching Galaxy Note 7 cost Samsung $17bn. That said, many more get it amazingly right.

Most leaders want to hear others' opinions. With so many voices, the choice is overwhelming. Most people tune in and out. Like radios, you can't listen to every station so you tune in to a select few. When unsure, people stick to familiar stations. If you never change stations, perspective shrinks. What you hear becomes all there is. Smart leaders tune in to stakeholder voices selectively.

Hearing others is a consummate organisational and social skill. Sir Winston Churchill's mother, Lady Randolph Churchill sums it up well:

When I left the dining room after sitting next to Gladstone, I thought he was the cleverest man in England. But when I sat next to Disraeli, I left feeling that I was the cleverest woman.

In Part Two, we encounter a wide spectrum of voices that are heard and unheard. We unconsciously tune in or tune out these voices. Only by being much more deliberative and intentional about who we hear will we improve our problem-solving and decision-making, getting closer to what we want and who we want to be.

I depict these in the schematic below, which is indicative as influence varies with context, time, technology, social norms and culture. I think it's an interesting way to think about who we listen to. A useful exercise might be to populate your own spectrum.

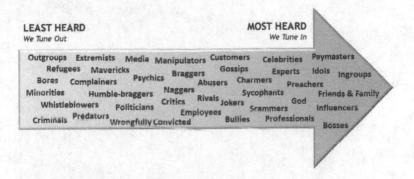

LEAST HEARD
We Tune Out

MOST HEARD
We Tune In

Outgroups Extremists Media Manipulators Customers Celebrities Paymasters
Refugees Mavericks Gossips Experts Idols Ingroups
Bores Complainers Psychics Braggers Abusers Charmers Preachers
Minorities Humble-braggers Naggers Sycophants Friends & Family
Whistleblowers Politicians Critics Rivals Jokers God Influencers
Criminals Predators Wrongfully Convicted Employees Scammers Bullies Professionals Bosses

It's nearly 50 years since Jonestown demonstrated how context can derail individuals. Tim Stoen and Thom Bogue reinterpreted their beliefs, changed their view and survived. Stoen accepts his mindset was swept up by context.

Every human being is responsible to do their own thinking... There are no Messiahs, no gurus... no matter how selfless they appear.[29]

Members had sacrificed too much. The social cost of back-tracking was high, so they clung to existing beliefs.

The Decision Ninja is now well-positioned and well-prepared to reinterpret meaning, messages and motivations. Understanding how potential human error spans the PERIMETERS traps starts with the Power you crave and ends with the Story you choose to hear. That's the focus of Part Two.

THE DECISION NINJA
WHAT TO REMEMBER

- Don't trust all you hear because what matters isn't always obvious. The PERIMETERS Effect occurs when multiple judgement traps limit what we hear, shaped by where we are, who we're with and what's in our head.
- Interpretation is an integral but neglected part of judgement. It's the middle step between receiving information and confirming decisions.
- Misjudgement is not about too much encoding of data, it's about too little decoding of data.
- Interpretation matters because you can't trust what you hear. Silos, subtext, euphemisms, pronunciation, accents, echo chambers and culture ensure what-you-hear-is-NOT-all-there-is.
- Motivated reasoning threatens likelihood of reinterpretation, activating deaf ear syndrome. We tune out discomfort and hear what matches our preconceptions and expectations.
- Tuning out is incremental. Don't be like the boiling frog.
- Opportunity exists. PERIMETERS traps can be mitigated with reflective reasoning, intentional listening and intelligent decoding of biases.
- Reasoning from first principles can broaden horizons and limit the force multiplier effect.
- Understanding the complexity of behaviour and tuning in to maverick, alternative or dissenting voices can save individuals time – and organisations millions.
- Tune in selectively to relevant voices, like a pre-selected radio channel.

PART TWO

THE PERIMETERS™ JUDGEMENT TRAPS

"Thinking is difficult. That is why most people judge."

Carl Jung

NVESTOR WARREN BUFFETT tells how he met a Polish woman who escaped a Nazi concentration camp. She still struggled to trust people, having seen too much and lost too much. She said something unforgettable: "When I look at people, the question I ask is 'would they hide me?'"

That's a bounded perimeter view.

We all have filters for viewing the world, assessing situations and reading people. It's neither right nor wrong. How you judge people is simply a product of what you've seen, what you've heard and how you've lived.

In Part Two, we delve into the bias-triggered PERIMETERS traps to highlight the effect of narrow thinking on judgement. Each trap draws on examples at three levels: individual, organisational and societal. Each trap binds our thinking, so we tune out, risking misinterpretation of a situation, strategy or stranger.

Each trap will be explored with a dedicated chapter. We'll interpret a reservoir of modern scandals and historical successes with a behavioural lens. We'll meet various characters that tuned in to different voices as their decision sources.

For instance, when hunting power, we elevate the voice of authority, idols and experts (*Power*, Chapter 4). Tuning in to our own voice drowns out others (*Ego*, Chapter 5) and we negate real risk probability (*Risk*, Chapter 6). We desperately crave ingroup acceptance (*Identity*, Chapter 7) and rarely consider recall might be inaccurate (*Memory*, Chapter 8). When tempted, we discount conscience (*Ethics*, Chapter 9). We overweight the present, underweighting the future or the past (*Time*, Chapter 10). In a hot state, we bury reason over logic (*Emotion*, Chapter 11) and tune in to the crowd for guidance (*Relationships*, Chapter 12), not challenging popular narrative (*Stories*, Chapter 13).

The PERIMETERS Judgement Traps are summarised as follows:

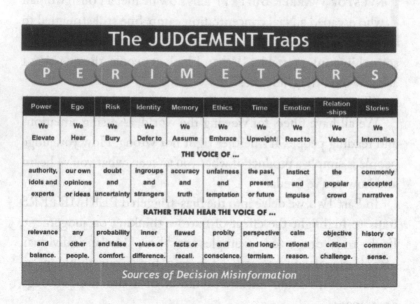

The JUDGEMENT Traps

P E R I M E T E R S

Power	Ego	Risk	Identity	Memory	Ethics	Time	Emotion	Relation-ships	Stories
We Elevate	We Hear	We Bury	We Defer to	We Assume	We Embrace	We Upweight	We React to	We Value	We Internalise
THE VOICE OF ...									
authority, idols and experts	our own opinions or ideas	doubt and uncertainty	ingroups and strangers	accuracy and truth	unfairness and temptation	the past, present or future	instinct and impulse	the popular crowd	commonly accepted narratives
RATHER THAN HEAR THE VOICE OF ...									
relevance and balance.	any other people.	probability and false comfort.	inner values or difference.	flawed facts or recall.	probity and conscience.	perspective and long-termism.	calm rational reason.	objective critical challenge.	history or common sense.
Sources of Decision Misinformation									

This section can be read in its entirety or revisited in bite-sized chunks. I encourage you to keep in mind a high-stakes decision you want to make or a past mistake you want to understand.

CHAPTER 4

POWER-BASED TRAPS: CHARGING AHEAD

"I listened to my father his whole life, but I never heard him until he was dead."

Gabriel Byrne

"**T**HE ECOSYSTEM IS neither sophisticated nor fully functioning… we need to build a sound financial system… not regulations in the old-fashioned way… China needs a lot of experts in policies not experts in paperwork."

This was the voice of China's most successful businessman, Ant Group and Alibaba co-founder Jack Ma, making a 20-minute speech at the Shanghai Bund Summit in October 2020.

Ma dismissed his doubts. "I'm so torn between whether to come here and give this speech today."[1] He continued, "In the future, I believe reform will come with sacrifices. It will come at a cost."

It did come at a cost: his own.

A Western audience might have interpreted these words as standard leadership rhetoric but in China, criticism is sacrilege. Ma crossed the boundary and stepped outside an accepted political perimeter. Days later, Chinese regulators suspended Ant Group's $34bn fintech IPO. It was to have been "the biggest IPO in human history."

Ma disappeared from the public eye for nearly two years.

China made its voice heard. Regulators have since cracked down on large internet platforms, pressuring Ant Group to overhaul its operations for governance reasons. A change in structure was announced in 2023 followed by Alibaba's split into six independently run groups, reducing Ma's power. Decision-making responsibility is now devolved in a company once worth $800bn.[2]

One thing is sure. Under a myriad of circumstances, power is always lost or reduced. The first rule of leadership is to respect hierarchy and know your place in it. As Ren Zhiqiang and Peng Shuai learned, Ma forgot about the nature of power and the boundaries of the Great Wall of China.

Lesson one: there's always a bigger bear!

Jack Ma tuned out. When hunting or holding power, tuning in when it matters limits self-sabotage.

Among the PERIMETERS judgement traps, power-led biases are the most destructive, cancelling careers prematurely and wreaking havoc on businesses, industries, communities and countries.

This chapter doesn't tell you how to gain or keep power. Thousands of books do that. Instead, I focus on six ways our preoccupation with hunting and holding power derails our judgement. Little is written about power-seeking derailers in the form of psychological deaf spots, until now.

For instance, obsessively hunting power can reduce your power base rather than enhance it (narrow focus). When we obey the voice of perceived seniority (authority bias), overly admire others (halo effect) or defer to experts (champion bias), we concede power. People wrongly deduce status from tone, pitch and pace of voice (contrast effect). Moreover, we naively think our supreme talent, effort and sacrifice will be rewarded and wrongdoers punished (just world hypothesis).

That said, strategic use of power is a tremendous asset. Let's explore the power conditions that help or hinder what we hear on our judgement journey.

THE HUNT FOR POWER

In *The Matrix*, Neo asks the Oracle, "What does he want?" The Oracle replies, "What do all men with power want? More power." Of course, it's not just gender-specific. While not everyone craves the hassle and responsibility power brings, many ladder-climbers covet the associated recognition, status and wealth. After all, giving orders feels a lot better than taking them! It's why powerholders are typically more fulfilled than non-powerholders.

Do newly titled leaders soar in your estimation? Research finds we overly admire successful seniors, idols or experts and behave differently towards them.

Power is context specific. In some situations, you're the powerholder, but in others, you're not. Power might belong to the assistant upgrading your hotel room, the banker approving your mortgage or the traffic warden clamping your car. If you think about it, when a pilot is flying Air Force One, in that moment, they have more power than the president of the United States.

As Jack Ma learned, power always shifts.

Our decision mindset depends on whether we hunt power, hold power or fear losing power. While not everyone holds positional power, few want to lose it. Once CEOs, politicians or athletes have trampled their way to the top, they rarely let go voluntarily.[3] It's a drug-like addiction.

Peacocks who suspect a crumbling empire evaluate with a short-term lens, often making self-serving, reckless decisions. Remember how Donald Trump's obsession with a second term led to violence at the US Capitol? He tuned in to the voice of ego and tuned out the voice of legal and political sanity.

Goal-setting has long been encouraged in aspiring students, recovery patients, ambitious entrepreneurs and medal-hunting athletes. It has tremendous utility, purpose and value, having fuelled historic empire-building from Alexander the Great to the Ming dynasties. During Covid-19, aggressive R&D goals facilitated the rapid development of vaccines within months rather than the usual years.

If growing a power base or gaining a promotion is your end goal, you'll fall into a dangerous trap. Mental perimeters narrow. You're more likely to tune out contradictory evidence, counterarguments or conscience. When hunting power, leaders tend to lose perspective and decide with a myopic lens.

GAINING POWER, LOSING PERSPECTIVE

Every week a new scandal hits our screens. I remember one in particular with a ridiculously unrealistic revenue target that led to a pressure-cooker environment.

In 2016, Wells Fargo hit the headlines when 5,200 employees knowingly fabricated millions of fake customer accounts. Leaders had instructed teams to achieve eight accounts per customer. For context, an average customer might hold two bank accounts from the available range of mortgage, savings, deposit, business or credit accounts. So why eight? When CEO John Stumpf was interviewed by the Senate Banking Committee, he explained that "eight rhymes with great."[4] Err! Blinded by ego, he blamed his employees rather than a toxic culture.

With salaries at risk and jobs on the line, leadership turned a deaf ear to stressed sales teams, customer welfare and regulators. On quarterly earnings calls, Stumpf bragged about sustained growth and pocketed a $19.3m bonus the prior year. This laser-focused revenue target cost the bank $3bn and Stumpf his career, plus an estimated $70m in clawbacks and lost earnings.[5]

A repeat offender, Wells Fargo didn't learn. Seven years later, executives in Wells Fargo's auto division overcharged loan fees, implemented unwarranted home foreclosures and illegally repossessed vehicles. This time, it cost the bank $3.7bn.[6] Too often, hunting power, position and profits annihilates rational perspective and balanced judgement.

Some fight back. In the line of fire at Number 10 for allowing "partygate" during lockdown, Britain's Boris Johnson dubbed his PR survival strategy 'Operation Save Big Dog'! But desperation isn't funny for those involved.

·ı||ı·|ı|||·|ı·

What voice do cost-saving leaders tune in to? Under pressure, thinking can degenerate and rational perspective dissipate.

Following the 1997 privatisation, France Télécom CEO Didier Lombard needed to relocate 10,000 employees and downsize 22,000 unionised employees. Deaf to decency, he approved intimidating tactics such as demotion, unmanageable workloads, employee surveillance and firing competitions.

Between 2006 and 2009, 60 France Télécom employees committed suicide in the most horrific ways – hanging, self-immolation, jumping from windows, highways and onto train tracks. With acute deaf ear syndrome, Lombard labelled this a "fad" on national television. One victim blamed him for "management by terror." The courts found him guilty of institutional harassment.

Toxic cultures are common. Extreme pressure also exists at the top. In Swiss-based Zurich Insurance Group, CFO Martin Wauthier took his own life in 2013 and left a bitter note, pointedly blaming an aggressive culture and "the worst chairman I have ever met." A regulatory investigation concluded "no unreasonable pressure" was exerted.

Over two years later, Zurich CEO Martin Senn committed

suicide after steeping down for no discernible reason.[7] At that stage, Swiss companies had seen five executive deaths by suicide within eight years.

It's not only profit-hunting organisations who exhibit deaf ear syndrome but individuals and nations. For example, online trolls, bullies, scammers and hackers frequently tune in to the voice of evil.

Consider 24-year-old romantically scorned Hunter Moore who built a revenge porn website called Is Anyone Up. The site earned $20,000 in monthly revenue by posting nude photos and linking them to the victim's social media account. Moore called himself "a professional life ruiner." He wasn't wrong. *Rolling Stone* magazine called him "the most hated man on the Internet." Eventually, the FBI charged Moore with hacking, identity theft and conspiracy. Moore's narrow focus ruined his own life.

There's always a bigger bear!

Just as Moore sought power, sexual predators overpower helpless victims for an adrenaline rush. Serial killer Ted Bundy beat and butchered 36 immobilised girls with a crowbar. In those moments, he held ultimate power, drowning out the voices of begging victims.

"The sex was merely perfunctory," he told colleague Ann Rule. Bundy valued possession over gratification. Fantasies that were "taking over" his life became "a downer," fuelling more sadistic goals. This type of single-mindedness can warp rational thought.

Nations aren't immune from single-mindedness either, whether competing in the space race, nuclear race or Olympic race. Throughout history, tyrannical dictators have ensured citizens hear their message. Vladimir Putin's invasion of Ukraine exemplifies a destination-driven decision. Uganda's Idi Amin, Zimbabwe's Robert Mugabe, and Taiwan's Chiang Kai-shek thrived on repression. North Korea's Kim Yong Un publicly executed his uncle to gain compliance. Joseph Stalin exploited the Russian Gulag concentration camp system. And in Cambodia, Pol Pot's regime wiped out 20% of a seven-million-strong population.

Like in Jonestown, these powerholders relied on conformity to maintain top-dog position.

COMPLYING WITH VOICES OF AUTHORITY

Unlike Jack Ma's willingness to criticise his government, most people conform to the voice of authority even when it contradicts their intuition, expertise or values. This is *authority bias*. We follow rules, orders and instructions from those senior or uniformed. Co-pilots defer to captains, junior officers to lieutenants, managers to CEOs. Who do you listen to? Power, social class and wealth create a natural hierarchy of who gets heard.

Holding power is the ultimate responsibility, akin to the 12th juror. You have the power to be a happiness – or misery – superspreader.

Although mass compliance aids effective social and organisational functioning, authority bias is so innate that even caring professions succumb to its tentacles and follow rules without thinking. In an Ohio hospital experiment, 95% of nurses willingly complied with doctors' instructions to administer drugs against established practice.[8]

Your personal power is mitigated under two conditions: (i) when you overly admire those who are an authority; or (ii) when you fear those who are in authority. We're people-pleasers, wanting to curry favour and circumvent hassle even though powerholders can challenge our rationality or even our morality.

When you hold power and are admired, your power exerts a subtle silencing effect.

One of the most famous experiments in social psychology illustrates the nature of hardwired hierarchical conformity. The

US Office of Naval Research wanted to test the effect of perceived power. In a 1971 mock simulation, Professor Philip Zimbardo recruited 24 students for two weeks. He allocated students to roleplay prisoners or guards as he played superintendent.

Uniformed guards were to be addressed as "Mr. Correctional Officer" and carried wooden batons. After a few hours, they got bored and became progressively more tyrannical. They locked rebellious 'prisoners' in cupboards, removed beds, threatened food deprivation, made them strip naked, recite poetry backward, bark like dogs and simulate sex. What's worse, prisoners gradually stopped resisting each more ludicrous instruction.

After six days, Zimbardo listened to his girlfriend's growing disgust and halted the experiment.[9]

Some scientists contest the Stanford Prison Experiment's robustness. Despite the controversy, it demonstrates how situational forces lead people astray. It fascinated millions, later becoming a Hollywood movie. When guards and prisoners were later interviewed, few could logically explain their choices.

Years later, US guards brutally tortured Iraqi prisoners at Abu Ghraib. This was no experiment. Major General Antonio Taguba's report notes:

> Punching, slapping and kicking detainees… forcing groups of male detainees to masturbate while photographed and videotaped… pouring phosphoric liquid on detainees… sodomising a detainee with a chemical light and perhaps a broom stick… simulating electric torture.

Zimbardo attributes Abu Ghraib to situational rather than dispositional factors.[10] Soldiers had tuned out.

The tired excuse "I was obeying orders" or "The boss told me to do it" is often trotted out. Court-martialled soldier Chip Frederik blamed his commanders for encouraging rough prisoner treatment. This excuse was rejected in the Nuremberg and Rwanda tribunals. Why? Military law advocates soldiers engage in reflective thinking rather than mindless order-taking.[11]

Lessons weren't learned in the US about prisoner treatment. In 2010, teenager Kalief Browder was incarcerated for a ridiculous three years in Riker's Island awaiting trial for an alleged backpack theft.[12] During this time, he spent 700 days in solitary confinement, and graphic video of him suffering violent abuse went viral. Abuse of power occurs at every level.

⫸⫷⫸⫷⫸

Nearly a decade after the Stanford Prison Experiment, the trial of Nazi Adolf Eichmann disturbed Zimbardo's classmate Stanley Milgram. Testing obedience to authority, Milgram recruited male students to roleplay a teacher and for each wrong answer, administer fake electric shocks to a 'learner' in a room next door. Each mistake increased shocks by 50 volts, up to 450 volts, enough to kill the subject.

Forty psychologists were asked to estimate how many teachers would administer full voltage. They estimated a mere 0.1%. Not so! Prodded by the experimenter, an overwhelming 65% administered the maximum 450 volts, despite hearing anguished cries. There were no rewards, punishments or anger towards the learner. This was pure authority bias.

I wonder if teachers would have administered fewer volts if they saw rather than heard the learners?

The power of the briefcase, crown or white coat pervades relationships. Obedience is a shortcut that saves mental effort. We're cognitive misers, after all. It's why most of us agree with the boss. And the boss likes compliance.

Rather than embracing dissent, Wharton professor Adam Grant contends, "Too many leaders shield themselves from dissent. As they gain power, they tune out boat-rockers and listen to bootlickers. They surround themselves with agreeable yes-men and become more susceptible to seduction by sycophants."[13]

When discussing leadership, Olympic medal-holder and World Athletics president Sebastian Coe reminds rugby's Sam Warburton, "Weak leaders love weak people around them." Weak leaders also love compliant people. When I joined the gender leadership taskforce to help build parity, reform meant tuning in to dissent and difference. Fast forward to 2023. World Athletics boasts the first 50/50 gender-balanced international federation in sport.

At times, it may be strategic to withhold opinions, but by doing so, you concede power. Silence gradually becomes habitualised in boardrooms, newsrooms and courtrooms.

As power can be ceded through fear of authority, it can also be ceded through admiration.

CONCEDING POWER TO ADMIRED VOICES

When we like or admire someone, we disproportionately overweight their opinion. Sinéad O'Connor once wrote about her admired manager:

Whatever Fachtna thinks is a good idea is a good idea. Whatever he loves I love. What he hates I try to hate. All I want to do is keep impressing him. I say whatever I imagine will impress him. I become whatever I imagine will impress him. Sometimes, I think I'm more like him than me.[14]

Whatever the subject, we nod along and don't filter misinformation. We assume expertise is transferable across domains in the *halo effect*. Would you expect Usain Bolt to give political advice or Joe Biden to give fitness tips? Nevertheless, we concede power to the popular, wealthy or good-looking expert.

Well-capitalised brands have long exploited this halo effect to sell celebrity-endorsed products. George Clooney's association costs Swiss coffee company Nespresso an estimated $40m a year. Does he even make coffee?

As a former chief marketing officer, I actively leveraged the power of association.

For example, over many years, I sponsored the high-profile ATP Tennis tour, the Ryder Cup, and the British and Irish Lions to symbolise team-based performance. I also invited prominent world figures to events, including President Bill Clinton.

Fusing power with expertise, when he spoke, people listened. Clinton achieved the gold standard for economic progress yet is most remembered for the 1998 Monica Lewinsky scandal. But Americans forgave him and admired his fortitude.[15] His approval rating was 71% post-scandal, ten points higher than before. His secret was making others feel good. And I learned this first-hand.

Before I interviewed Clinton onstage in Vienna (that's another story!), I was reminded how much a powerholder's sycophantic entourage hears only the paymaster and concedes their professional power and, sometimes, dignity. Only one opinion matters, and it's not yours. It bore echoes of the Memphis Mafia – and most workplaces! How bizarre is the mad-dash scramble when HQ is visiting? I've seen many a dignified leader reduced to an approval-seeking toddler! And I've probably been one too!

When clients hold advisors or agents in excessive esteem, clients tend to accept information at face value and gloss over the fine print. After Elvis Presley's death, his estate filed against Colonel Tom Parker for "mismanagement, self-dealing, overreaching and breach of trust."[16] The complaint argued he breached "fiduciary obligations and his duty of loyalty and reasonable care," causing detriment to his client through "exploitation of Elvis in a manner designed to maximise his own private financial gains and profits."

For instance, 65-year-old Parker took an extortionate 50% commission of total earnings, ahead of the 10% industry average. Bad deals and bad advice left millions on the table. The 1973 back catalogue deal with RCA generated a one-off $5.4m payout, with half going to Parker.[17] Elvis received an estimated $2m after tax. Yet his 1972 net earnings after Parker's take, taxes and expenses were $4m. In other words, he earned twice as much the previous year than the total gained from selling the rights to a lifetime's work of 650 recordings.

At just 38, he forfeited all future revenue benefits. It was a car crash deal.

Disproportionate admiration of others is a red flag. Don't assume your admired heroes, co-dependent advisers or industry experts are infallible or acting in your best interests. Often, they're not.

Experts as oracles

Most people tend to trust professional voices "because they're the experts." But allocating monopolistic power to anyone can be a judgement killer. Making decisions based on an individual's track record and wall-hung diplomas is known as *champion bias*. We've all fallen into the trap at some stage, whether with a money-grabbing builder, fee-hunting lawyer or upselling mechanic.

Experts rarely have perfect knowledge. They misread clues, misread markets and misread trends. Rational thought distorts under pressure. It's why mergers still fail and start-ups still implode. It's why regulators misinterpreted Madoff and the Global Financial Crisis. Or the FBI dismissed verbal warning about school shootings. Political scientist Philip Tetlock found even novice newspaper readers outperform experts when making predictions.[18]

Yet our trust in experts is absolute. When we hear a medical prognosis, most of us shut down our minds as suddenly as a blown fuse rather than challenge or seek a second opinion, even for critical conditions. Regardless, human error is the fourth leading cause of death – most malpractice cases cite "missed, failed or wrong diagnosis."

Take prescribing antibiotics.

The Centers for Disease Control and Prevention estimates 30% are unnecessary and 50% are inappropriate. I've seen the default tendency to prescribe myself.

At 85, my mother takes a cocktail of 18 tablets daily including some to sleep, some to stop sleeping! Like many patients, she awards a pill-dispensing doctor the status of high priest and naively assumes good judgement and accurate diagnosis. Little is challenged. The more ailments, the more prescriptions. Her bounded reasoning sustains the myth of expert infallibility.

Like Dr Feelgood, too many oath-taking practitioners dispense antibiotics for minor illnesses. Why so? One US study finds that some tune in to the cash register, others patient-please or fear malpractice.[19] It's a combination of reasons.

Similarly, lawyers acquire glorified status. In many cases, their services are a distressed purchase from fraught clients in crisis. It's a delegated decision – sue or settle, jury or bench trial, plea deal or pot luck?

One study of negotiated financial settlements compared rejected pre-trial offers with post-trial outcomes.[20] In 61% of cases, the plaintiff's lawyer misjudged the trial outcome and rejected a more favourable pre-trial settlement. This cost plaintiffs an average of $43,100. Defence lawyers performed no better. In 24% of cases, lawyers rejected favourable pre-trial offers, costing corporate clients an average of $1,140,000.

Experts aren't always right, but we depend on them. And trust them.

This is especially the case with financial matters. For instance, research found 94% of wealth managers claim "top quartile" performance, i.e., among the top 25% of peers. But this is based on self-serving selective time periods. The *Financial Times* reports instances where one fund manager boasted "top quartile over ten years but actually bottom quartile over one, three and five years." Some are "good performers over one year, but poor performers over the long term."[21] Unsuspecting investors default to believing the experts. It's a mistake.

As decision-makers, we're obliged to look beyond misleading claims or certificated awards and to conduct much more due diligence than a noisy world often allows.

Don't assume expert infallibility because of misplaced admiration, or worse – tone of voice.

DECEPTIVE POWER SIGNALS: TONE OF VOICE

Sometimes, we intuit power from tone. It's as instant as first impressions. Fifty studies analysed presidential debates, concluding that low-pitched male voices won more debates than high-pitched counterparts, and with wider margins.[22]

Testing the same message, 70% voted for the lower-tone candidate who was perceived as more leader-like.[23] It's more psychological than logical and partly explained by the *contrast effect*. A loud voice makes a softer voice appear even softer – with all the irrational associations that may bring. And vice versa.

Psychologist Nalini Ambady cites evidence of the effect of verbal tone on behaviour. She interpreted doctor-patient tapes to predict which surgeons would be sued. Specifically, she assessed extensive 40-second clips for warmth, hostility, dominance and anxiety, concluding that dominant power-wielding doctors had greater legal risk of being sued. Why? We ooze respect – or lack of respect – through tone of voice, and with it, likability. Tone of voice shaped patients' decisions.

Verbal tone can be a decision asset or liability. The wrong tone on a Samaritan call or during sensitive negotiations can yield disaster. The right tone can talk someone off a bridge or broker a peace agreement.

Tone is a false signal that communicates superficial gravitas. It's a "supposedly irrelevant factor" as Thaler would say. But it's not. And it directly affects gender disparity.

High-pitched, fast-talking women are rarely present at board tables or presidential podiums. Former prime ministers Margaret Thatcher and Theresa May felt it necessary to undertake special vocal training. Even Elizabeth Holmes acquired a baritone voice to penetrate Silicon Valley. Tone and vocal pitch amplify inequality, penalising high-pitch employees and ignoring soft power. Being talked over and unheard is not exactly breaking news.

As Mary-Ann Sieghart rightly states in *The Authority Gap*, "Men are assumed to be competent until proven otherwise, whereas a woman is assumed to be incompetent until she proves otherwise." We'll revisit the consequences of this later when we discuss the *beauty bias*.

Even pace affects interpretation and credibility.

ılı|ı·|ıı|ıl|ı·

As a fast talker, I know that to be heard I must consider how others interpret my words. I knew I had a challenge when someone digitally slowed down my speech for their webinar! Vocal pace can be distorted when technology edits sound or voices get cloned by AI deep-fakes. Musicians digitally remix their tracks to sound better all the time, just as movie makers alter tone to suit characters. While manipulation is done for commercial reasons, we're still deceived by what we hear.

Conversations are rarely explicit, often punctuated with double-edged rhetoric. When President John F. Kennedy received feedback on his 1961 Bay of Pigs plan to invade Cuba, his chiefs of staff gave it "a fair chance of success." They meant a 30% chance but didn't state that explicitly.

Kennedy interpreted this favourably, likely hearing "success" rather than "fair" and pushed ahead. Hundreds died, carving repercussions for the Cold War.

The tone Kennedy publicly expressed to the communist Soviet Union was one of force and intransigent resolve. The administration had invested $185bn in the space race, building military might to support Asia and Western Europe. What Soviet Union leaders and American citizens heard wasn't reality.

After all, what you hear is never all there is.

For years, successive administrations sustained this show of foreign policy force. Yet declassified historical recordings now reveal that the Kennedy tone was more conciliatory behind closed doors. He had secretly engaged with former Soviet Union premier Nikita Khrushchev to avoid nuclear war, advocating peace and signing the Partial Test Ban Treaty for disarmament. This outward display of national force and power concealed an inner lack of confidence, as is often the case with business and world leaders. Calculated optics tend to overshadow the truth.

Clearly, word selection plays a critical component in messaging.

Words as weapons of power

Are you successful because you warrant it or because you sound as if you warrant it? It's an important distinction.

We know language conveys power and aggressive tones tend to silence dissent. When I worked in the City, a serial acquirer would frequently raise his voice, bang the table and storm out of negotiations. People feared poking the bear, so conceded. He won many "non-negotiable" deals. It's a tactical power play, like "best and final offer" or deadlines to force concessions.

An irate or angry tone captures attention and can intimidate others. What matters to the Decision Ninja is how this influences their ideas, evaluations and choices.

Using US software data, psychologist Larissa Tiedens demonstrated how angry co-workers are perceived as having more status and being better role models than sad co-workers.[24] She showed participants Clinton's Lewinsky testimonial video in which his gestures varied between anger and contrition. Participants concluded that Clinton exuded more power when angry.

While anger displays aren't for everyone, some bulldozing bosses lead by fear and employees become frozen in subservience. Amazon's culture is "notoriously confrontational." Founder and executive chairman Jeff Bezos's tirades are infamous. "I'm sorry, did I take my stupid pills today?" or "If I hear that idea again, I'm gonna' have to kill myself."[25] In contrast, affable corporate rock star Jack Ma was known for an intelligence that crossed cultures, even if the context became anti-capitalist.

Anger is latent, affecting unrelated future decisions. If you're angry in the morning, it affects what you decide in the afternoon. Maybe you're less generous or more critical? This latency heightens misinterpretation. It's never about what it's about.

The order in which you speak also affects how much you're heard, especially in business.

Like seating plans at weddings or events, the order suggests ranking. When I was invited to the White House Correspondents' ball in DC to hear Barack Obama's final address, I was super excited at the privilege. But when my table was located practically in the corridor at the furthest point from the presidential podium, I learned my true place pretty quickly!

Early speakers are typically perceived with higher status than fast followers. However, if you're the most senior individual, beware giving your opinions first. Most conform to the leader's voice. Anti-apartheid advocate Nelson Mandela always admired how his mentor and tribal chief Jongintaba Dalindyebo spoke last.

Using words positively accelerates power. For instance, Zappos. com founder Tony Hsieh built his online retail shoe empire with the happiness mantra, "Create fun and a little weirdness." It worked. Amazon bought Zappos for $1.2bn in 2009.[26]

When I met Frank Maguire, founding senior executive at Federal Express, he regaled how he told employees the same three words for years: "You're the greatest." I never forgot it. In his book of the same name, he recounts how this not only validates employees but improves profitability. From 1980, FedEx went from losing $1m a month to growing at 40% a year. Now FedEx is a verb. Maguire rightly argues that motivation lasts a short time while validation lasts a lifetime.

However, pseudo-validation always needs reinterpretation, especially in a merger situation.

POWER PLAYS IN AN UNFAIR WORLD

Former Bank of America CEO David Coulter orchestrated a $64bn merger with NationsBank in 1998. With a military-type culture, NationsBank CEO Hugh McColl had completed over 30 acquisitions in a slash-and-burn style, almost "keeping a hand-grenade in his desk."[27]

In comparison, Coulter was "a mild-mannered intellectual who likely believed he would succeed McColl." After all, good gets rewarded and evil punished – reflecting the so-called *just world hypothesis*.

Coulter failed to reinterpret the pseudo-message of unity. Warning signals should have flashed when McColl kept him in the townhall shadows on integration day. Or when top jobs went to NationsBank and the board was stacked in NationsBank's favour. Former Bank of America board member Sanford Roberts said Coulter's days were numbered, "They were looking for an excuse."

They got it. When extensive trading losses emerged, McColl's heir-apparent had to go.[28]

Like Jack Ma, did Coulter misread the situation? Was he inattentionally deaf? Most employees think the world is fair and hard work will be rewarded. But this is delusional!

It's also pervasive. The biggest lesson for Tesla co-founder Martin Eberhard was getting ousted by the board. He later sued Elon Musk for libel. He told India's *Economic Times*, "I did not see it coming at all. I have learned to distrust people a bit more. It is a sad reality, but true." Similarly, OpenAI founder Sam Altman was sacked over safety concerns but hired by Microsoft within days, only to return to OpenAI within a week!

The day I reached the C-suite, a CEO told me not to expect fairness. He hadn't got there "by playing nice." Indeed, he hadn't.

Positional power is only ever on loan in the corporate game of thrones anyway. Real power lies within.

Every year, CEOs depress stock prices, leave with massive severance packages and complicit board members escape without penalty. Yet loyalists and dissenters get squeezed out for bogus reasons. Sacked opinion leaders send a message. And the politically naive are caught in the crossfire.

Regardless of fairness, prescient leaders proactively preserve power. Consider Meta founder Mark Zuckerberg who can never be fired. "I kind of have voting control of the company, and that's something I focused on early... without that... I would've been fired."[29]

Governments change policy for the same reason. Chinese president Xi Jinping will rule for life as the National People's

Congress abolished term limits. And Russian citizens amended the constitution, allowing Putin to rule until 2036.

It's common for powerholders to be treated with kid-gloves. Former Southern Florida district attorney Alex Acosta gave paedophile Jeffrey Epstein a sweetheart deal in 2008 despite identifying 30 underage victims. The Office of Public Responsibility admitted "poor judgement."[30] Former lead prosecuting attorney Marie Villafaña claims "deep implicit institutional biases" prevented justice. This reinforces the delusion of invulnerability.

Stanford professor of organisational behaviour Jeffrey Pfeffer suggests power carries an inherent forgiveness ticket. "Once you acquire power, what you did to get it will be forgiven and forgotten."[31] All evidence suggests he is correct.

Some leaders are too big to jail!

Some leaders willingly accede power, retire or join the Great Resignation. But in most cases, power is lost through bad luck, timing, transactions, changes in control or board arm-twisting. As someone once told me, "Maybe your face just doesn't fit." Whatever the reason, loss of salary, title and routine feel traumatic. A study of displaced Swedish workers concluded higher risk of death after job loss.[32] In such moments, the voice of doom reverberates loudly.

Many years ago, I attended a tremendous course on leadership authenticity by ex-Medtronic CEO and Harvard professor Bill George. He argues for values-led leadership and following your true north. It sounds cliché, but how many people do it? It made me want to resign that week! Changes in power status give you that opportunity.

REDEFINING POWER

Like businesspeople, musicians, academics and actors, athletes navigate a win-lose pendulum throughout their careers. With a lifetime in the spotlight, some seek to recreate the adulation and adrenaline high. Once power is lost, some fear anonymity. Others reinvent themselves.

Iconic tennis player John McEnroe knows how to win, earning 155 combined ATP singles and doubles titles including seven Grand Slams. His legendary rivalry with Bjorn Borg and Jimmy Connors entertained millions of superfans in the 1980s.

Millions wanted him to win. And he did, for a while.

True to his own voice, McEnroe's trademark on-court outspokenness disproportionately defined him. Was his voice an asset or liability? Did people see him or hear him? Unlike Tiedens's findings, the media decided anger was not a source of sporting gravitas.

Like most high-achieving perfectionists, perhaps his biggest misjudgement was listening to criticism, his own voice or that of others. Gradually, his marriage crumbled and the tennis spotlight faded.

McEnroe knows how to lose the hard way – in the public eye. In *You Cannot Be Serious*, he writes, "For anyone who's ever been at the top, when you lose that, everything spirals out of control, and it's hard to find your way back."[33]

Far from perching on the pity pedestal, he tuned in to his own voice to move forward. He jokes 37 psychologists helped! So did savvy agent Gary Swain who was plugged into delivering what his client wanted for three decades, in contrast to Colonel Parker. A series of shrewd judgements solidified McEnroe at the forefront of his industry, decades after the game ended and the crowds went home.

When I asked him about the drag of endless autograph hunters, he told me he never tires of it. "Who doesn't want to be told they're loved?" One of the most popular sports personalities, his career trajectory rocketed from US Open ball boy to four-times US Open winner to Emmy-nominated commentator for the US Open.

He learned how to reinvent his career and not be defined by a single identity. A musician, best-selling author, art gallery owner, philanthropist, proud husband and parent, he found a way back.

His voice inspires generations – he was the first athlete invited to give the 2023 commencements address at Stanford since 1891 in the footsteps of Oprah Winfrey and Bill Gates.

In this address, McEnroe advocates perspective. Despite losing the 1980 Wimbledon final, he gained something greater. He learned Mandela had watched the battle against Bjorn Borg from prison.

> That we gave Mandela a brief respite from the excruciating hell of 27 years of political imprisonment meant more to me than any award I've ever won.

His point was this: "You don't have to win to be part of something that is truly magical."

The bad boy has come good. By any ranking, that's advantage McEnroe.

TUNING IN: THE VOICE OF RESPONSIBILITY

Loneliness shouldn't be a virtue. Jeffrey Pfeffer urges leaders to secure power by building alliances and networks. Loneliness shouldn't be a virtue. He argues power can be an ugly game, but it's not a dark art and must be used responsibly.

"To be used for good, more good people need it."[34]

Throughout history, leaders like Nelson Mandela, Abraham Lincoln and Martin Luther King Jr. have been applauded for using their voice to advance democracy and human rights. Every day, leaders of corporations, clubs and communities use their influence for good. Some do it at scale.

In the 1980s, Larry Fink was a hot-shot fixed-income trader at First Boston, its youngest ever managing director. But markets turned and millions were lost. He recalled, "My team and I felt like rock stars. Management loved us. I was on track to become CEO of the firm. And then...well, I screwed up. And it was bad."[35]

He went on to establish BlackRock with seven colleagues using a serial acquisition strategy and commitment to data-driven technology. When BlackRock acquired Merrill Lynch Investment Managers in 2006, I observed three things as an employee: a willingness to listen, a relentless focus on team culture and commitment to long-term investing.

"BlackRock is a firm that tries to sell hope because why would anybody put something into a 30-year obligation unless you believe something is better in 30 years?"[36]

Fink tunes in to the market, savers and clients. In 2004, he walked away from a Barclays Global Investors deal, not "quite confident enough."[37] By 2010, the deal was done. Consultant Casey Quirk observes, "Looking back over 10 years, the deal looks great. But at the time, during the [financial] crisis, it was a large, scary deal." Shares rose from $178.52 to $443.81 over the period.[38]

When Fink speaks, governments, the Fed and think tanks listen. Echoing Milton Friedman's social responsibility mandate, Fink uses his voice to urge captains of industry to promote sustainable investing in his annual letter. "I've long believed that it's critical for CEOs to use their voice in the world." He tells McKinsey:

> There is a need for a responsible voice. There's a need for a voice for savers. There's a need to speak up—to speak up to a politician, speak up to a regulator—but not to speak *at* them, but to speak *with* them.[39]

Fink speaks of being permanently a little paranoid. In *The Psychology of Money*, Morgan Housel describes a barbelled personality as vital to investing success, being "optimistic about the future but paranoid about what will get you to the future."[40]

Optimism is reflected in BlackRock's former tagline, "Opportunity favours the prepared mind." Today, BlackRock is approaching a $10trn Wall Street investment powerhouse.

Great organisations have a voice, but the greatest leaders use their voice for good.

Presidents construct libraries, sporting legends build academies, and foundations distribute wealth. Manchester United striker Marcus Rashford was once reliant on social welfare. When the British government stopped providing free school lunches during the summer holidays, he successfully lobbied parliament to reverse this decision. That's using power for good.

᠁᠁᠁᠁

"People are more impressed by the power of our example rather than the example of our power," Bill Clinton once said. His combination of diplomacy, nuanced thinking and patience enabled him to achieve world peace. He brokered the historic 1993 Middle East Peace between sworn enemies, Israel's Yitzhak Rabin and Palestine's Yasser Arafat, symbolised by the infamous handshake on the White House lawn. Twenty-five years ago, he facilitated the Good Friday Agreement in Northern Ireland, in what he now describes as "one of the greatest blessings of my life."[41]

In 1998, George W. Bush invested in a generous emergency AIDS relief plan to curb a growing epidemic. By 2023, this foresight is estimated to have saved 25 million lives.[42]

Whatever power you hold, it should be used for good.

Whatever power you want, hear what voices matter.

A major driver of using power for good is of course ego and the desire to self-congratulate. Just as ego can be a force for good, ego is one of the most toxic and least acknowledged decision derailers.

THE DECISION NINJA
WHAT TO REMEMBER

- Identify when you're in or out of power to ascertain misjudgement risk and adverse power plays.
- Be careful what you wish for. Single-mindedly chasing power narrows perspective. You jeopardise hearing what matters and risk encoding falsehood rather than decoding truth.
- Whether you're in authority or an authority, it triggers deaf spots. While others hear you, it not only limits your receptivity to alternative voices but can intimidate some into silence.
- Excessive tuning in to admired idols or experts reduces critical thought and personal power. When others control your voice, you've already lost power and compromised integrity.
- When assessing or attributing power, don't overvalue tone, pace, posture or pitch. Tone can be artificially created and digitally remastered.
- It takes effort to build a powerful leadership position. Taking the easy option is a fast route to mediocrity, not a route to power.
- The more you win, the more you fear losing. That is precisely when judgement is most threatened. Fear of loss triggers short-term destructive decisions that crater reputations, revenues and relationships.
- The world isn't fair, so be prepared to lose power. It can always be repositioned, rebranded and redefined.
- When you gain power, it's a temporary privilege. Make decisions responsibly and use it for social good.

CHAPTER 5

EGO-BASED TRAPS: NOTHING COMPARES TO ME

"When the ego dies, the soul awakens."
Mahatma Gandhi

VENTURE CAPITAL FIRM Sequoia Capital described Sam Bankman-Fried, founder of the cryptocurrency exchange FTX, in messianic terms. His "intellect is as awesome as it is intimidating." Bankman-Fried says of himself, "I was on the cover of every magazine, and FTX was the darling of Silicon Valley."

Reputable investors like Sequoia, BlackRock and SoftBank piled into the bitcoin frenzy. "Politicians flocked and NFL quarterback Tom Brady was a glowing fan."[1] Bankman-Fried appeared alongside world leaders and even took out a Superbowl ad.

Billed as the ethical safehouse of crypto, by October 2022, FTX's value had risen to $32bn. A week later, Bankman-Fried filed for US bankruptcy amid allegations of misconduct and governance failure. In panic, he naively tweeted from the Bahamas:

I f***ed up, and should have done better... I'm piecing together all of the details, but I was shocked to see things unravel the way they did earlier this week.

Explaining matters further: "We got overconfident and careless." He explained his potential misuse of customers' funds to jaw-dropped journalists. "I don't know of a violation of the terms of use... I don't know every line of the terms of use. I can't confidently say there wasn't."[2] With a bad case of verbal diarrhoea, he couldn't stop himself, admitting millions in illegal political donations. NPR called it a "gift to prosecutors."

Gift unwrapped, the Department of Justice charged him with 12 counts of fraud and misappropriating $8bn in customer funds. He was later found guilty on all counts.

The peacock cares about the peacock. They care about who's right not what's right.

It's easy to feel invulnerable when seduced by your pseudo-brilliance or surrounded by sycophantic voices. Ego is a dangerous three-letter word, threatening powerholders and power hunters.

Egotism operates on a spectrum. In small doses, idle boasting and displays of vanity are harmless. We all do it to feel good. In larger doses, the hunt for recognition and reward can be career kryptonite.

This chapter builds on the PERIMETERS power-based traps to illustrate how six ego-related biases derail judgement when least expected. It doesn't explore ego fragility or self-esteem per se but rather, how overreliance on your own voice is a perilous source of misinformation, mishearing and misfortune.

I draw on stories of journalists, joggers, scientists, explorers and innovators to depict how our judgements feel infallible (illusion of validity), our views accurate (overconfidence) and better than others (illusory superiority). Because they're ours, we feel immune from error (illusion of invulnerability), convinced everything will work out. We don't recognise our own incompetence (Dunning–Kruger effect). After all, talent explains our success (false attribution) which is why we think everyone's watching our slip-ups as if we're Truman Burbank.

As a result, powerholders underestimate risk, reject advice and don't hear timely criticism. Being a Decision Ninja means learning how to temper ego.

EGO FM

Ego-centric deafness is pervasive in well-meaning, if misguided, leaders. History is littered with high-consequence examples. Pacifist Mahatma Gandhi donated one million Indian lives to the British Empire's World War I effort without negotiating any reciprocal goodwill. Neville Chamberlain vainly believed Hitler's false promise not to declare war.

Too often, we think our interpretations and predictions are valid. This excessive confidence in judgements is an *illusion of validity*.[3] Every day, professionals fall victim to these illusions and tune out counterfactual thinking.

When Frenchman Thierry de La Villehuchet of Access International Advisors invested billions in Bernie Madoff's fund, he turned a deaf ear to Markopolos's evidence. He believed what he saw, not what he heard. He didn't question the uni-directional charts or 1–2% average monthly return for seven years. Madoff's sophisticated split strike conversion strategies were market-driven, yet correlation with the S&P 100 index was a staggeringly low 6%. It didn't make sense. Markets are volatile. Yet Villehuchet conducted only minor due diligence on Madoff's transaction statements.

Why did this well-educated professional not interpret a mathematical impossibility as an anomaly?

Villehuchet heard the voice of an industry titan over a geeky nerd, convinced by what he saw – Santa Claus investment graphs, Madoff's charm and Wall Street reputation. His misjudgement erased his entire personal savings and cost his investing clients between $10bn and $35bn.

It cost more than money. Tragically, this proud Frenchman took his own life.

As Markopolos deduced, sometimes the simplest solutions are obvious. Occam's Razor is a 14th century philosophy that states simpler explanations are more likely to be true than complicated ones. In this case, it holds true.

There's more pressure than ever to be bright and right, especially if you're paid the big bucks – or charge them! If you're like most ladder-climbers or leaders, you want to be seen as smart. And companies expect it. Avoiding stupid mistakes is the quickest way to be seen as smart.

While trying to be *a* smart person is wise, trying to be *the* smart person is foolish.

Media glamorises industry titans as wizards, oracles, geniuses or saviours. Warren Buffett is the 'Oracle of Omaha,' Elvis was 'the King,' Steve Jobs a 'genius' and Elizabeth Holmes a 'wunderkind.' Idolatrous labels reinforce delusions.

It's an impossible ideal in today's culture of low forgiveness and low tolerance. There's nowhere to hide on social media. If others don't punish your mistakes, the persecuted punish themselves – except those who tune into their own station, Ego FM.

The mountain monologue

We all know people who love the sound of their own voices. Sometimes it's our own! It's more enjoyable to talk about yourself than listen to others, whether clients, colleagues or strangers. Here's one of my favourite examples:

As the oldest man to climb Mount Everest at age 55, Texan

Dick Bass was a local celebrity. During a cross-country flight, Bass passed the time and regaled a passenger about his mountaineering prowess. As the plane touched down, he formally introduced himself.

The polite passenger reciprocated, "Hi, I'm Neil Armstrong. Nice to meet you."

Bass was aghast. Before Armstrong died, I spoke with him in-depth and share some of his insights in Part Two. When you only hear yourself, you miss valuable voices.

Wisdom is talking less about yourself and listening more to others when it matters.

Listening in high-fidelity all the time isn't realistic, but it makes sense to at least ensure there's low distortion and a low signal-to-noise ratio.

When you think you might be over-talking, a useful coaching acronym is W.A.I.T. or "Why am I talking?" If you really can't stop, try W.A.I.L. or "Why aren't I listening?" The WAIL–WAIT duo is doubly effective!

ılı|lı·|ılı|ılı·

Sometimes leaders need to hear themselves speak. When Tony Hayward was appointed CEO of BP, he referenced performance as "dreadful" with "massive duplication," and claimed BP cared about "the small people." Eh? Unsurprisingly, shares plummeted.[4] After an offshore explosion, 100 million gallons of oil spilled into the Gulf of Mexico for 87 days. Eleven workers died.

Narcissism can destroy reputations overnight.

Interviewed by *ABC*'s Dianne Sawyer, among his apologies Hayward said, "There's no one who wants this over more than I do. I would like my life back."

The self-pity continued, "What the hell did we do to deserve this?" he moaned.[5] A decade later, BP still hadn't compensated Gulf fishers.[6]

When leaders believe their own spin, Professor David Collinson calls this "Prozac leadership."[7] One of the best ways to counteract ego-centric bias is to seek contrary views. But we don't take advice. We've invested too much in forming and confirming our sacred beliefs. Extensive advice-seeking is often misinterpreted as weak or "a confession of ignorance."[8]

When you solicit another opinion, do you adjust your views? Experts don't. Boards don't. And lawyers certainly don't. One study found 82% of lawyers claim to seek second opinions when predicting jury verdicts. In practice, they neither valued nor used these opinions.[9]

Listening to advice can reorient your life or business. That said, *unrealistic optimism* and *self-belief* fuel many an entrepreneur.

THE DOCTRINE OF SELF-BELIEF

In the late 1990s, Marc Benioff left his Oracle vice-president role to launch a business in a one-bedroom San Francisco apartment. At the time, few venture capitalists believed in the potential of cloud computing. "When we were raising money, no one would give us money," he told TechCrunch. So in 1999, he partly funded a start-up with $500,000 called Salesforce.

When Benioff bought the email app Slack for $27.7bn, investors thought it nuts and the stock fell 8%. Pre-deal eulogising is common. COO Bret Taylor said, "There could not be a more relevant product at a more relevant time for every single one of our customers."[10] The rapture factor continued. Commentators described Benioff's earnings call as a "lovefest of bedazzled proportions."

Benioff listened to his inner voice. "We believe so strongly that the world has changed, that the past is gone, and that we are in a new world." As at December 2023, Salesforce was worth $253bn.

Like entrepreneurs, investors and venture capitalists such as

Benioff or Bankman-Fried exhibit extreme self-belief. Takeover titan Carl Icahn is a hugely successful investor, despite his father's cynicism, "You have no talent, go be a doctor." Icahn tuned out that particular message! A corporate raider, he made billions speculating on TWA, Netflix and Apple.

His trick? He frequently adopts contrary positions against established voices.

For instance, Pershing Square CEO Bill Ackman took a $1bn short position in nutrition-supplement firm Herbalife before calling it a pyramid scheme. Ackman hoped the stock would sink. Icahn deliberately adopted the reverse position. A public vitriolic spat ensued. As traders tuned in to CNBC to hear it, NYSE trading dropped 20%. Icahn was right. Herbalife survived.

However, it's a balance. The smartest leaders misjudge when they don't listen to their own voice. Since 2017, Icahn estimates losing $9bn for betting against the market. He told the *FT*, "Maybe I made the mistake of not adhering to my own advice in recent years."[11] This reminds me of Oprah Winfrey who said, "I've trusted the still, small voice of intuition my entire life. And the only time I've made mistakes is when I didn't listen."[12] Knowing how to listen selectively to the right voice is a skill.

One industry that does this well is entertainment. Musicians exhibit tremendous capability to reinterpret what they hear.

Take cover versions. Over 1,600 artists have covered the Beatles hit 'Yesterday,' now a Guinness World Record. Artists master the ability to tune in to complicated arrangements, chords, harmonies and tempos, adding dimensionality to convert these into a unique sound. This requires innate self-belief. Nevertheless, some suffer temporary imposter syndrome. John Lennon famously said, "Part of me suspects that I'm a loser and the other part of me thinks I'm God Almighty."[13]

A dangerous ego-based bias challenging the Decision Ninja is *overconfidence*.

Above-average dancers and decision-makers

The more successful we are, the more we tend to think we're right, as Icahn, Kennedy, Ma and Bankman-Fried illustrate. Like owners of property or pets, people disproportionately value their own ideas and creations. If you paint a picture, do you value it more than one you buy? Most certainly.

This *endowment effect* leads to overconfidence and a false sense of security. What's worse, it weakens rational judgement.

Not to be confused with confidence, *overconfidence* is the unjustified belief in the supremacy, validity and accuracy of your ideas, usually without substance.

In a Wright State University survey of 8,000 business, hospital, university and government employees, most respondents scored themselves as *above-average* listeners compared to co-workers.[14] Consistently, Accenture surveyed 3,600 professionals in 30 countries and found 96% self-reported as good listeners.[15] That's almost everyone surveyed!

Not only do people self-report as better listeners but also better decision-makers, dancers, lovers and teachers.

Overconfidence is pervasive. A 1997 U.S. News & World Report study asked 1,000 Americans, "Who is most likely to get into heaven?" They chose between Bill Clinton, Michael Jordan, Mother Teresa and themselves.

Whom would you pick?

Over 87% selected themselves, ahead of Mother Teresa at 79%.

Overconfidence renders us psychologically deaf in seconds.

Golfer Rocco Mediate faced Tiger Woods in the 2008 US Open play-off. Mediate rocked with optimism, convinced of victory. Why? Woods had surgery for a double-stress knee fracture two months before. Mediate's overconfidence was misplaced. "Everybody and their mother knew that I was going to get killed, except for me."[16] We're all a bit like Mediate at times.

Overconfidence tempts us to underestimate downside risk and overestimate upside risk. A sense of *illusory superiority* leads to prediction inaccuracy. Professor Itzhak Ben-David of Ohio State University found CFOs miscalibrated forecasts of the S&P 500 returns. Claiming 80% confidence, in reality, only 36% of CFO projections were accurate.[17] A massive gap.

Overconfidence has been shown to impact financial regulation,[18] accountancy misstatements,[19] over-trading[20] and shareholder value.[21]

It's also a judgement killer in courtrooms.

The voice of OJ Simpson prosecutor Marcia Clark fell on deaf ears when she couldn't prevent Chris Darden from showing the jury a glove found at the murder scene. In an unforgettable moment, it didn't fit. The latex had shrunk as the gloves had been frozen and unfrozen. In 2016, she told *ABC News*, "I knew it was a mistake... I objected." After 253 days and 156 witnesses, Simpson went free.[22]

Some leaders are consistently overconfident in communications, forecasting and strategic planning. If you think you're always right, why listen to others?

Mergers and mind-readers

Successful M&A is grounded in strategic fit. Good complementarity will deliver economies of scale, fill capability gaps and accelerate access to products, channels or markets. It's why Proctor and Gamble acquired Gillette, why Morgan Stanley merged with Japan's Mitsubishi UFG, and why Microsoft sought Activision Blizzard for its cloud gaming capabilities.

Egotism deafens dealmakers about what constitutes good fit. It's easier to justify product or market fit and postpone the complexity of culture fit. For example, Laidlaw CEO James Bulloch believed ambulances and emergency services aligned well with its bus transportation business. This peculiar business mix and a $4.6bn debt resulted in bankruptcy.[23] Even when there is strategic fit, deal fundamentals may be wrong.

Hunting a trophy deal, Royal Bank of Scotland (RBS) CEO Fred Goodwin ignored concerns about the $49bn acquisition of ABN Amro. By 2007, RBS had completed 26 acquisitions so a complacent board predicted another success.[24] Like idealistic gamblers, they extrapolated luck would simply continue.

It seems reasonable, but it's irrational.

UBS banker John Cryan advised against the deal, "There's stuff in here that we can't even value."[25] Despite limited due diligence, Goodwin reportedly replied, "Stop being such a bean counter."

Even rival Barclays backed out. "We weren't prepared to secure a win at any price."[26]

Chairman Philip Hampton later told shareholders, "With the benefit of hindsight, it can now be seen as the wrong price, the wrong way to pay, at the wrong time and the wrong deal."[27] After posting a £28bn loss, the government bailed out RBS at a cost of £45bn and Queen Elizabeth II stripped Goodwin of his knighthood. Ordinary taxpayers still pay the price.

Ego-based biases dominate pre-deal thinking. A study of 1,000 CEOs and CFOs concluded that most make capital allocation decisions in relative isolation.[28] Disproportionate overconfidence and self-belief triggers leaders to suppress doubt and reject contrarian advice.

Instead of instinctively discounting contrarian arguments, humble leaders highlight some aspect of value with two words, "You're right." The mood always shifts!

·ı|ı|ı·|ı|ı·|ı|ı·

How often do we think others can read our mind when we communicate ideas?

Elizabeth Newton's experiment proves how much overconfidence is inbuilt. Subjects tapped out 120 tunes such as 'Happy Birthday' or Queen's 'We Are the Champions.' They guessed 50% of listeners would accurately identify their selected melody. Like a bad game of charades on Christmas day, only 2.5% guessed accurately.[29]

Do you think you understand a subject's complexity only to find you don't?[30] Most of us have a superficial knowledge of many topics yet think we know more than we do. Scientists coin this the *illusion of explanatory depth*. It's related to how well we think of ourselves and how little we accept our shortcomings. And it's a crucial derailer for those in power, the Decision Ninja or aspiring leader.

Overconfidence generates misinformation and false conclusions, whether about M&As, trial evidence, golf prowess, tapping or quiz answers. It's compounded when we think we're immune from error. It stunts what we hear and reduces inclination to course correct. That's why it's a fatal judgement killer.

IT WON'T HAPPEN TO ME

In Yellowstone National Park, notices are placed on forest treks highlighting the presence of black bears and warning unsuspecting tourists not to frighten them with sudden noises. During a vacation, I learned a jogger had been tragically mauled to death. I assumed it was a tourist. It wasn't. It was a local young man wearing earphones. He knew both the area and risks involved but irrationally ignored the warnings.

A vastly neglected bias can help explain this tragedy: the *illusion of invulnerability*.

Speeding teenagers think they'll never crash. Homeowners on the San Andreas Faultline think earthquakes won't happen. Drug users think they control cocaine. Ted Bundy thought

Utah, Washington and Florida police would never catch him. Bankman-Fried, a modern-day Madoff in cargo pants, denies charges yet his CEO, CFO and engineering director admit fraud.

This illusion is rampant, from journalists to socialites, royalty, innovators or sports stars.

When six-time Grand Slam winner Boris Becker declared bankruptcy, he proceeded to hide £2.5m worth of assets, despite having narrowly avoided a prison term. When he later exhibited no remorse, Judge Deborah Taylor sentenced the German star to over two years in prison.

> You did not heed the warning you were given and the chance you were given by the suspended sentence and that is a significant aggravating factor.[31]

When diagnosed with rare pancreatic cancer, Apple founder Steve Jobs engaged in unconventional therapies with macrobiotic dieticians and spiritualists for nine months. He rejected traditional treatment but eventually had the necessary surgery. He admitted to his biographer Walter Isaacson that this delay was a mistake. "I should have gotten it earlier."[32]

According to Isaacson, "I think that he kind of felt that if you ignore something, if you don't want something to exist, you can have magical thinking."[33]

Board directors think companies will never go bust yet the average lifespan is dropping. In the mid-2010s, Yale's Richard Foster reported that the average S&P 500 company's lifespan had fallen from 67 years in the 1920s to 15 years. Moreover, 76% of FTSE 100 firms have disappeared since the early 1990s. Nevertheless, smart well-meaning professionals still think themselves immune and make myopic decisions.

Being single-minded and deaf to risk stops us appraising true vulnerability.

In the 1990s, *Sunday Independent* crime reporter Veronica Guerin investigated Dublin's biggest drug barons and underworld criminals. She received death threats, a bullet in the leg, a warning shot through her front door and her son was threatened with rape. She also dismissed a police escort, telling local media *RTE*, "That's what I do. Somebody has to do it."

In June 1996, 37-year-old Guerin sat in her red Opal Calibra at the Naas dual carriageway traffic lights. Two motorcyclists roared up and shot her six times.

As her name was added to the Freedom Forum Journalists Memorial for those who die in the line of duty, her husband said, "Veronica stood for freedom to write... Veronica was not a judge, nor was she a juror, but she paid the ultimate price with the sacrifice of her life."[34] Thinking the worst was over, "She didn't want to stop, but she didn't really think that things were going to get any worse."[35]

It was a single-minded misjudgement with unintended consequences.

TOO BIG TO FAIL, TOO BIG TO JAIL

Another population that believes themselves immune is privileged powerholders and wealthy socialites. Why? Because they're usually protected and escape recriminations.

Daughter of media baron Robert Maxwell, Ghislaine Maxwell, was hunted in connection with trafficking minors for Jeffrey Epstein. She eluded detection for a year, moving locations and concealing her identity. Having bought a 4,365-square-foot New Hampshire property, she returned to the US and was apprehended. She thought herself invincible. This regret was bigger than "ever meeting Epstein." Today, there are few rays of sunshine for the woman whose name means 'ray of sunshine.'[36]

The overconfident dismiss the voice of common sense, forgetting what you hear isn't always reality.

Barclays CEO Jes Staley caught my attention when I was doing whistleblowing research at the London School of Economics, exploring what factors differentiate the bystander from the whistleblower. In 2018, regulators fined him nearly a million dollars for a conflict of interest after he hunted down a whistleblower who complained to the board about a close colleague.

Three years later, Staley resigned when regulators found him guilty of mischaracterising his relationship with Epstein. Prior to this, he spent 30 years in JP Morgan running asset management and banking. When compliance placed red flags against Epstein following the 2006 sex crime charges, Staley vouched for Epstein. JP Morgan subsequently sued Staley for "misrepresenting the true facts." Like Maxwell, Staley "deeply regrets" the friendship and "didn't know about crimes."[37]

People with power think they're invulnerable, partly a function of ego and systemic privilege but also a history of limited consequence. The powerful rarely pay. Different rules apply and failures are excused because few want to take on a Goliath. This is slowly changing as demand for justice and fairness grows louder as cases against Theranos and FTX substantiate.

·ıl|ı·|ıl|ı|ıll|ı·

Countries also exhibit the illusion of invulnerability.

Remember when Saudi Arabian journalist and dissident Jamal Khashoggi was forcibly restrained, drugged and brutally dismembered in the consulate in Istanbul? The Saudi government overestimated its infallibility and underestimated global outrage. This sense of mutual invulnerability led to flawed choices by the perpetrator and victim. Although Khashoggi took precautions before entering the consulate, he tuned out the voice of intuition.

His fiancé wrote, "He didn't believe something bad could happen on Turkish soil."[38]

Countries regularly miscalculate decisions. For instance, the US underestimated the peacekeeping fallout of prematurely withdrawing troops from Kabul. After years of protection, Afghanistan fell to the Taliban within hours.

In the same way, China miscalculated the horrified global response to self-immolation images of "Free Tibet" and later, the disappearance of outspoken tennis star Peng Shuai.

Trying to build an empire like the Romans doesn't always auger well.

IS THERE SOMETHING I SHOULD KNOW?

As power rises, so does ego. The more successful you are, the less likely you are to doubt yourself or hear shortcomings. Our overconfidence makes us poor at spotting or accepting incompetence.[39] Fawning fans, employees, acolytes and sycophants merely reinforce our Svengali status.

Merryck & Co and the Barrett Values Centre compared the self-assessments of 500 leaders with 10,000 peers over 15 years.[40] Leaders' self-assessments rarely overlapped with their executives. In fact, 84% of assessors disagreed with leaders' self-reported listening skills.

Similarly, Deloitte found that 90% of CEOs think their employees rate them as doing a great job, but only half of employees believe CEOs care about their well-being.[41]

Recall how most employees considered themselves better than average listeners and decision-makers? It's easy to miss our incompetence.

After reading about a bizarre case in Pittsburgh, David Dunning coined the inability to spot our own incompetence the *Dunning–Kruger effect*. In 1996, McArthur Wheeler robbed two banks at gunpoint. Wheeler thought rubbing lemon juice on his face made him invisible to the bank's security cameras. Why? Lemon juice had apparently concealed his face when he took Polaroids. "But I wore juice," Wheeler explained deludedly.[42]

How can we make good decisions if we don't realise, let alone accept, our own failings?

There's no shame in not knowing something. Shame is assuming or pretending we know everything.

At sports press conferences, you might hear winning players attribute success to practice. Their opponent might blame the club or rowdy crowd.

Excuses are frequently heard on earnings calls when profits fall below expectations or during scandals. John Stumpf blamed fraudulent employees rather than culture, in what Elizabeth Warren called "gutless leadership."

It's common for people to attribute a successful outcome to personal skill over luck, timing or other situational factors. It's called *fundamental attribution error*. You only need to watch the movie *Sliding Doors* to appreciate how life is shaped by random events, like which subway train you catch.

It takes time to go from bad to good decisions but just nanoseconds to go from good decisions to bad.

If you spot incompetence in others, you can use it as a source of advantage. This week, try to notice if others attribute failure or poor performance to external forces rather than themselves.

Everybody's watching me

If you're like most people, you probably think everyone notices your Pulitzer-worthy post or cringeworthy faux-pas. When we think others pore over our every mistake, paranoia stops us from thinking clearly. In reality, people don't notice us half as much as we think.

Like unrequited lovers, we obsess about others who don't obsess about us.

We all have a public and a private face. Most people change behaviour when they think they're being watched. It's the *Hawthorne effect*. In the quest to be accepted, promoted or popular, we may offer more collaborative insights or work late when bosses are watching. It's why managers get so easily duped by optics and smooth-talking employees!

Visibility yields moral advantages. Science tells us we donate more and are less anti-social when we know we're being watched. Take washing hands. Kristen Munger and Shelby Harris wanted to see what bathroom users did when they thought they were alone.[43] So they placed a visible attendant in a public restroom.

What happened? Some 77% washed their hands. When no attendant was seen, handwashing halved to 39%. In other words, being observed doubled compliance.

Visibility is effective in law enforcement settings. It turns out British and US police officers were less likely to use force when trialling body cameras. Use of force dropped 37% when cameras were on but soared 71% when officers were allowed to turn them off at will.[44] Barak Ariel's global research indicates complaints directed at wearers fell by 93% in what they termed "contagious accountability."[45]

Charities use this insight to boost donations. In a six-month Dutch experiment across 30 churches, when a donation basket was left open and each congregant's contribution visible, donations increased by 10%. Just-giving sites and fund-raising coffee mornings with glass jars visibly perched in the centre of the host's kitchen table exploit this effect as a shaming tactic, knowing ego encourages us to maintain appearances and conform to social norms.

TUNING IN: THE VOICE OF OBJECTIVITY

Ego-based biases are to be nurtured and managed. When they exist in moderation, the world wins. Admitting error or climbing down from public pronouncements, projects and predictions takes courage. So does turning around a failed project. It may appear backwards, but leaders who set aside ego can propel nations forwards.

NASA engineer Greg Robinson inherited a project that was $9bn over budget, 15 years late and nearly killed by Congress several times.[46] According to a *Wall Street Journal* report, it had a 50% schedule efficiency. In other words, the project spent half of its lifespan dysfunctional. It featured 300 single-point failures. Putting that in context, "on a Mars landing mission, you might have 70 single-point failures."

Robinson turned the project around. When it completed, schedule efficiency was 95% and incorporated ten critical technologies.

The project constructed the largest optical telescope in the world. In partnership with European and Canadian agencies, the James Webb Space Telescope was designed to study galaxies, one of the most complex and ambitious scientific instruments ever.

The lesson? Breakthrough progress is possible with a balanced ego and broad perspective.

Ego is context specific. Great partnerships mean setting aside ego, at least temporarily. Consider one of the greatest songwriting collaborations of all time, Lennon and McCartney. As young Liverpudlians, the pair agreed to equal credit. Each contribution was respected, even if it was just changing a chord or a lyric. The reward for offsetting relative capabilities was over 180 jointly credited Beatles songs and 600 million record sales.

Sentiments change. After the Beatles split, acrimony set in. Legal disputes arose about whether the order of credits could be reversed. The lesson? Even world-class partnerships have a shelf life.

As Fred Goodwin, Tony Hayward and Bankman-Fried have demonstrated, when ego and power blend, the scale of risk-taking and damage can be commercially and morally catastrophic. Vanity often trumps sanity.

Regardless of industry or life stage, you can stem bullish tendencies and shrink ego by collecting disconfirming data, alternating views and recalibrating expectations. When big brains surround themselves with bigger brains to raise the bar, everybody wins.

If ego is the enemy of good judgement, then humility is the hallmark of good judgement, making us more willing to ask questions and question answers, assertions and beliefs.

When ego dominates decisions, rational calculations of risk evaporate. Individuals and organisations are so convinced by the sound of their own logic that overestimation of reward and underestimation of regret results.

That's the focus of the Risk-based PERIMETERS traps.

THE DECISION NINJA

WHAT TO REMEMBER

- Ego-based self-belief is a double-edged sword: both power-charger and source of career kryptonite.
- We default to ego but fail to recognise its decision contamination until it's too late.
- Overconfidence is closely linked with extreme optimism and a deluded sense of invulnerability.
- Listen in high-fidelity as much as possible and choose when to WAIT and when to WAIL!
- Ego is a dangerous three-letter word. We care too much about being heard and not enough about hearing others.
- When obsessed with yourself, there's no room to hear rational or independent voices.
- Unmanaged self-belief and illusory superiority lead to underweighted risk. Thinking you're always right means you don't hear who or what's wrong.
- Assigning probabilities to outcomes at pre-decision stage will reveal overconfidence as inaccuracy usually emerges after the fact.
- Knowing we're being watched creates contagious accountability as our ego craves others' approval. It's a valuable behaviour-modification tool.
- Ego-based judgement traps are manageable with effort. Humility is not a foreign science or dark art. It can supercharge innovation, artistic differentiation and social good, especially when combined with power.

CHAPTER 6

RISK-BASED TRAPS: DECISION ROULETTE

"If nature has taught us anything, it is that the impossible is probable."

Illyas Kassam

ORMULA ONE DRIVERS, fire crews, suicide bombers, skydivers, hunger strikers and mountain climbers all have one thing in common. They risk their lives for ideologies, causes or dreams.

As the tallest peak in the world, it presents a challenge that draws people like no other mountain ... for some people, the risks actually add to why they want to climb it rather than detract from it – if there were no risk, it wouldn't be the prized challenge that it is.

That's the voice of Sarah Arnold-Hall, whose father, experienced Adventure Consultants owner Rob Hall, died with seven other climbers during the 1996 Everest expedition. Case studies, books, memorials and movies have been dedicated to untangling the judgements involved.

In 1996, overcrowding in Everest's 'death zone' was a

rising hazard.[1] Hall's clients underwent a month's intensive acclimatisation from base camp. With five successful climbs, he knew that reaching the summit by 2pm ensured safe descent. On this expedition, Hall joined forces with a less-experienced team. Thirty-three climbers set off but when they reached the hazardous Hillary Step, no fixed line ropes were in place to ascend the vertical rock face, causing a critical one-hour delay.

Some climbers turned back. One client, Doug Hansen, was desperate to complete his second attempt and refused. The prize was a once-in-a-lifetime opportunity with bragging rights. Hearing his client's desperation and tuning out his own rule, Hall waited to help Hansen reach the summit. Was this empathy, client service or irresponsibility?

An unexpected blizzard blocked their visibility to descend safely. Without any tent, water or oxygen, both climbers perished from frostbite and hypothermia.

Few decisions are risk-free. Most people want maximum reward for minimum risk. Yet reward-seeking distorts rational judgement in the moment, increasing unwanted risk.

This chapter doesn't explore risk management. Instead, it focuses on seven risk-based deaf spots that lead decision-makers astray. To some people, the thrill attracts (sensation-seeking) while others are driven by low risk (certainty bias). Like the Everest climbers, we evaluate situations based on perceived risk rather than actual risk (availability bias) and miscalculate likelihood of adverse outcomes (probability neglect). Miscalculation occurs when we fixate on the first message heard (anchoring) and strive to limit loss (loss aversion), reflecting the climbers who turned back. Like Doug Hansen, those committed to a path can't stop (commitment escalation).

The good news is risk perception and risk preferences evolve and can be managed (preference reversals). Understanding how appetite affects people's choice is not just a source of relative advantage but a contributor to outperformance and economic success.

Like each PERIMETERS trap, perceived risk can work for or against you. A confluence of factors shapes individual and organisational risk assessment. It starts with preference and personality.

TO THRILL OR NOT TO THRILL

While some personalities are extreme thrill-seekers like escape artist David Blaine, most people favour certainty, order and familiar processes. We tend to tune in to, marry, live and socialise with those who have similar appetites to ourselves.

There's no ideal or one-size risk appetite. It's context-dependent.

German psychologist Gerd Gigerenzer advises against categorising people as either risk-seeking or risk-averse, arguing we acquire the social habits of our peers because appetite is fluid.[2] For instance, you can be a gambler (risk-seeking) yet refuse to carry guns (risk-averse). Equally, you might never gamble (risk-averse) but happily carry guns (risk-seeking).

Take Swiss surgeon Johannes Fatio who performed the courageous first separation of conjoined twins in 1689. Two years later, Fatio took a different type of risk as a rebel in the Basel Revolution, eager to rewrite the Swiss Constitution. It wasn't to be. He was executed for treason.

Culture shapes risk appetite. For example, in Spain, bullfighting and bull-running are hazardous; tourists are trampled, matadors gored and 250,000 bulls die every year. Yet it's local entertainment.

Culture and the company you keep shapes whether you take shortcuts, gamble, speed date or shoplift.

Mood shapes risk appetite. Research finds people in a good

mood typically make optimistic judgements while those in a bad mood make more pessimistic judgements.

Risk consequentiality exists on a spectrum. Apollo 11 astronauts spent most of 1964 compiling thousands of questions with unknown answers. In his memoir, Michael Collins tells of the "enormous reservoir of doubt to be drained before the task could be considered a reasonable possibility."[3] He asked, "Would the dust layer on the moon exceed the height of the lunar module? Would static electricity obscure the astronauts' view from the windows?" Safe return was riddled with risk.

On the return, the atmospheric 're-entry corridor,' or zone of survivability… was only forty miles thick, and hitting a forty-mile target from 230,000 miles is like trying to split a human hair with a razor blade thrown from a distance of twenty feet.

That's risk!

Risk consequentiality also shifts over time. Coming out as gay was a lot different in the 1940s for mathematician Alan Turing than it was for Billie Jean King in the 1980s, singer George Michael in the 1990s, All Blacks player Campbell Johnstone in the 2020s, or 95-year-old baseball player Maybelle Blair in 2022.

Every day, businesses combine known and unknown risks, making decisions about hiring, compensation, cybersecurity, regulations, R&D and safety. Consequentiality is as much a collective responsibility as an individual one. Choices often boil down to sensation-seeking appetite.

The sensation rollercoaster

In the 1994 World Championship, Formula One Brazilian driver Rubens Barrichello hit the wall and flipped his car, escaping with his life. Twenty-four hours later, a minor incident damaged the front wing of Austrian Roland Ratzberger's car. As he approached the Villeneuve corner on the same track, Ratzberger crashed at 195mph and died on impact.

Organisers decided the race would go ahead.

These freak accidents rattled racers onsite including Ayrton Senna, Alain Prost, Niki Lauda and Michael Schumacher. Seeing Senna distraught, neurosurgeon Sid Watkins suggested the three-time world champion could retire. Senna replied he couldn't stop racing.

Was he obsessed with winning, glory-hunting or just committed to his chosen career?

On Sunday, a shaken Senna lobbied Prost and others to improve the sport's safety. Video footage shows a pensive Senna settling into the Williams car. On the seventh lap, Senna smashed into a wall at 131mph. An investigation ruled the cause was failure of the car's steering column which snapped, rendering Senna helpless. The column had been rewelded for extra cockpit space days earlier. Massive mourning followed, with three million Brazilians attending his funeral.

The sensation rollercoaster pervades many domains.

Adventure tourism is trending, whether to space, the Antarctic, Everest or the ocean floor. Much of this is unregulated. In 2018, 38 experts warned OceanGate owner Stockton Rush that the submersible firm needed certification to avoid catastrophic problems. Untested carbon-fibre materials had been used to manufacture the hull of its *Titan* vessel which would descend to view the wreckage of the *Titanic* 12,000 feet below the ocean's surface.

A former passenger described the experience as "learning as they go along."[4] When the vessel's PlayStation controller malfunctioned, one expedition missed the Titanic's bow completely. But a confident Rush believed its adventures to the shipwreck were "way safer than flying in a helicopter or even scuba diving."[5] Minimising risk and safety concerns, he fired vocal whistleblowers.[6]

In July 2023, the *Titan* vessel imploded shortly after submersion, killing all on board, including its owner. Blind spots and deaf spots likely prevented hearing what mattered or asking enough probing questions on this $250,000-a-seat, once-in-a-lifetime escapade.

When *tunnel vision* combines with *sensation-seeking bias*, it can literally be a judgement killer.

For some, money is the motivator for risk-taking rather than the adventure. According to the 2021 World Economic Forum, the Covid-19 pandemic created over 3,300 billionaires, one every 30 hours.[7]

Long before that, risk-takers piled into bitcoin, dogecoin and non-fungible tokens, thinking exotic instruments would facilitate fast money. Many had no idea what they were buying. Get-rich-quick Ponzi schemes and start-ups are attractive but high risk.

Some don't mind. Risk is relative: what's risky for a retiree may be thrilling for a millennial. And vice versa.

The antithesis of thrill-seeking is certainty-hunting, and induces bias in its own way.

CRAVING THE CERTAIN BET

What's happening? Who's that? Where are we going?

We don't like the unknown. Humans prefer certainty to ambiguity and chaos. The market doesn't like fifty shades of grey either. Immediately after 9/11, almost $1.4trn was lost as the Dow Jones dropped 14% and Standard & Poor's 11.6%.[8]

Few decisions are risk-free. High-stakes decisions are characterised by complexity, uncertainty and incomplete data. For instance, when boards replace a CEO, any candidate may perform, but which will outperform? Political donors invest millions, but will their party win? Parents choose schools, but which will secure top results?

You can't know everything for certain, but you can certainly estimate its probability.

Certainty obsession is a decision risk in itself. It narrows thinking in *certainty bias*. For example, when Spotify introduced music streaming to counteract illegal downloading, rather than course correct, dismissive record companies sued entrepreneurs for copyright infringement. That only heightened momentum among music fans tired of being fleeced for CDs.

Ironically, demand for streaming grew in a classic *Streisand effect*. By blocking publication of photos of her home, Barbra Streisand increased public curiosity in precisely what she was trying to prevent. The same thing happened with streaming. Spotify now boasts over 225 million subscribers.

Organisations can be deaf to ideas perceived as far-fetched, expensive, disruptive or psychologically remote. Such cynicism isn't new. In 1876, Alexander Graham Bell failed to sell a telephone patent to Western Union for $100,000. Executives didn't think consumers were smart enough to use phones! They heard the voice of familiarity.

In the early days of the auto industry, Gottlieb Daimler concluded one million cars would never exist globally due to a "lack of capable drivers."[9] Yet pre-pandemic sales reached 90 million vehicles.

And Microsoft CEO Steve Ballmer famously told a press conference in 2007, "There's no chance the iPhone is going to get significant market share." A career-defining comment.

Of course, consumers embrace change or disrupted industries wouldn't exist, such as Uber's hail and ride, Airbnb properties, Audible books, Robinhood trading and TripAdvisor's travel. Toy manufacturer Mattel once manufactured Barbie dolls, now it's in the movie business and breaking all-time records.

Certainty is a billion-dollar business. Knowledge-based industries commercially exploit the human craving for *regret aversion*. Just as the cosmetic industry sells hope, consultants, financial advisers, coaches and therapists sell hope for a fee. Leaders gratefully delegate tough decisions to independent third parties. Why?

The delusion of false certainty feels better than the dilemma of certain doubt.

Probabilistic thinking is a handy way to communicate ideas and improve judgement accuracy. To avoid ambiguity, Annie Duke suggests calibrating events in terms of probabilities. For example, "There's a 95% chance it will rain" communicates a more realistic assessment than "I think it'll rain."

That said, the data available reinforces the delusion of certainty, throwing us off course.

PERCEIVED VS ACTUAL RISK

Just as Senna's accident antennae must have increased that fateful weekend, if you hear about two air crashes in a week, your sensitivity to travel risk will rise disproportionately. Similarly, if you hear about a technology hack from a trusted colleague, you recall it quicker, thinking it's accurate.

The illusion of accuracy occurs because individuals decide based on perceived risk, not actual risk. *Availability bias* suggests we rely on whatever information immediately springs to mind. We use mentally available information rather than the right information. This derails us because even the sharpest minds don't suspect it's happening.

For example, a market-sensitive trader may pick biotech stocks based on news stories about biotech.[10] In fact, INSEAD professor Joel Peress tested trader susceptibility to news flow when choosing stocks. Would trading volume shift on days newspapers went on strike?

On strike days with no news, trading dropped 12%, suggesting professionals in a noisy world rely on what's easily available rather than what's accurate.

Leaders who have never gone bust ignore profit warnings. Homeowners defer security until they're burgled. It's easy to discount what isn't imagined or outside your frame of reference. Just as a Ponzi scheme seemed remote to Villehuchet, Jack Ma seemed destined to be China's lifelong poster child.

When we construct narratives from available data, we suffer bounded attention in the PERIMETERS Effect. What's more, we miscalculate true probability.

A 'one in a million' chance

In the movie *Dumb and Dumber*, goofy Jim Carrey calculates his prospects of winning over a super-hot girl. His friend points out his one in a million chance. Carrey bounces up shrieking, "I have a chance, I have a chance." When we overestimate small probabilities, it's termed *probability neglect*.

Every day we unconsciously neglect true risk. We overspend and undersave, drink too much and drive too fast. Passengers may fear plane crashes even though there's a greater chance of being knocked down on the road, according to accident statistics. It's irrational but feels real.

Dread risk exacerbates this further. For months after 9/11, Americans were understandably afraid to fly and drove instead. Gerd Gigerenzer found "the number of Americans who lost their lives on the road by avoiding the risk of flying was higher than the total number of passengers killed on the four fatal flights."[11]

Similarly, sunbed users discount the risk of skin cancer. Expense-abusing employees ignore the risk of termination or prosecution. The *Titanic* adventurers knowingly signed a liability waiver not thinking they'd ever need it.

In politics, outspoken Russian critic Alexei Navalny underestimated the cost of violating probation in 2021. Having survived an assassination attempt, he returned to Russia only to be sent to a penal colony. "They imprison one man, as a means to intimidate millions of people," he said.[12] Authorities subsequently added 19 years to his 11-year sentence.

Former prime minister of Pakistan Benazir Bhutto was warned not to return home after eight years of self-imposed exile. Distrusted by the military, corruption allegations had removed her from power. Campaigning for justice and re-election in 2008, she was assassinated in a jihadist attack.[13]

It's a surprise when these things happen. It's a surprise when we're scammed, fired or dumped but it shouldn't be. The signals are usually there, we're just tone-deaf, hearing what's comfortable and convenient.

Our greatest fears fund lucrative businesses. Some exploit the fact we underweight large probabilities (being scammed) and overweight small probabilities (winning the lottery). For instance, lottery companies know a 1% chance of winning $1,000 is more attractive than a guaranteed $1 reward. They know our minds are often more illogical than logical.

Human delusions are big business. Loss adjusters and risk managers pump millions into the economy. According to SwissRe Institute, global premiums passed $7trn in 2022 and are forecast to rise. That's a lot of anxiety! In most cases, the insured risk never materialises.

Nevertheless, we want to be sure.

Hollywood's Robert De Niro had to put on 50 pounds to play middleweight boxing champion Jake LaMotta in 1981's *Raging Bull*. Putting on weight was "One of the toughest career things ever," he said. Hmm. I know an easy way! It involves a third tub of Häagen-Dazs! In case he couldn't lose the weight, he took out insurance with Fireman's Fund.

Fox Studios insured Betty Grable's legs for $1m. Thereafter she was promoted as "the girl with the million-dollar legs." That's a lot less than David Beckham's $195m footballer legs!

Some go to extremes. According to an insurance historian, in 1938, actors Priscilla Lane and Wayne Morris insured their relationship against "subversive influences of Hollywood, scandal-mongers and other vicious forces." Their love was valued at $50,000![14] Cheap!

Even brands encounter unexpected black swans. During the 1990s cola wars, Pepsi underestimated one of its adverts being taken literally. Executives had advertised the top prize of a harrier fighter jet for 7,000,000 loyalty points but forgot to include the risk-free disclaimer. Ambitious student John Leonard interpreted the offer as legitimate and liaised with a businessman to secure the jet. Pepsi scoffed, saying it was a joke. A bitter battle ensued. Leonard rejected a settlement offer but lost the case.

When black swans occur, typically the client, investor or shareholder pays.

For prescient organisations, risk paranoia can pay off. After the 2003 SARS outbreak, the English Lawn Tennis Association insured against the remote risk of a pandemic. For £25.5m in premiums, they collected £114m when they cancelled Wimbledon in 2020.

॥|॥·|॥|॥·|॥

Professionals are paid to take calculated risk, not compromise client safety. On 20 January 2020, Ara Zobayan piloted a helicopter with his client and seven passengers. The night before, he thought conditions were "not the best." Before take-off, Los Angeles County fog was hovering, but he concluded it "should be OK." Shortly after take-off, he advised air traffic control he was climbing.

In fact, the helicopter was descending. Breaching rules, Zobayan had ascended into clouds without a visual reference. The Sikorsky-76 crashed into a hillside killing all on board, including five-time NBA champion Kobe Bryant.

The National Transportation Safety Board concluded flying with limited visibility "resulted in spatial disorientation and loss of control."[15] It referenced "self-induced pressure" from Bryant's presence. The charter company also lacked governance with "inadequate review and oversight."

This wasn't a black swan as it was predictable, but the probability of an accident was neglected just as it was with the *Titanic* adventurers.

Zobayan exemplified pilot pride, something Apollo 11's Michael Collins relates to.

> Death before dishonour is replaced by death before embarrassment… accident files are bulging with cases in which a pilot's professional pride, or obstinacy, caused him to choose an ultimately suicidal course of action rather than admit a mistake.[16]

When we neglect probability, we pay over the odds for insurance, extended warranties or premium branded equipment. But more importantly, we endanger lives – ours and others'.

Rational thinking is impeded by another silent judgement killer: loss aversion.

IT'S BANANAS. I CAN'T LOSE

In 2006, Caesars Palace in Las Vegas published the tournament results of René Angélil, an experienced poker player and Celine Dion's husband. His losses were estimated at $230,300, with winnings marginally higher at $259,079.[17] According to Kahneman and Tversky, "Losses loom larger than gains."[18] In other words, losses likely hurt Angélil far more than the gains. It's *loss aversion*.

Do you default to safe options? Do you always swipe left on Tinder? Or have the same breakfast every day?

Your loss aversion radar is one of the most underestimated sources of misjudgement. Loss aversion is rationalised as "better the devil you know." We disproportionately overweight decisions where we won't lose.

The oddest things can be interpreted as a loss. Many firms provide perks like free coffee, snacks and fruit. In 2009, when markets turned, many firms slashed jobs. In a bank close to where I worked, the daily free fruit was cancelled. Employee revolt ensued. Management was baffled. What upset the well-paid employees wasn't unemployment risk but loss of entitlement to free bananas! It became known as 'bananagate.'

Loss aversion dictates which risks you're willing to take. This aversion can spark or stagnate a business. Science finds the older, richer and more successful you are, the more loss aversion kicks in.[19] At board level, it's common to hear well-off powerholders vote for decisions protect their privilege and prioritise self-interest. Is that loss aversion combined with greed?

Some people really do suffer from feeling like they messed up, especially professional firefighters, emergency services, protection services, investigators and counsellors. To combat fallout from loss aversion, it's better to focus on what you achieve, not what you miss, mess up or miss out on.

Closely related to loss aversion is FOMO, or fear of missing out. That could consume a full chapter in itself. Many retailers successfully leverage this to sway impressionable and gullible customers to overspend in annoying "going, going, gone" campaigns. And we still tune in every time, wasting hard-earned cash!

Loss aversion triggers our inbuilt desperation to not lose time, money or energy invested. It reminds me of the *Mastermind* quiz line, "I've started so I'll finish."

I'VE STARTED SO I'LL FINISH

Do you watch the end of a dull film because you started it? Some stay in jobs, theatres and relationships too long.

In 1956, my own mother and father attended a compulsory Catholic pre-marital course to ascertain partner suitability. My mother suspected long-term incompatibility but ignored the warning signs. Separation followed five children later!

Clinging to what we've started is a side-effect of loss aversion. Our inclination to hear reason diminishes when we've invested time, money and effort. In business, firms persist with failing or resource-draining initiatives. Vain leaders hate to admit mistakes so escalate commitment rather than call it a day. That's the *sunk cost fallacy*.

Like SoftBank, several venture capitalists invested in WeWork. One investor, Benchmark partner Bruce Dunlevie sat on WeWork's board and grew increasingly concerned about Neumann's investment patterns and erratic demands. He told a reporter:

> We get paid to deal with these wild and crazy entrepreneurs… we're expected to remain in the ring and keep swinging, even when we're getting our ass kicked.[20]

Despite the voice of doubt, Dunlevie tuned out concerns. It made sense – until it didn't. Sunk costs irrationally escalate commitment.

It's the same with pet projects.

McKinsey estimates 98% of construction projects overrun.[21] While it's better to kill your own project than have others do it, it's hard. Tim Koller proposes 'mandating objectivity' by designating an independent 'Project Killer,' citing how an ingredient producer streamlined its portfolio from 560 to 200 products over three years.[22]

On the Everest expedition, Doug Hansen knew the risks. Close to his dream, he couldn't quit and wouldn't descend. So what made fellow climber US reporter Jon Krakauer turn back?

Krakauer explains, "A perilously thin line demarcates laudable perseverance from reckless determination." It was part financial and part psychological.

Three of the surviving climbers in his group had one thing in common:

> [They had] spent as much as $70,000 and endured great hardship to have this shot at the summit. All were driven men, unaccustomed to losing and even less to quitting. And yet, faced with a hard decision, they were among the few who made the right choice that day.[23]

This fallacy explains why people stubbornly progress along their chosen path, despite warning signs and alarm bells.

Let's explore another insidious risk-related bias that traps the smartest decision-makers. You'll never negotiate the same way again.

Anchored to what you first hear

When a politician's aunt was kidnapped in Haiti, hostage-takers demanded a $150,000 ransom. In *Never Split the Difference*, veteran FBI negotiator Chris Voss tells how he dropped this to $4,751 plus a CD stereo.[24] He told the kidnappers three things.

Firstly, "We don't have that much money." This anchored expectations. The family offered $3,000 then $4,751. The precision communicated a methodical calculation, gaining trust as people view round numbers cynically.

Secondly, Voss reminded them, "We can't pay if you hurt her." Ransoms aren't paid on dead people.

Thirdly, Voss offered a CD, reinforcing their inability to pay with such a frivolous gesture, "This is all we have," reinforcing a low anchor and building rapport.

The aunt was released unharmed within six hours. The lesson? Always pitch first to anchor others to your range!

How does this work? Anchors act like primes that stick in the memory. Like first impressions, we overweight whatever word, phrase or number we first hear.

Think about when you're choosing wine in a restaurant. The first option on the list is Saint-Emilion-Grand-Cru costing $66; the second, a Chianti, costs $27. The Chianti looks relatively cheap, so most people order it even if they usually only spend $18. They've been anchored!

While anchors defy logic, they're an important deaf spot affecting everything from negotiating to buying, selling, lending, project forecasting and sentencing.

Here's one of my favourite experiments that demonstrates the power of anchoring.

Prosecutors gave judges hypothetical sentencing recommendations that ranged from two months to 34 months. Would this matter? It did. Judges given the higher anchor awarded an average sentence of 28.7 months. In comparison, judges given the lower anchor awarded an average of 18.78 months.[25] A life-altering difference.

Lawyers exploit this insight and typically sue for high amounts to anchor juries.[26] However, fair-minded juries tend to reduce awards for greedy plaintiffs and prosecutors.

How often do you spot anchoring? When deciding your pay rise, bosses and recruiters tend to anchor to your current salary not your market value. I once interviewed a man who boasted how he used to earn twice his current salary. The anchor backfired. He became half as valuable and wasn't hired!

For the salesperson, it's a common ploy. For the buyer or employee, it's an Achilles heel. Monitoring this PERIMETERS trap gives you the chance to reverse decisions and win negotiations.[27]

Another source of advantage is understanding the nature of risk preference reversals.

CHANGING YOUR TUNE: RISK REVERSALS

Every day, people change their minds about everything from careers to consultants or concubines. It's normal. Since the mid-2010s, growing divorce rates in OECD countries have been matched by declining marriage rates. Not all have love insurance! We all change our minds whether about people, situations, habits and hobbies. China handcuffed its biggest billionaire, and Sinéad O'Connor sued her once-sanctified manager Fachtna.

While U-turns are often ridiculed as flip-flopping, strategic reversal signals strength. It took courage for the three Everest mountaineers to turn back.

In 2015, former German chancellor Angela Merkel guaranteed Syrian asylum seekers safe passage. Confronted with a practical rehousing challenge, she listened and reinstated border controls.[28]

Under political and media pressure, individuals increasingly swing with the tide, especially in response to social outrage and cancel culture. At the 2023 World Cup award ceremony, a Spanish Football Federation president planted an unwanted kiss on a female player. Initially, FIFA backed Luis Rubiales then suspended him until he resigned and was subsequently banned from the industry for three years. Initially, Jenni Hermoso said she didn't like the gesture, then she issued an exculpatory statement to AFP about "a natural gesture of affection and gratitude" based on their "great relationship." It was shortly followed by claims of feeling pressurised, vulnerable and a victim of aggression.

Public commitment makes reversals difficult, especially in visible situations. Take M&A. As deal teams dash towards filing deadlines, momentum builds. Decision-makers bury doubts instead of cutting losses. Occasionally, a third-party regulatory voice can force termination. For example, after 16 months of an impasse and market monopoly concerns, insurance giant Aon called off its $30bn Willis Towers Watson deal.[29]

Some leaders redefine deal-breakers and shift the moral high ground, especially with millions involved. Two years after the PGA Tour publicly battled the Saudi-backed LIV tour and proclaimed human rights concerns, they announced a lucrative merger.[30] Loyal PGA players like Rory McIlroy and Tiger Woods learned that what you hear is rarely all there is.

While a judge may reverse a verdict, sometimes opinion reversal occurs too late.

In 2000, a federal jury found Brandon Bernard guilty of carjacking and the murder of two ministers in Indiana. Reflecting on post-trial evidence, five of the nine jurors reassessed and concluded punishment was warranted, just not the death penalty.

Huffington Post writer Jessica Schulberg spoke to juror Gary McClung, "I've had a kind of struggle standing up when an opinion is different from mine... I regret that now."[31] Former prosecutor Angela Moor agreed after learning about evidence concealment. President Trump didn't reverse the decision or issue a pardon. Bernard was put to death by lethal injection in 2020.

Fortunately, people change their mind about important decisions including enacting end-of-life treatment. In California's doctor-assisted suicide programmes, 1,270 people received the fatal prescription in 2022 under the End-of-Life Option Act. While 853 people exercised this option, a third changed their minds.[32]

Tuning in to conscience matters.

TUNING IN: THE VOICE OF PROBABILITY

The reward for those who recalibrate risk is significant. It's the foundation for every confident entrepreneur, investigator, diligent scientist or medal-hunting athlete who doesn't give up. It can be the difference between life and death, success and failure, progress and stagnation.

Consider the risks rescue workers face when dealing with tornados, bombsites, earthquakes or mines. Before the Copiapó copper-gold mine collapsed in 2010, local Chilean miners predicted it. Gino Cortés said, "All the workers knew something was going to happen. They heard strange sounds in the Atacama Desert mine."[33] They were right. Thanks to government and NASA co-operation, 33 men were rescued after 69 days at a cost of $20m.

In disaster recovery situations, saving lives depends on workers accurately hearing the voices of trapped victims and mitigating anticipated hazards.

Risk assessment is a finely tuned skill essential for professional success. Suicide call lines, victim counselling and FBI negotiations are life-and-death situations for which agents are trained in exceptional listening. They know miscommunication, disrespect or an unintentional adversarial tone risks lives.

Voss suggests, "You can lie 15 different ways, but each of those is still different from when you tell the truth."[34] He advocates communicating with a "late-night FM DJ voice" and listening intently to spot words used or omitted, like a human lie-detector.

·ı|||ı·|·ıı|ı·|ıı·

Throughout this book, I explore how context shapes emotional or complex decisions. In every situation, you might think, "What would I have done?" It's usually not what the protagonist decided.

Atop Mount Everest, Rob Hall and his clients suffered oxygen deprivation.[35] This chemically disoriented their judgement. Context matters.

Decision-makers make the best risk–reward choices they can with the best intentions, information, time and capacity available. If you haven't climbed in their boots, moral judgement is best avoided.

For some, risk-taking is an essential part of their DNA and personality. People pride themselves on the title of risk-taker, worn like a badge of honour. Like power, ego and risk, even unmanaged identity can contribute to misjudgement. That's the focus of the Identity-based PERIMETERS traps, discussed next.

THE DECISION NINJA

WHAT TO REMEMBER

- No decision is risk-free. The trick is to accept that and know what you don't know.
- Decisions vary on a spectrum, from sensation-seeking to certainty-craving. Our position fluctuates over time, life stage and context – there's no ideal risk appetite.
- Companies invest billions in managing risk while consumers spend billions preventing risk, hearing the voice of catastrophe. Most overpay for security via insurance or premium brands.
- Motivation to minimise loss is rooted in rational self-interest yet it severs useful decision options.
- Anchors are irrational reference points that distort logical decisions until too late.
- We dislike abandoning public commitments, relationships or promises after investing time and money. Yet adherence costs time, money and lives.
- Decision U-turns and preference reversals signal confidence not cowardice. Some consider changing your mind the highest form of intelligence.
- Decision risk is calculated based on available rather than accurate information. Successful professionals feel morally obliged to relentlessly decipher data.
- Our deepest fears are improbable, yet we neglect true probabilities which derails judgement. Evolved leaders learn to live with uncertainty and black swans.
- Sophisticated decision-makers recalibrate risk appetite to selectively hear the voice of opportunity, even when it's inconvenient or costly.

CHAPTER 7

IDENTITY-BASED TRAPS: PHOTOSHOPPED LIVES

"Be yourself; everyone else is already taken."
Oscar Wilde

BUZZ ALDRIN WAS the second man to land on the moon. Nearly five decades later, when asked whether this upset him, he said, "At the time, not in the least. As the senior crew member, it was appropriate for him [Neil Armstrong] to be the first." Things change:

> After years of being asked to speak to a group of people and... introduced as the second man on the moon, it does get a little frustrating. Is it really necessary to point out to the crowd that somebody else was first when we all went through the same training, we all landed at the same time, and all contributed? For the rest of my life, I'll always be identified as the second man to walk on the moon.[1]

You can empathise with Aldrin's disappointment. NASA's associate administrator for manned space flight had announced Aldrin as first man to the press.[2] Who wants to be second? It's the understudy, backing singer, vice-chair or royal 'heir as spare.'

Mountaineers want to be 'the one that climbed Everest' not the one that turned back. Michael Collins observed:

> Fame has not worn well on Buzz. I think he resents not being the first on the moon rather than he appreciates being second.[3]

In compensation, Aldrin likes to joke he achieved other lunar firsts – snapping a selfie, celebrating Holy Communion and taking "one great leak for mankind"![4]

This chapter examines six core identity-based biases as sources of mishearing, misinformation and misjudgement. I explain how individuals and brands go to extreme lengths to curate identity (impression management) and remain consistent with it (consistency bias). But we lose ourselves in narrowly defined identity, leading us to gravitate towards braggers, rivals, retailers, psychic mediums, critics or con artists. Typically, we don't hear different identities (outgroups), only resonant voices (ingroups), reinforced by convenient social labels (representativeness bias). Frequently, we lose our identity in national, political and organisational groups (false consensus effect). Identity obsession contaminates interpretation, especially when fused with ego or emotion. Conversely, curated identity is a tremendous source of impact for the confident Decision Ninja.

A 3D perspective that considers blind spots, deaf spots and dumb spots helps us decode what we hear rather than encode what we think we hear.

Many stories in this book illustrate that what we hear is not all there is. It starts with impression management.

OBSESSED WITH CURATING IMPRESSIONS

Buzz isn't alone in his sentiments. Relative positioning significantly influences our self-image. Using photos from the 1992 summer

Olympics, psychologist Tom Gilovich analysed the facial expressions of silver medallists.[5] In terms of a happiness average, silver medallists ranked 4.8 compared to bronze medallists at 7.1.

Athletes at the 2004 judo Olympics revealed similar results. While 92% of gold winners smiled, no silver winner did. In fact, 43% looked sad.[6] Why? Silver medallists compare themselves upwards.[7] It's the near miss that hurts. Bronze medallists feel grateful. However, people neglect probability. An average of just 11% of competitors win medals.

How you rank yourself in relative terms impacts your approach to solving problems and making decisions.

Much of what we achieve, earn, drink, buy and post is driven by our desire to impress. It's the essence of *impression management* and typically converts into Thorstein Veblen's *theory of conspicuous consumption*.[8] We're preoccupied with who we are and what we present, online or offline.

US philosopher J. David Velleman writes, "We invent ourselves... but we really are the characters we invent." We do it to impress and lose ourselves in the process.

For better or worse, more channels exist to express identity than ever. Billions engage on Instagram, TikTok and LinkedIn to be heard. But we hear less than ever in a noisy world.

A German heiress unmasked

Some take identity curation to extremes. From humble origins, immigrant Anna Sorokin invented herself as the $50m heiress Anna Delvey. Her New York networking started small, cultivating high rollers. Sorokin's seductive German accent also carried subliminal weight.

Over time, well-connected socialites and gullible hoteliers were conned into funding her lavish lifestyle. Posing as her own financier, she applied for a $40m loan to build a Soho arts club and forged documents for Wall Street bankers, advisers and real estate gurus. Days before securing $22m, Sorokin was arrested. *New York* journalist Jessica Pressler later exposed her story of exploitation, grandiosity and manipulation to the world.

Despite conviction on multiple counts for grand larceny and theft, Sorokin sees nothing wrong with shameless self-confidence. "I don't see myself as a con woman... I just asked them for things and they said yes." She adds, "I have no patience for people's stupidity." She asserts most brands fake it until they make it. "So many businesses are just a house of cards, you just don't know about it."[9] She's not wrong.

·ıllı·|ılı·ıllı·

Desire for a flattering self-image extends beyond German fraudsters and disappointed Olympians. Illinois's John Wayne Gacy received the death penalty for raping and murdering 33 men and boys. Yet Gacy was adamant he was no "fruit packer." In his view, it was okay to be known as a serial killer but not gay.

In comparison, serial killer Ted Bundy was comfortable in his own skin.

> I haven't blocked out the past. I wouldn't trade the person I am, or what I've done, or the people I've known, for anything.

He described himself proudly as "the meanest son-of-a-bitch you'll ever meet."

He used his law student identity, good looks and charm to lure victims. Yet he stripped them of their identity, many dumped nameless on bleak mountainsides. Bundy maintained his curated image of composure all the way to Florida's electric chair, drowning out chants of "Burn Bundy Burn."

Vain parents aren't immune from impression management either. Take college admissions. Exclusive Ivy League entry requirements are tough. Although universities preach inclusion, they favour ingroups – some reserve 15% of places for children of donors or alumni, regardless of grades.[10]

Although the US court has now banned legacy admissions, a study found that in Harvard, 43% of white students are either legacy, athletes or related to donors and staff.[11] This might explain why Hollywood's Felicity Huffman paid a stranger $15,000 to sit her daughter's entrance exam to the University of Southern California.

When I guest lecture alumni, I'm always struck by their pride in the affiliation. A Harvard Business or Kennedy School graduate might introduce themselves as "I'm Jo Abrams, AB '92" or "Mahood Amir, MBA '06." It's a badge of honour. While the network benefits are significant, privilege is maintained with perspective narrowed to the Cambridge campus boundaries.

When our need to impress fuses with desperation, ethical judgement gets crowded out.

We all want to impress. When I did my first TEDx talk on *How to Overcome Indecision*, my nerves were shot.[12] It didn't impact my career or wallet, yet I dreaded the cyber permanence of a stutter or mind freeze. There were no second takes. I really believed the message would help people escape dreaded indecision but what if I only got 100 YouTube views? I had seen TEDx speakers waltz to 10 million. What number would make me happy? I was anchoring with a narrow perimeter view.

In reality, what made a difference was the effect it had – a Muslim mother who said it helped her teenage daughter struggling with anxiety, the bullied technologist who finally left his toxic job or an executive search CEO's decision to close his board practice. Sometimes, impact trumps vanity.

Once we curate our professional, political or national identity, adhering too consistently to it can become a judgement minefield.

I WANT TO BREAK FREE

Preconceived identity can be a trap no matter how successful you are or what profession you hold. When discussing role choices open to female actors, Reese Witherspoon suggests, "There was a lot of talk about who we were supposed to be for other people... It was like we're supposed to only create fantasy people."[13]

We have pre-formed impressions of actors, moms, teachers, junkies and traders. We don't expect the king to curse, presidents to 'grab crotches' or leaders to embezzle funds. We like people to stay consistent with their words, appearance and positions in *consistency bias*. That's why images of OJ Simpson as a throat-slashing murderer and Michael Jackson as a child molester clashed with fans' preconception.

If people, processes and systems are consistent, it makes the world more stable and controllable. It provides elusive certainty and comfort in a type of mental sorting.

This desire for consistency simplifies reality but omits complicating shades of grey. Employees, customers, voters and viewers value the predictability of products and promises. Yet this desire to satiate what others want is a mental trap that stifles creativity and evolution. It holds you back.

Ozan Varol writes, "When you turn down the volume of other voices, you'll begin to hear... the whispers of a new voice... you'll recognise it as your own. The path to tuning in to the genius within begins by tuning out the noise without."[14]

After her Harry Potter blockbuster, JK Rowling published under the pseudonym Robert Galbraith. Trapped in character, she wanted "a liberating experience... without hype or expectation, and pure pleasure to get feedback under a different name."[15] If success means tuning out your voice, why chase it?

Identity gets lost when we let our co-workers, competitors or fanbase define who we are and what we believe.

Some escape. Neil Armstrong shunned the media circus. Describing himself: "I am and ever will be a white sock, pocket protector nerdy engineer." After Apollo 11, he became a professor of engineering at the University of Cincinnati. He knew who he was.

Meanwhile, Buzz Aldrin battled alcohol addiction, craving the limelight his comrades shunned. Describing the moon as "magnificent desolation," it reflected his mind. "There was no goal, no sense of calling, no project worth pouring myself into."[16]

Like Armstrong, some people are clear about their identity. Russian mathematician Grigori Perelman certainly was. He rejected the Fields Medal and a $1m Millennium Prize, stating:

> I don't want to be on display like an animal in the zoo. I'm not a hero of mathematics. I'm not even that successful; that is why I don't want to have everyone looking at me.

⑈⑊⑈⑊⑈

At an organisational level, consistency becomes suboptimal when firms need to shift direction. For example, most fund managers boast high-conviction stock-picking techniques. It's an identity trap. When markets crash, many disregard the admonishing voice of economist Paul Samuelson: "When the facts change, I change my mind. What do you do?"

Change becomes an admission of error. I've worked with hundreds of fund managers and no matter how low equity performance dropped, most tweaked rather than reallocated assets. And clients lose.

Ralph Waldo Emerson rightly deduced that "consistency is the hobgoblin of little minds."

From analysts to movie producers, we want to be consistent with our definition of perfection. For instance, when *Titanic* director James Cameron learned that the night-time stars were misaligned on the famous sinking ship scenes, he reshot them post-release. Similarly, innovator James Dyson invested 15 years and developed 5,127 prototypes perfecting the first upright vacuum cleaner.[7]

Trying to impress others can mean you inadvertently lose yourself and, sometimes, even depress yourself.

Part of impression management is the curse of perfectionism. Top performers are closet perfectionists even though perfectionism is an identity trap. Many wrongly conclude that anything less than perfect means you're flawed – that's not how you define yourself or justify fees.

Although it has its virtues, the voice of perfectionism deafens us to logic. How many different ways can I write this sentence? Which sentence sounds more perfect? We need to listen to the voice of sanity not vanity.

IDENTITY GIVERS AND IDENTITY TAKERS

Who are you really? In the 1970s, Henri Tajfel coined *social identity theory* as the idea we belong to groups based on shared values, social class, beliefs and allegiances.

Identity is nuanced. An engineer might be a mechanical, electronic or civil engineer. A Jew may be German, Hungarian, Israeli or Polish. Do you define Elvis as the 1950s hip-shaking jailhouse rocker, the 1960s beach movie crooner or the 1970s flamboyant Vegas cape-wearer? We're a composite of multiple selves.

We are what we do. And we do what we want to be, hoping to convince others of who we are.

Other people shape our self-image – dangerously so. In your curated workplace and social channels, do negative views, likes or comments ruin your day or disproportionately damage your confidence? What about Reddit's karma counter? All is fist-pumpingly good when you get upvotes but thumbs down and vitriolic comments crater self-esteem.

No one is immune, whether adult or child, senior or junior, celebrity or stranger. Hollywood producer Hal Wallis remarked, "In order to do the artistic pictures, it is necessary to make the Presley commercial pictures." Parker commented to the *Los Angeles Times*: "All they're good for is making money." Elvis was shattered. "They couldn't have paid me no amount of money in the world to make me feel self-satisfaction inside."[18]

Identity can get lost in close relationships. When Priscilla Presley met her future husband, she was 14 years old. She married at 21 and had no idea who she was for over a decade. "I just kind of followed what he did. I mean, you lived his life... You really kind of lost yourself."[19] His wishes, moods and insecurities became hers. She existed only to please her idol as a "living doll."

Recognising gradual loss is tricky when living in a frenzied circus and hankering for others' approval. Divorced after four years, Priscilla found her voice, reinventing herself as an actress and businesswoman. She subsequently raised Graceland from a $1m to a $100m property.[20]

What if you're a seven-year-old boy who loses his identity?

In 1972, paedophile Kenneth Parnell abducted seven-year-old Mormon boy Stephen Stayner on the ruse he was looking for help with church donations. It was a tragedy that shook the small town of Merced, California. Parnell even convinced Stephen that his economically stretched parents approved his legal adoption. Distraught Stephen became a sex slave for over seven years until Parnell recruited a five-year-old replacement, Timmy White.

Teenage Stephen grabbed the opportunity to escape and

fled with Timmy. Both families were reunited, giving hope to relatives of missing children everywhere.

With his self-worth in tatters, a confused and angry Stephen never discussed this formative experience with his mother, father, therapist or brother Cary. And they never asked. Theirs was a family destroyed by self-imposed silence. Stephen struggled to adjust to his new life. He was jeered and ostracised in school, his sexuality constantly queried. He told *Newsweek*:

> I returned almost a grown man and yet my parents saw me at first as their seven-year-old… Would I have been better off if I didn't [come home]?

This victim narrative defined his life, yet he was a hero. It didn't help that his captor spent just five years in prison. A decade later, Stephen was killed in a freak motorbike accident. A tragic end to a tragic life.

It's easy to lose your identity in any circumstance but especially within groups.

LOSING YOUR IDENTITY IN GROUPS

Most people are proud of where they come from. You likely cheer for your country in the World Cup, Ryder Cup or Eurovision Song Contest. Like professional identity, national identity is an ingroup mindset. We hear only its boombox voice. Is it a product of history, teaching and conditioning rather than independently formed views?

At the extreme, it can spark intolerance, hate crimes and violence.

You might think Jonestowners, hunger strikers, suicide bombers, Scientologists, QAnon or Ku Klux Klan members are irrational. They disagree. Like any team, the group validates beliefs so members assume everyone shares their loyalties and welcomes its voice. It's the *false consensus effect*. It's why you think everyone wants the same sale item, hotel booking or concert ticket as you.

When we want our ingroup to tell us what's true, our mental perimeters shrink. Experts call this *epistemic closure*.

At a national level, extreme ingroup loyalty is polarising. Take Northern Ireland. In 1969, 'The Troubles' began. The colloquial label belied a bloody daily reality. Two tribal factions were at war, the independence-seeking Irish Republican Army (IRA) and Unionists battling to remain in the UK. War-torn images flooded the news: Lord Mountbatten's murder, Bloody Sunday, long-haired rebels and emaciated Bobby Sands' 66-day hunger strike. My uncle was stationed in a Belfast monastery. No one could cross the border for fear of random petrol bombs and brutal sectarian massacres. Over 3,500 victims died in a three-decade conflict.

In 1998, the violence ended with the Good Friday Agreement. Instead of proposing the binary options of independence or unionism, a devolved power-sharing government was formed. Despite the ceasefire, scars lingered.

This period moulded everyone's life, including my 96-year-old grandmother who survived the hardship of two world wars. When hospitalised in 2005, she warned bemused nurses that IRA soldiers were hiding under her bed, an assertion we attributed to medically induced hallucinations. However, "in morphine veritas" – as splinters of truth resurface in memory.

When writing this book, I learned her father's police station was bombed by the IRA, with bullets fired into their home. His 13 children were forced to flee for safety. One sister was sent to a South African Dominican convent. Another was sent to Australia to avoid possible IRA conscription. Neither came home.

Seventy years later, my ailing grandmother fretted that the

defunct IRA was imminent and hunting down her sister. She died shortly after, never quite at peace despite a lifetime of sacrifice. In many respects, she represents a lost generation, one that had no need of iPads and iPhones, just the art of conversation, a voice of compassion and kindness towards others.

Not everyone shares our national, professional or religious views. Diluting your adhesion to a single identity can facilitate life transitions. Just this week, when discussing retirement, a former colleague and vice-chair of a Wall Street empire asked me "What if this is just who I am?" It's sensible to build associations with groups now that define you as more than your job title, marital status, racial identity or political affiliation.

HEARING AND HELPING INGROUPS

For 13 years, a reserved German lived with a Hungarian family in Brazil. When Gitta Stammer stumbled across a photo of her house guest in a magazine article, he confessed his identity.

It was Auschwitz's most notorious doctor, Josef Mengele, the 'Angel of Death.'

From the outset, Mengele desired Nazi approval. With a research grant, he amputated limbs and infected Jews with typhus.[21] His depravity grew, allocating prisoners to the gas chamber, supervising the administration of Zyklon-B pesticide and conducting horrific and deadly experiments on live twins.

The Stammers immediately sought Mengele's eviction, to no avail. His concealment was subsidised by his family in Germany, enabled by a local go-between. Fearful, the Stammers felt silenced. With little in common, Mengele grew more dictatorial on the modest farmland, effusing Aryan superiority.[22] He stayed in situ for over a decade. When the Stammers's sons became teenagers, Mengele helped fund a new home nearby.

Wolfram Bossert, an Austrian expatriate and army corporal, was introduced to "Peter" who became his regular guest. They drank Riesling and debated philosophy, politics, music and post-war German injustices.

Then, like Gitta, Wolfram discovered that Peter was the most wanted Nazi fugitive in living history.

Psychologically blind, Wolfram saw Mengele as a fellow ingroup member. He closed his eyes to the horrific images. After all, they shared identity, interests and an anti-Semitic bias. Unlike the Stammers, they had formed an ingroup.

Psychologically deaf to ample evidence, Wolfram said:

He was not an evil person. He always had the greatest respect for human life. I believe only a fraction of all the things he is accused of.[23]

Psychologically dumb, Wolfram's wife Liselotte justified her silence:

For humanitarian reasons we simply went along with it. Although the man was being sought, we only knew him as a highly cultivated gentleman. And we carried on as if we didn't know anything.[24]

The Bosserts misjudged Mengele and themselves. Neither spoke out. Deaf to the truth, they tuned out in complicit and narrow thinking. They exemplify the PERIMETERS Effect.

We tune in to voices with which we feel in tune; we tune out of voices with which we feel out of tune.

It's easy to condemn bystanders. Would you have acted differently? Recall how regular students in the Stanford Prison Experiment were driven to abnormal behaviour in an abnormal setting?

Most of us feel a responsibility to help who we perceive as 'one of us.' We hire, help and support people like us rather than strangers. As Steve Martin and Joseph Marks suggest in *Messengers*, we listen to ingroup voices:

> When we feel we are linked in some way to someone else
> – we tend to listen more and assign greater importance to
> what they have to say than if no bond existed.[25]

This ingroup favouritism is used pro-socially. Savvy charities exploit the *identifiable victim effect*. For example, following the 2004 Asian tsunami, urgent appeals were directed to donors who shared the same nationality as victims. Compatriot donations significantly surpassed non-compatriot donations.[26]

It's not unusual to pigeonhole your own identity. It's why people struggle to change careers. When seeking board positions, I assumed my best prospects lay within the investment industry where I had worked. Not so. I discovered unrelated industries value unrelated skillsets. Some open-minded chairs embrace diverse voices. For example, I have been the only non-footballer and non-coach on the Football Association's inclusion advisory board; one of the few non-Olympians on the World Athletics gender advisory group; and currently the first and only female independent British and Irish Lions board member.

At times, we constrain our self-image and short-change ourselves when lateral thinkers do the opposite.

THE HEARDS VS THE HEARD-NOTS

"He's an engineer." "They're Mexican." "She's not our sort." We choose to hire, promote, marry, socialise and emulate people like us. We also ask them for advice more than the outgroup member. When recruiters mention 'fit,' it's code for 'someone like us.'

When we try to fit in, we just become like everyone else.

Despite best intentions, we don't hear marginalised or unfamiliar voices – the 'heard-nots.' It works both ways. White people struggle to buy houses in Harlem while black people struggle to access houses outside Harlem.

Ironically, exclusion strikes those who need inclusion most.

For every winner, there's a loser. If we tune in familiar ingroups, we tune out unfamiliar outgroups.

Three years before Elvis was born, 340 miles from Graceland, Alabama's Public Health Service initiated a study at Tuskegee University to record the natural history of syphilis in low-income African American men. Without informed consent, these men swapped blood samples for meagre incentives such as free meals and insurance.[27] This study continued for four decades.

In 1943, Penicillin treatment became available. However, researchers never disclosed the diagnosis or provided Penicillin. Only when a whistleblower made public this devaluation of black lives did the study end. Some 128 men died of syphilis or related complications. Many of them indirectly contaminated families and children. In 1997, President Bill Clinton made a public apology to the untreated syphilis victims. Ironically, this parallel universe took place over the same period as pill-popping Graceland.

Immoral actions don't stem from discriminatory, exclusionary or cruel intentions; but this doesn't lessen the devastating impacts they can have.

Mergers are another breeding ground for exclusion. Having been through numerous, a 'them or us' mentality flares up despite the 'merger of equals' rhetoric. They invite rejection, even if you're part of the same profession, function or race. Under threat, sentiments change. People retreat to familiar colleagues. Suddenly the irritating salesperson or specialist becomes your best ally and ingroup member.

Over two decades, MIT analysed 4,000 high-tech start-up acquisitions and found that 33% of acquired employees voluntarily departed within the first year.[28] Tuning in to the other side partially stems flight risk. Ninety-two percent of leaders admit they would have "substantially benefited from greater cultural understanding prior to the merger."[29] It's too late to blame mismatched culture post-deal.

More broadly, individuals become victims of unintended discrimination for multiple reasons. We tune out the voice of injustice when it's psychologically distant. Most of us will never know what it's like to be famous for the wrong reasons.

One mother learned the hard way.

Deaf to difference and dissent

Injustice is not a distant phenomenon to Julia Rea, separated mother and former PhD candidate at the University of Indiana. In 1997, a serial killer broke into Rea's home and murdered her ten-year-old son, Joel. Despite her providing the attacker's description, having no motive and there being no evidence against her, Rea was sentenced to 65 years by a conservative jury. The jurors were outraged by prejudicial information about Rea's abortion deliberations, revealed by her ex-husband. Rea flouted their preconceptions about motherhood. Remember consistency bias?

Thanks to the Innocence Project, Rea's voice was heard, exonerated after the intruder confessed. On Wrongful Conviction Day 2022, I heard her story first-hand.

It's hard to go on… I had been a doctoral candidate before this doing a dissertation with two masters. I can't get back to work since exoneration in 2006. I have no retirement.[30]

Rea isn't alone. She's in the ingroup of an outgroup.

Some people neither fit in on the outside nor the inside.

When police tune out difference, it costs disproportionately. In Milwaukee, officers ignored the voice of African American Glenda Cleveland despite her repeatedly reporting suspicions about a neighbour. When a drugged 14-year-old Laotian boy fled the neighbour's apartment, police returned him to the same neighbour who joked about his 'drunk' 19-year-old boyfriend. White police believed white serial killer Jeffrey Dahmer over a black female. His victims paid the price of prejudicial judgement.

It's a daily occurrence.

In Philadelphia, when coffee shop managers called the police to arrest two black customers waiting for a friend before ordering, Starbucks later closed 8,000 outlets for anti-bias training.

When spotted prising open a jammed back door, black Harvard professor Henry Gates was arrested entering his own home. Cambridge police fixated on what they saw, not what they heard. Barack Obama hoped it would become a teachable moment. It wasn't. His comments about this event marked a larger decline in white citizen support than any other event in his presidency.[31]

Dissenters quickly become outgroup members. Recall how Sinéad O'Connor was vilified for ripping up the pope's picture in protest against Catholic Church abuse for over a decade? Yet she spoke the truth.

Celebrity status affords no immunity from bias deaf spots. In a 1971 interview, heavyweight boxer Muhammed Ali recalled how he asked his mother about white people:

Why are Jesus and the angels white? Why is Tarzan, King of the African Jungle, white? Why are Miss America, Miss World and Miss Universe white?

He noted that everything good is portrayed as white – the White House, White Swan soap, white cigars and Angel's food cake. Yet everything bad is portrayed as black – blackmail, black sheep, black swans and the Devil's food cake.

His questions are still valid today.

Labels as lazy stereotypes

In organisations, stereotypes such as nerdy techs, balloon-blowing marketers or nit-picking auditors prevail. Maybe you work with a quiet Asian colleague. Are all Asians quiet? Stereotypes generate false assumptions as we extrapolate from the specific, failing to adjust for difference. Behavioural economists call this *representativeness bias*.

Police, prosecutors and politicians fall into this trap. Because there are more black than white people in prison, it's assumed all black people are criminals. And because white people think black people look alike, a rush to judgement follows.

Stereotype labels are identity sources. They're evident in everyday parlance as people refer to "the short guy," "the black girl" or "the weird one." When repeated, they reinforce misperceptions and fuel misjudgement. Former US president Donald Trump used these for political gain. He referred to himself as a "wartime president" while Hillary Clinton was "Crooked Hillary" and Joe Biden was "Sleepy Joe Biden."[32]

Glorified titles such as 'Dame,' 'Colonel,' 'Reverend' or 'Sir' are power signals. In the documentary *Savile: Portrait of a Predator*, Sir Jimmy Savile remarked, "Getting the knighthood was an enormous relief... as it got me off the hook." He hid behind a label with a veneer of respectability and trust.

Labels are a handy, if biased, mental shortcut. It's not unusual to hear managers label employees as 'trouble' or 'lazy.' This becomes self-fulfilling. The converse is also true. The 'talented' or 'safe pair of hands' becomes the star.

In *Apollo 11: The Inside Story*, NASA director Chris Kraft

explained why Aldrin wasn't selected to lead the mission: "Armstrong was calm, quiet and had absolute confidence... He had no ego. On the other hand, Aldrin desperately wanted the honour and wasn't quiet in letting it be known."

I understood the choice when I met 78-year-old Armstrong. He hadn't changed. Armstrong was still curious, detailed and unflappable – a handy trait during Apollo 11 given there were just 20 seconds of descent fuel left before landing on the moon, side-stepping craggy craters the size of football fields. But identity is not necessarily fixed. Reinvention is becoming increasingly common.

REBRANDING AND REINVENTION

When couples decouple or a parent dies, identity changes. The spouse becomes a 'one parent family' and the children 'from a broken home.' It's just a stage that can be an opportunity. Individuals and firms escape trapped identities by changing what they call themselves.

Name changes can occur for religious, career, strategic or personal reasons. They feature in witness protection programmes and undercover operations. Czech-born Jan Ludvik Hoch was so poor his six siblings took turns wearing shoes. He became media mogul Robert Maxwell. Change can also be more fundamental.

Perceived reinvention can be surprising in a given context or time period, like when Olympian Bruce Jenner was introduced as transgender Caitlyn Jenner, yet this was just her true self. People judged what they saw. And what you see dominates who you hear. Visually adding pronouns 'he/him', 'they/them' or 'she/her' to emails lends voice to a minority and is a fast-embedding social norm.

Sometimes changing your name is symbolic. When Cassius Clay converted to Islam, he declared his name "a slave name" and changed it to Muhammad Ali. Resisting Vietnam conscription resulted in the removal of his heavyweight title. He was unrepentant.

> I don't have to be what you want me to be. I don't have to say what you want me to say. I don't have to do what you want me to do. I'm free to be who I am.[33]

That's freedom. Bill Clinton remarked at Ali's funeral:

> He decided that not his race nor his place, the expectations of others, positive, negative or otherwise, would strip from him the power to write his own story.

Employees can expand their mental perimeters by moving functions or switching careers. For example, Ronald Reagan and Arnold Schwarzenegger both swapped Hollywood for governorship of California. Jorge Mario Bergoglio was a bouncer by night and janitor by day before leading the Catholic Church as Pope Francis.

An aspiring skater didn't qualify for the 1964 Olympics. "I had a nervous breakdown and ended up doing a semester in Paris."[34] Today, Vera Wang is a global fashion icon. Remember the satellite career path of John McEnroe, not defined by a single identity?

ılı|ı|ılı|ılı

Countries rebrand like Brexit Britain or Ukraine under Zelensky's leadership. I think of Tanzania where I worked on a World Bank project for a year. Its first president, Julius Nyerere, ruled 125 tribes, including the largest Maasai tribe. To avoid identity politics, Nyerere emphasised being Tanzanian over tribal allegiances. Today, Tanzania is a country of peace.

Brands love to rebrand. Having managed multiple global

rebrands in my career, I find too many fail for silly reasons. Decision-makers don't understand the brand essence or bother to reinterpret the customer voice. Equally, vanity trumps sanity as new CEOs love to stamp their imprint like Yellowstone cattle ranchers sear livestock.

More and more brands invest in sonic identity. In 2018, Mastercard invested $15m in its audio brand, now its most valued brand asset. Professor Kai Wright suggests "audio is the most underleveraged part of brand building." Sound engineers estimate it takes only three seconds to recognise a tune. Can you hear the James Bond theme, the McDonald's "Loving it" or Coca-Cola's "The Holidays are coming"?

As brands fight to differentiate identity, sonic branding is a growing marketing mechanism.

During Covid-19, government, telephone companies and scientists chose a clever sonic solution to reach 113 million Pakistanis.[35] Sound was the preferred medium rather than written leaflets or educational posts. As 90% of the population used mobile phones, citizen ringtones were centrally changed to deliver a preventative health message within 15 seconds. Citizens heard it!

Some 71% of citizens were found more likely to identify symptoms correctly, 31% interpreted Covid as a threat and 43% planned to use sanitisers or wear masks. This aural medium is set to grow as a means of influencing behaviour.

TUNING IN: THE VOICE OF ACCEPTANCE

Behavioural scientists help organisations to achieve their goals by leveraging desire for identity. In one case, the 2012 US elections tested a high-frequency online campaign with 61 million Facebook users. Rather than being asked to "Please Vote," voters were asked to post "I'm Voting" or "I'm a Voter."

We all want to be a somebody. Actively self-labelling as "a voter" rather than passively declaring "I voted" added an identity label. This sticker-wearer strategy generated 60,000 additional votes.[36]

Anyone can use this noun-based behavioural hack.

When I advised World Athletics about how best to encourage sports participation during Covid-19, this birthed the successful campaign in Ireland, "I am a Runner."

As a '12th juror,' you might label yourself a decision 'provocateur,' 'disrupter' or 'dissenter.'

Despite self-labelling as an expert in orbital rendezvous, Aldrin felt like a fraud after the moon landing. Having lost his identity, he suffered mental health issues, telling the BBC in 1980, "I was concerned I wouldn't measure up to my own standards. It's a self-directed concern… a very inflated ego."[37] He won out by listening. At 93, Buzz Aldrin married for the fourth time. For this dreamer, the sky was not the limit.

When you tune in to others, others tune into you.

The best asset you have is yourself so be yourself. "Those who mind don't matter and those who matter don't mind."[38] Being yourself means you don't have to curate or rebrand yourself to fit in with others.

It's worth remembering a fabulous quote from Kurt Cobain. "They laugh at me because I'm different; I laugh at them because they're all the same."

Knowing who you are and what you stand for enables freedom of expression. It allows you to speak up and have voice, engrained in your DNA and your memory. Sometimes, unconscious memory interferes in your judgement. That's the focus of the next set of decision derailers: memory-based PERIMETERS traps.

THE DECISION NINJA
WHAT TO REMEMBER

- Identity traps are as much about curating impressions as about rejecting difference.
- We're multiple conflicting selves. Which voice do you hear? Which voice do you want to be heard? Prioritise your most important self and listen selectively.
- Rigidly striving for consistency doesn't just prevent opinion reversal, it hampers creativity and accuracy.
- Everyone wants to be heard yet the world bifurcates into identity-based ingroups and outgroups. This segregation amplifies deaf ear syndrome and contributes to culture wars, conflict and violence.
- Humans are contradictory, attracted to what's both familiar and novel. We want to stand out but fit in; we remember what we hear first and hear last; we want what we don't have yet stick to what we do have.
- Extreme allegiance to a cause, company or ideology hinders rational perspective, dangerous at scale.
- Online and offline, individuals and brands obsessively curate identity to impress others and secure bragging rights. It's a trap – one that is avoided if you're authentic and comfortable in yourself.
- It's easy to lose identity in groups or moments of panic but identity isn't fixed at an individual, brand or societal level. Reinvention is always an option.
- Boosting others' identity is a kindness that costs nothing. Remember the power of "You're the greatest."

CHAPTER 8

MEMORY-BASED TRAPS: RECALL ROULETTE

"Memories are thoughts that arise. They're not realities. Only when you believe they are real, they have power over you."

Eckhart Tolle

O N 6 MARCH 1987 at 18:05 GMT, the MS *Herald of Free Enterprise* ferry embarked on its routine crossing between the Belgian port of Zeebrugge and Dover. It carried 539 crew and passengers, 81 cars, 47 trucks and three buses. Twenty-three minutes later, the MS *Herald of Free Enterprise* destabilised and capsized, flooded by 11,000 gallons of water per second. In one of Britain's worst maritime disasters, 193 lives were lost. A court of inquiry concluded that human error was responsible.[1]

What happened? The 28-year-old assistant boatswain Mark Stanley forgot to close the bow door. Asleep in his cabin, he didn't hear "Harbour Stations" over the booming Tannoy. Compounding this error, Chief Officer Leslie Sabel forgot to check the doors.[2] And Captain David Lewry assumed the doors were closed.

The memory of previous close calls was forgotten. "In October 1983, the assistant bosun of the *Pride* had fallen asleep. He neglected to close both the bow and stern doors."[3]

Context matters. A crown report concluded an operating climate of lightly enforced processes and fast turnarounds contributed. It referred to "staggering complacency" and a top-down "disease of sloppiness." Whose responsibility was it? A general instruction prescribed it was the duty of the officer loading the vehicle deck to ensure doors were "secure when leaving port."

Was it a misinterpretation of roles and responsibilities? The report continued, "That instruction was poorly worded, but, whatever its precise meaning, it was not enforced. If it had been enforced, this disaster would not have occurred."[4] The bosun officer who pulled the chain after the last car "took a narrow view of his duties." While memory played a part, it was compounded by stressful context.

When individuals forget processes, misinterpret conversations or recall fictitious events, misjudgement cascades. Lives are lost, money squandered and relationships cratered. Yet memory is the least acknowledged PERIMETERS trap.

What we hear is what we remember. If we mishear, we're more likely to misremember.

This chapter may feel unpalatable because we think what we remember is accurate. I show how six memory-related psychological concepts impact our judgement. For instance, new information is forgotten within hours (forgetting curve). What we remember isn't necessarily accurate (misremembering self) as we omit important details (recall bias), recall events that never happened (false memory) and are influenced by hinted hearing (power of suggestion) and data planting (misinformation effect). It's understandable as we're seduced by salient images, gossip or shock – and overloaded with so much information we can't process it into memory. When we misremember, forget, repress and distort data, decision risk accelerates, contributing to human error. It's a fact worth remembering.

Memory-based misjudgement is best considered alongside the temporal traps, amplified by nostalgia and hindsight. The most easily identifiable decision derailer is *recall bias*.

FORGET ME NOT

Who doesn't want to preserve memories? Minutes after his trip to space on *Blue Orion*, 90-year-old *Star Trek* captain William Shatner gushed, "I hope I never forget it." But the romance of autobiographical memory crowds out reality. Despite best intentions and professional oaths, we forget what clients, colleagues and loved ones say, especially in a noisy, distracting world.

Underpinned by neurological processes, memory is based on distorted recollections that form in our neural networks. Memory operates like a highlights and lowlights movie reel with missing scenes. We unconsciously edit the movie and replay certain narratives – a snarky comment, rude remark or insensitive statement. Sometimes it's our wittiest moments too!

How often do you misquote someone or misrecall conversations? It's counterintuitive that brands invest millions in customer feedback yet neglect recall bias. "Did you enjoy your flight?" one airline emailed me a month later. I can't remember yesterday! But minutes after an Amazon package arrives, I'm prompted to evaluate the service. Delayed recall leads to expensive mistakes. An irritated customer always remembers. What brand have you recently cancelled?

Irish author Colm Tóibín puts it well: "Memory has its own weather. There are days it's cloudy and days it's clear."[5]

German psychologist Hermann Ebbinghaus argues we only retrieve 50% of information an hour after encoding it in the *forgetting curve.*[6] While it's normal to forget keys, wallets, dates, postcodes or numbers, it's harder to understand forgetting guns, children or safety.

Forgetfulness can have fatal consequences. In the US, an average of 492 people under 25 die annually from accidental gun shootings.[7] Owners forget to check if guns are loaded.

In the summer of 2019, New York experienced a heatwave. After a late shift, social worker Juan Rodriguez left for the Virginia Medical Centre. He usually dropped his one-year-old twins off to creche. That day, Rodriguez took a new route in his silver Honda Accord. Following an eight-hour shift, he reminded his wife to pick up the twins. Having driven several blocks, Rodriguez spotted his children still strapped against the seat, lying limp.

Distracted and tired, he forgot his routine. Luna and Phoenix died from exposure to 108 degrees heat. It takes less than 60 minutes for a car to transform into a deadly oven. In the US alone, a child dies every nine days from hot car syndrome. Bereft Rodriguez was charged with manslaughter and negligent homicide. Was it his fault? Was he negligent or just overworked? Isn't that all of us?

Operating context affects how we retrieve information to do our jobs, like closing a ferry door. Stress-induced forgetfulness is an underestimated decision derailer. Under pressure and public scrutiny, practice-perfect footballers miss World Cup penalties, actors fluff lines and exam students clam up. Even surgeons cut off the wrong limbs.

᙭᙮᙭᙮᙭᙮

In medicine, the Society of Anaesthesiologists estimates surgeons leave a dozen implements inside patients every day – scalpels, scissors, sponges, needles, gloves or clamps. According to the *New England Journal of Medicine*, a gauze sponge remained inside a woman for six years after two caesarean sections, risking infection and sepsis. Device manufacturer Stryker calculates each implement retrieval costs $600,000, including legal bills and corrective surgery.[8] This mistake incurs not only financial and reputational costs but emotional consequences for patients.

One solution that process- and system-driven industries use to reduce memory reliance is checklists.[9] It limits the risk of patients waking up with a scalpel stitched to their stomach!

In *The Checklist Manifesto*, Atul Gawande writes, "In high-stress circumstances like emergency situations or where there is an unexpected change in procedure, you have a ninefold increase in risk that this kind of case will occur."[10] He estimates checklist use reduces trauma error by a third.[11] In another study, Dutch anaesthesiologists found checklists eliminated wrong-site surgery by 50%.[12]

Checklists can even boost your salary. When researchers gave checklists to a team of mechanics, revenue grew by 20%, earning each an average of 10% more commission.[13] While valuable to industry, value assumes they're comprehensive and employees are trained to remember to habitually use them.

Such tools help avoid decision damage, especially when you consider the added problem of the difference between the experiencing self and the remembering self.

THE EXPERIENCING VS (MIS) REMEMBERING SELF

As the world watched Armstrong and Aldrin make history on the lunar surface, Michael Collins was alone in the Columbia spacecraft for 21 hours. He admits sweating "like a nervous bride" for confirmation the Eagle had lift-off.

My secret terror for the last six months has been leaving them on the Moon and returning to Earth alone; now I am within minutes of finding out the truth of the matter.[14]

Forty years later, Collins recalled the experience at an event.

I was not lonely. I had a happy little home in the command module. Behind the moon, it was very peaceful – no one in Mission Control is yakkin' at me and wanting me to do this, that, and the other. So I was very happy.[15]

Unconsciously, he edited the 'secret terror' in his mental movie. It's easy to redefine our memories when the *experiencing self* differs from the *remembering self*.

In this regard, I've always been struck by Elizabeth Kendall's story.

In 1981, Elizabeth Kendall wrote her first semi-autobiographical novel, *The Phantom Prince*. Described by critics as "surreal and brave," it centred on a divorcee's search for romance, punctuated by struggles with jealousy, insecurity and alcoholism.[16]

She wrote of her great true love, once voted the shyest boy in Tacoma High School. "Part of me will always love a part of him." Four decades later, in the 2020 edition, she regretted that single sentence.

Elizabeth was Ted Bundy's long-term girlfriend, enthralled by his charm, intellect and good looks. She buried her suspicions about his absences on dates that coincided with missing girls, his crutches and yellow Volkswagen Beetle that matched witness reports. Yet over time, her inner voice grew louder and more overwhelming. Like Bundy's co-worker Ann Rule, she reluctantly reported him to the police.

Time helped her reinterpret a one-dimensional perspective beyond poems and romantic declarations. She recalls his "dead, hate-filled eyes." With confusion subsided, she reframed idealised memories. Our *experiencing self* is not the same as our *remembering self*.[7]

In comparison, Elizabeth's daughter Molly can't remember loving Bundy despite living with him for years. She once thought him "bright and shiny," polished and well groomed, a "golden saviour that entered their lives." Now she's sickened and depressed at who he really was. "I can recall the things we did together but not the feelings of love that went along with them."

What we experience isn't always what we remember. But what we remember shapes life's decisions. As Stephen Stayner discovered, trauma can shrink our mindsets and memory.

One hidden factor that affects our recall is the subtle *power of suggestion*. It's one for every Decision Ninja to monitor and master both in the home and workplace.

THE POWER OF SUGGESTION: HINTED HEARING

Hollywood loves to commercialise memory by depicting amnesia, memory erasure or microchip planting in blockbusters such as *The Bourne Identity, Inception, 50 First Dates* or *Total Recall*. Even *Barbie* triggers our childhood memories. Creative movie directors then use the *power of suggestion* to strategically move audiences to make them laugh or cry. Similarly, retailers use suggestion as a magic wand, manipulating product placement and online pop-ups to make consumer buy.

As consumers, we're vulnerable. It's why we buy more expensive vodka, hotel rooms and airline seats. Of course, Red Bull won't "give you wings" yet the idea of flight is suggestive. It resonates, reinforced by sponsorship of extreme sports like cliff diving, windsurfing and rock climbing.

Brands act like insulating placebos. For example, researchers found people who were told they were wearing high-quality 3M headphones heard more words through noisy construction than those who were told they were wearing lower-quality sets.[18] The brand literally affected what people heard and how they heard it.

As citizens, we're also vulnerable to suggestibility. Politicians hint at lower taxes, economic incentives or social housing developments – and secure votes. Brexiteers suggested immigration would be a massive problem – and secured 51.89% of votes.

In organisations, the ambitious exploit the power of suggestibility to get ahead. A senior executive once told me they would drip-feed poison about a rival. It's a nasty trick. Moreover, poison and propaganda communicate misinformation to the unsuspecting decision-maker.

The power of suggestion is dangerous in newsrooms, boardrooms and particularly courtrooms. Neuroscientist Elizabeth Loftus is a memory expert and former witness at the Ted Bundy, OJ Simpson and Harvey Weinstein trials. Curious to test whether the power of suggestion extended to eyewitness sensitivity, she assembled five groups to watch a simulated traffic accident. Subjects were asked to estimate the average car speed. In each condition, Loftus changed one word in the question. Estimate the speed before the cars 'hit,' 'smashed,' 'collided,' 'bumped' or 'contacted.'[19]

Would one word matter? It did.

People estimated higher speeds on hearing the suggestive word "smashed" (49.8%) compared to "contacted" (32.8%). Days later, the group bizarrely reported seeing broken glass, yet no glass featured in the simulation. The *misinformation effect* evidences how we incorporate redundant information into events prompted by suggestion. We substitute the data we expect to see and hear.

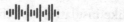

In 1979, Fred Clay experienced the cost of memory fallibility and the misinformation effect directly. Boston cab driver Richard Dwyer turned away three suspicious black passengers and watched them get into another taxi. Minutes later, 28-year-old driver Jeffrey Boyajian was robbed and murdered execution-style. When interrogated, Dwyer apparently remembered 16-year-old black Fred Clay as a passenger.

But Clay was neither in the taxi nor the Roslindale neighbourhood.

Clay went on trial as two witnesses testified against him. At the time, Massachusetts used scientifically unproven and hypnotically elicited testimony, despite its ban in 33 States. Dwyer claimed the memory "was clear to me... like a TV screen."

A confident, articulate eyewitness is a compelling tool in any prosecution toolkit. And courtroom contexts prime juries to think memory is robust. If an expert scientist or etymologist testifies, it's weighted higher, like Dr Patrick Barnes's testimony in Louise Woodward's case. Dwyer relied on intuition that night, but how clear were passengers' faces?

Neuroscience suggests that white people struggle to differentiate between individuals within ethnic groups. Equally, ethnic groups struggle to differentiate between white populations. For some, Katy Perry and Demi Moore look alike; others confuse Morgan Freeman with Samuel Jackson. It's the *other race effect*, attributed to rapid brain processing and low racial familiarity. Stereotypes don't help. All blondes aren't Swedish, and all moustache-wearers aren't Mexican!

Corroborating Dwyer's account was intellectually disabled Neal Sweatt. It later emerged that police tried to persuade him four times to pinpoint Clay in a line-up. Clay was convicted based on mistaken identity. It took 38 years to secure his release. The Massachusetts settlement was $3m, or $0.33 for every hour of incarceration. Our unshakeable faith in memory costs morally and financially.

Ten years later, a Georgia jury sentenced Troy Anthony Davis to death for murdering an off-duty police officer. There was no evidence. Davis fought to clear his name for 20 years. Seven of the nine eyewitnesses eventually recanted their testimony. Amnesty International, Pope Benedict XVI, President Jimmy Carter and a million signatories supported a clemency petition, but the Board of Pardons and Paroles tuned out all appeals.

On 21 September 2011 at 22:53 EST, Davis became the 52nd man executed by lethal injection in Georgia, uttering the last words, "For those about to take my life, may God have mercy on all of your souls."

He understood the cost of misinterpretation, deaf spots and a judicial rush to misjudgement.

The cases of Fred Clay and Troy Davis are common. The US Registry of Exonerations attributes 69% of overturned cases to misremembering witnesses. Flawed memory combined with a rush to judgement easily lead to the miscarriage of justice. It's not just planted evidence that destroys lives but planted memories.

A FAMILY AFFAIR: DON'T TRUST WHAT YOU REMEMBER

Like Elizabeth Loftus, for years psychologists and neuroscientists wanted to know if pre-defined ideas could be remembered, so experimenters deliberately implanted false memories into subjects' minds. These planted memories started small like getting lost in a shopping mall, releasing handbrakes or spilling drinks at weddings.[20] Over time, implants escalated in severity to false memories of near drownings, punching other people or being attacked by animals.[21] Subjects were convinced these fabricated events had occurred.

Alas, planting false memories isn't restricted to experiments.

In 1994, an executive at the Robert Mondavi winery, Gary

Ramona, launched a landmark case. His teenage daughter Holly had sought counsel for depression and an eating disorder. Her therapist had an unusual diagnosis: incest. Tenuous links in literature had been mooted. The therapist administered sodium amytal to recover the alleged missing memories. Despite pushback, Holly claimed her father raped her from age five to 18. Even his wife "believed her gut" despite lack of evidence.

A disbelieving father sued the therapist and won. He lost his 25-year marriage, his career and his reputation. Deaf to any alternative interpretation, Holly sued her father and lost.

Whose voice did a broken family tune in to? A fallible expert with a loose theory over reliable proof?

We seek logical explanations – and false memories provide convenient but illogical answers.

Oath-taking professionals are dutybound and paid a lot of money to use their best judgement. Most do but when diagnosis fails, malpractice results with reputations, businesses and lives destroyed.

Our desire to forget traumatic events can be strong. Not everybody can. Boatswain Mark Stanley suffered extensively after Zeebrugge. Local media reported the sinking "severely affected his health, working life and family."[22]

Shankar Vedantam considers, "a generous sprinkling of positive delusions can help us perform better, stay happier and avoid the pitfalls of depression and low self-esteem." Even mild self-delusion and false memories help the traumatised avoid cognitive dissonance and build mental resilience to cope. Sometimes, it saves our lives.

Little house on the prairie

In 1991, 11-year-old schoolgirl Jaycee Lee Dugard was dragged into a Ford Granada by convicted sex offender Phillip Garrido and his wife. In one of the longest known abductions, Dugard spent 18 years captive a mere 170 miles from her South Lake Tahoe home. Repeatedly raped, she had two daughters with Garrido. The backyard became her mental and physical perimeter, with the Garridos' voices all she heard.

In 2006, a neighbour warned police a sex offender had children living in the backyard. A deputy spoke to Garrido for 90 minutes, suspecting nothing. Three years later, Garrido wanted to hold a religious event, so he visited the University of California at Berkeley with his daughters.

Officer Ally Jacobs was suspicious of the homeschooled children's demeanour, drab attire and reference to a 28-year-old sister. She thought them programmed "almost like *Little House on the Prairie* meets robots."[23]

Jacobs tuned in to her intuition and alerted authorities. Garrido was arrested. The Sheriff later admitted, "We should have been more inquisitive, more curious and turned over a rock or two."[24]

Reframing bad events provides temporary relief. In an *ABC* interview with Barbara Walters, Dugard reframed her experience as "adapting to survive circumstances," labelling Garrido "my captor." She tells how the backyard memories never fade. Was her 18-year experience different from what she remembered? It's an event Officer Jacobs won't ever forget.

While the child bitten by a dog usually learns to avoid stray dogs, not everyone learns from history. Recall how Wells Fargo executives repeated poor choices? Some entrepreneurs launch a string of average start-ups. Their overconfidence embeds misplaced resilience. However, the majority of individuals learn from error and try to right their wrongs.

It doesn't help when professionals manipulate our memory frailty.

SOURCES OF FALSE MEMORY

Most people are savvy about disinformation but less so about how fake news creates false memories. We continue to believe fake news long after facts are disproved.[25] As professional communicators know well, this is due to how information is presented. Three bias-inducing factors aid recall but simultaneously threaten good judgement: information salience, information sequence and information repetition. These are particularly dangerous when not noticed, heard or decoded.

1. Information salience

Most of us think we remember where we were when hearing about an unexpected death or shock event. You would imagine 9/11 would qualify. Apparently not. A US survey showed that only 63% of individual recollections collated 11 months post-9/11 were consistent with versions given that day.[26] It's *flashbulb memory*. Our memory vividness and confidence are not related to accuracy.

Another survey showed that many Americans think they watched the Space Shuttle Challenger crash live, yet most networks didn't broadcast live in 1986. How does this happen? Two reasons explain this phenomenon.

First, what's mentally available is recalled quickly, like secrets or gossip.

Second, the crash felt familiar because networks replayed it extensively. It was *salient*.

The easily recalled voice can be wrong, yet people solve problems based on what springs to mind. A hard question tends to pull in easily available data. Imagine your boss asks you to nominate the best salesperson for an award. You heard Sam Silver landed a key account, so Sam is salient. But Prakash Singh won more deals year-to-date. You don't know Prakash. It's how managers form inaccurate views of talent.

Salient voices stick in the same way as breaking news or criticism. Leaders should note how harsh words linger. Manchester United manager Sir Alex Ferguson won 13 Premier Leagues and five FA Cups. Notorious for the 'hairdryer treatment,' he ranted into players' faces when annoyed. Even David Beckham received the trademark treatment following a 2–0 defeat to Arsenal in the 2003 FA Cup.[27]

As I watched a press conference for new Middlesborough manager and former Manchester United player Michael Carrick, he was asked if he would mimic Ferguson's leadership style. It was a decade later, yet he replied, "Do I look like an angry Scotsman?"[28] Experiences stick in memory.

We remember what shocks us. After 40 years on the run for armed bank robberies, Ross McCarty was apprehended by Australian police. It wasn't Ross who provided "clear and vivid" statements but the victims. Police remarked, "It's like they were recounting something that only happened to them yesterday."[29]

In politics and business, salience is used strategically. The most memorable ads are shocking, humorous or awe-inspiring. In Australia, a controversial 2018 TV ad created by Dying to Live featured Jesus on the cross, urging viewers to sign up for organ donation. While it generated Catholic outrage, its salience maximised attention as a message to save lives for a worthy cause.

2. Information sequence

The second major bias-inducing factor affecting recall relates to whether we hear information presented first or last. Ebbinghaus coined this the *serial position effect*.[30] It's why we're manipulated by clever communicators, politicians, preachers and retailers.

Imagine your manager describes a potential candidate.

"Hans is smart, diligent, and jealous."

Do you like Hans?

Now imagine the order of adjectives is reversed. "Hans is jealous, diligent and smart."

Do you like Hans now?

Researchers found people evaluated Hans more positively after the first description.[31] The *primacy effect* suggests we hook into the first piece of information heard. If Hans is first described as smart, we like him more than if he is first described as jealous. We recall what we hear last in the *recency effect*.

Warning! Human behaviour is contradictory – we remember what we hear first and last.

Sensitivity occurs with sentences too. Social psychologist Fritz Strack demonstrated sensitivity to wording sequence.[32] He asked students, "How happy are you with your life?" followed by "How many dates did you have last month?"

Strack then reversed the order. "How many dates did you have last month?" followed by "How happy are you with your life?"

Would question sequence matter? It did. People were five times happier when first asked about happiness. Being primed to think about dates prompted reflection and conclusions of lower happiness.

As an executive, I wondered if being interviewed first or last would affect my success rate. Having experimented, it's inconclusive! However, science does suggest timing matters more than sequence. If the hiring decision will be made quickly, try to be interviewed last.

Moreover, if you're asked to list strengths in interviews, announce the most important first. To build trust, introduce a weakness followed by 'but' and a counter-strength. It works. Think of Avis's message, "We're second but we try harder" or L'Oréal's blockbuster slogan, "We're more expensive but you're worth it."

Notice how others pitch messages to you. Don't be a sucker for a salient, well-sequenced story!

3. Information repetition

The third derailer influencing memory-based judgement relates to repetition. For decades, advertisers have combined salience with repetition to sell brands. Politicians repeat "Make America Great Again." Retailers repeat "Buy one get one free." Religions repeat "Praise be Allah" or "Amen."

Savvy lawyers use rhyming repetition to influence juries. In the Simpson trial, Johnny Cochrane coined, "If the glove doesn't fit, you must acquit." It stuck.

Like rhyming, simpler words are easier to process and recall than rare stimuli. You'll remember the name Billy quicker than Billilifrankodopolous. And you'll remember it quicker if it rhymes, like Billy Zillie or Jenny Penney, or if it is alliterative, like Mork'n'Mindy or Molly Malone.

How exactly does repetition and simplicity derail decisions?

Polish psychologist Robert Zajonc found the more you're exposed to a stimulus like an ad, idea or name, the warmer you feel towards it. And the warmer you feel towards it, the more you believe it's true. He coined this irrationality the *mere exposure effect*.

To illustrate, he issued adverts at two Michigan universities over several weeks. Intermittently, the front page featured Turkish words. He asked over 1,100 students to rate 12 unfamiliar words. Unsurprisingly, they didn't just recall the words they saw more often, but surprisingly, they preferred them.[33] There was a likability effect. This unconscious subjectivity becomes a derailing decision input. We vote for the politician, select a dentist, pick a movie, order a wine or buy a brand that sounds familiar and towards which we have developed an inexplicable warmth, even if it's not the best choice.

More importantly, this is the foundation of fake news which dictates what we perceive as true or false.[34] Gordon Pennycook and colleagues show how a single exposure to information increases the perception of accuracy. Moreover, the idea only needs to be mildly plausible to disrupt beliefs.[35] For instance, "the average size of Scottish dogs is shrinking," or "Australia has a wider surface than Jupiter."

These biases illustrate that we can't trust what we remember as much as we think. Conscious reinterpretation is required.

Knowing how your colleagues, clients or competitors process information in the workplace can increase your ability to decode potential misinformation and in turn, your persuasion ability. It's another source of advantage.

Don't forget the importance of organisation memory either!

In business, leaders underestimate memory-based misjudgement because it's not visible or quantifiable. Over my career, I've never heard employee, shareholder or customer memory cited as a decision risk. Maybe it's my memory? Operational, legal and market risks are measured. But what employees retain about products, services and customers constitutes the bedrock of its intellectual capital. And it matters. When someone quits, teams groan because years of intellectual property and process knowledge escape out the door.

A quicker way to stem flight risk and activism is tuning in to employee voices! Smart organisations protect memory via formal processes such as professional data archiving and recording critical conversations, interviews and meetings.

Organisations and nations maintain heritage by commemorating figures of significance. They celebrate landmark dates such as year of establishment or independence. In addition, towns erect statues, universities name wings, companies establish foundations and regulators pass laws. By honouring milestones, memory is better preserved.

TUNING IN: THE VOICE OF EXPERIENCE

Despite its flaws and limited visibility in decisioning, memory is a source of wonder. Who isn't impressed by the leader who remembers every name in the room? In 2020, Pakistani memory athlete Emma Alam broke the Guinness World Record by putting 218 names to faces in 15 minutes.[36] Could you?

Other exceptions exist. US autistic mega-savant Kim Peek inspired Raymond Babbitt in the 1984 Academy Award-winning *Rain Man*. Kim had near-perfect recall in 15 subjects, from music to history, literature and geography. He memorised 9,000 books, including phone books. His father recalled, "Kim could tell the day you were born and that day's headlines." Even NASA studied his brain.[37]

You can train memory by chunking information into bite-size pieces. Twenty-eight memory athletes were asked to memorise 72 words. After six weeks, average recall was 62 words.[38] It's a discipline.

To stop the spread of misinformation, simple fact-checking works. Voice-activated systems like Alexa or Siri do this in seconds. When scientists designed accuracy-checking habits and automated reminders like "Are you sure?", people's ability to discern mistruths trebled and willingness to overshare misinformation was deterred.[39]

Memories are important for building brand loyalty. Some brands retrigger memories by spending millions on free samples and giveaways. It's why hotels issue branded pens, fans keep ticket stubs and companies distribute logo-emblazoned t-shirts. Souvenirs act like fresh voices that replay experiences.

Psychologist Sam Gosling calls this *behavioural residue*. It's an effective memory trigger in any decision environment. On a more macabre level, it's why serial killers take victims' possessions and body parts from crime scenes.

Rewriting your history is a choice. Take the late rock'n'roll legend Tina Turner who shocked *People* magazine's 30 million viewers in 1981 when she admitted domestic abuse by her husband-manager, Ike. When she escaped, she was penniless. The only thing she asked for in the divorce was her name. She converted this asset into a multi-million-dollar career, staying true to her identity.

Forty years later in an *HBO* documentary, she reflected feeling caught between guilt and fear. "I promised him I wouldn't leave him, and in those days, a promise was a promise." It's a reminder of how consistency bias keeps us trapped.

> For 16 years, I stayed with a man I knew I'd never be happy with… I went through basic torture. I was living a life of death. I didn't exist. But I walked out and didn't look back.

In her eighties, Turner didn't relive the past. At the 2018 *Tina: The Tina Turner Musical* premiere, she told a probing journalist, "Why would I want to relive the beatings?" She preferred positive memories, like eight hard-earned Grammys.

> The goodness didn't outweigh the bad… you just want to leave the old memories in the past.

A born-again Buddhist living on Lake Zurich, she didn't want to be defined as an abused woman or rock'n'roll singer. She cultivated a perimeter perspective, controlling memory-based inputs for a better lifestyle and decision mindset.

The Decision Ninja leverages memory as an asset, recording important occasions and statements. Remembering your fiduciary responsibility and moral obligations boosts ethical decisions rather than derails them – discussed next.

THE DECISION NINJA
WHAT TO REMEMBER

- People discount memory-related error because it's hidden, intangible and uncomfortable to accept.
- We hear information that memory feeds us yet what we experience isn't always what we remember, exacerbated by overload, distraction and stress.
- Memory misinformation is reflected in amnesia, forgetting and false memory.
- As processing capacity is finite, memory is recalled selectively. Equally, selective filtering of voices avoids overload and filters what's useful.
- As the recency and primacy effects impact accuracy, we retrieve data in four ways, each inducing a form of bias:
  - *Repetition*: repeated information is believed, liked and trusted even if untrue.
  - *Salience*: the more vivid an image, advert or idea, the easier it is to recall.
  - *Sequence*: the information, dates and names heard first or last drive decisions.
  - *Suggestion*: memories can be manipulated through idea planting.
- Recall is teachable. Liability can be reduced with checklists, behavioural residue and mnemonics.
- Recreated memory isn't always bad; it's a coping mechanism for trauma victims to hear a better future.
- Age-related memory dysfunction is an underestimated liability that's taboo in some organisations. While it threatens sustainability, it requires genuine empathy.
- Like history, memory can be preserved to protect intellectual capital and facilitate learning.

CHAPTER 9

ETHICS-BASED TRAPS: CONSCIENCE CHAOS

"If you see fraud and don't say fraud, you are a fraud."

Nassim Taleb

"WHAT WOULD YOU do if you knew you couldn't fail?" That was the sign 19-year-old Theranos founder and CEO Elizabeth Holmes displayed on her desk.

Her idolisation of Steve Jobs led to a laser-like focus on creating the "iPod of healthcare." Theranos's finger-prick blood diagnosis was billed as ground-breaking: cheaper, smaller and less painful than competitors. Its progressive disease map would apparently detect cancer markers, HIV and hormones.

Relatives say Holmes always wanted to be a billionaire. She succeeded. Within a decade, the world's youngest self-made billionaire was valued at $9bn, dubbed by *Inc.* as "the next Steve Jobs."

Theranos's Silicon Valley office space at 1701 Page Mill Road became her mental perimeter. Mirroring Jim Jones's leadership style, Holmes demanded unbridled loyalty. Her team was "building a religion... if anyone didn't believe in it, they should leave." Dissenters at every level were shown the door.

Secrecy and paranoia defined the culture for 15 years. To protect proprietary information, visitors signed non-disclosure agreements and were escorted to the bathroom. Why? The Edison technology had failed in a spectacular way.[1]

Disregarding patient risk, Holmes continued to sell this technology as world-class microfluidics, misreporting reality to her highly decorated board of chairman, senators and former US secretaries of state, including George Shultz. Partnerships with distribution giants were fabricated on exaggeration and lies. Retail giant Walgreens ignored the expert warnings and invested $140m to outpace rival CVS. Meanwhile, many Theranos employees self-silenced to protect their jobs.

Wall Street Journal reporter John Carreyrou exposed the pseudo-technology following tip-offs from Adam Clapper MD and former employee Tyler Shultz, George's grandson. It was too late. Governance failure was colossal. Investors lost an estimated $804m. In 2018, Holmes was charged with fraud and conspiracy, and sentenced to 11 years in a Texan prison.

The voice of arrogance and ambition often supersedes the voice of conscience and compassion.

This chapter describes five deadly psychological blind, deaf and dumb spots that trigger individuals and organisations to ignore the voice of conscience, wasting billions and shattering lives. For instance, when we're too goal-focused, doing the right thing becomes fallacious (bounded ethicality). Many well-meaning leaders decide with a business lens rather than a moral lens (moral climate) and downplay conflicts of interest (moral dilemma). In the moment, doing the right thing gets tuned out and conscience relegated (ethical fading). Some compensate for wrongdoing by performing kindnesses (moral licensing), then justify wrongdoing as revisionist historians (moral disengagement). Examples from pharmaceuticals, banking, manufacturing, law and sports illustrate how easily misconduct fuses with power, emotion and ego to constrain the right voices.

When sentencing Holmes, Judge Davila wondered what motivated a "brilliant" entrepreneur. "Was it hubris… intoxication with fame… or loss of moral compass?" How did she seduce so many smart stakeholders? Why didn't more directors and investors spot it? Were they distracted by who they saw rather than what they heard? Multiple deaf spots combined in a force multiplier effect.

WHAT CONSCIENCE? I'M GOAL HUNTING

Investors, regulators and patients wanted to believe in the cutting-edge technology. They heard what they wanted in *bounded ethicality*. And deception was not on anyone's radar, reflecting Levine's truth-default theory. Tyler Shultz explained:

> She's really good at telling you what you need to hear to keep going. She did that a lot with my grandfather… she would just feed him… things that were factually not true.

Attractive Holmes didn't look like a typical fraudster either. People saw style so didn't question substance, validating Herbert Simon's concept of bounded rationality. Her Stanford pedigree cast a long shadow that impressed partners.

Governance was abysmally absent. In a deposition, former Wells Fargo chairman and CEO Richard Kovacevich recalls the board as more advisory than fiduciary. "I don't remember disapproving with anything that she did… ultimately, Elizabeth made the decisions."[2] Only Holmes had the full picture. This information asymmetry qualified her to control the message.

With little MedTech experience, the board gratefully

swallowed all scientific, operational and financial data at face value. The success story was too seductive to second-guess.

Like in Jonestown, context and timing contributed. The 1990s Silicon Valley dream was alive. Facebook, Uber, Spotify and Salesforce were making history. The media was romanticising leaders like Bill Gates and Mark Zuckerberg. Holmes wanted to be accepted into the Palo Alto bubble.

From peanuts to painkillers

Goal orientation characterises most business. But some take it too far. In 2015, CEO of Peanut Corporation of America Stewart Parnell sold salmonella-contaminated products with faked safety certificates. In a national outbreak, nine people died and hundreds fell ill. Following one of the largest US food recalls in history, the company was liquidated.[3] Parnell's attorney told *TIME* magazine his client was "doing exactly what the rest of the peanut industry was doing."[4] Responding to the voice of greed, Parnell was imprisoned for 28 years on 72 counts of fraud.

Parnell isn't alone. Owners of Purdue Pharma, the Sackler family donated millions to philanthropic institutions, lending their name to a Louvre wing, Washington gallery and Harvard museum. Yet they're indelibly stained as orchestrators of the opioid crisis, overselling pain-alleviating OxyContin. Salespeople were given uncapped bonuses, praised as pain-reducing heroes. Mismarketing a spurious 1% addiction risk over two decades led to an estimated one million deaths from overdose.[5]

Despite hearing about pill-dispensing stalls and rising addiction, the company tuned out. Richard Sackler blamed the users. "They are the culprits and the problem; they are the reckless criminals."[6]

Under duress, Purdue admitted it "knowingly and intentionally conspired and agreed with others to aid and abet" staff to dispense its products "without a legitimate medical purpose." Predictably, they claimed to "sincerely regret" that their most profitable drug "unexpectedly became part of an opioid crisis" and settled with the Justice Department for $6bn. Institutions like Oxford University have since removed the Sackler name from their hallowed halls.

Purdue had help. Distributors, pharmacy chains, physicians, executives and advisers were complicit. CVS and Walgreens paid $5bn each to settle thousands of lawsuits.[7] Two years earlier, Johnson & Johnson paid $572m in damages to Oklahoma. Nobody went to jail.

DERAILED BY CONFLICTS OF INTEREST

Grasping consultants contributed too. White-collar McKinsey advised Purdue about boosting sales. According to the *New York Times*, this was "even after the drug maker pleaded guilty in 2007... it misled doctors and regulators about OxyContin's risks."[8] Shockingly, McKinsey calculated potential compensation of $14,000 for each OxyContin overdose or addicted patient.

In an undeclared conflict of interest, 22 McKinsey consultants advised the Food and Drug Administration (FDA) to regulate OxyContin while advising Purdue how to promote it.

This conflict continued for 15 years. At one stage, anticipating regulatory oversight, McKinsey suggested "eliminating our documents and emails." House oversight members called them "drug traffickers in suits" as profits over "highest professional standards" infected this Hermes-attired clan. Managing partner Kevin Sneader admitted McKinsey didn't "adequately acknowledge the epidemic unfolding."[9] Predictably, they wanted to be "part of the solution."

Too little, too late.

Was this a moral dilemma? McKinsey earned a whopping

$86m from Purdue and $140m from the FDA. The voice of public opinion and the courts found them liable for $573m in damages, payable to various rehabilitation programmes.

Ethical misconduct isn't restricted to business, brown envelopes or government contracts. Scientists tune out conscience to achieve goals. It's similar to how the Tuskegee researchers mistreated African Americans.

In the 1960s, US psychologist Peter Neubauer separated twins and triplets at birth to explore how nature or nurture would affect social development. He never told the adoptive families and justified the cruel separation of siblings as advancing science. His actions were only discovered years later when twins met accidentally in nearby towns.

While clients are demanding, they don't expect unsavoury antics from professional advisers, agents, auditors, therapists, coaches or consultants. But policy violation and conflicts of interest are inevitable when big money, careers and high-profile initiatives are involved. Rules, fines and penalties only go so far.

This isn't new. Recall Elvis's complicated co-dependent relationship with Colonel Parker.[10] An illegal immigrant with a conflicted position, only three concerts were held internationally over 30 years.

You can't only rely on what you see. Ask questions and question answers.

When doing the right thing might be wrong

Contemporary customers, employees and citizens expect officers, advisers and CEOs to do the right thing by signalling zero tolerance of injustice. It's the role of regulators and agencies to hold errant firms and individuals to account. In many ways, they are as responsible as the 12th juror. Sometimes professionals face the toughest of conflicted dilemmas.

FBI Director James Comey confronted a Buridan's Ass dilemma. In 2016, a month before the presidential election, he learned that US Democrat president-elect Hillary Clinton had transgressed protocol by sending classified emails from a personal server.

The political stakes were high. Publicly all leaders are party-agnostic. If Comey stayed silent about the investigation, the Bureau would appear politically partisan. If the investigation was later discovered, he could reasonably be accused of covering up for Clinton.

Yet if Comey disclosed the investigation, a credible candidate's prospects would be jeopardised whether she was found in breach or not, and Republican rival Donald Trump would be advantaged. The office, and Comey, would invite scandal and be accused of a pro-Trump bias.

Three weeks before the election, Comey advised Congress and the investigation was leaked to the media.

Eleven days before the election, the FBI formally announced its investigation into Clinton.

Three days before the election, Clinton was cleared of any wrongdoing.

For many, it was the morally right decision with the politically wrong outcome. Comey was vilified as the architect of Trump's victory. Comey listened to his inner voice but underestimated the situation. He paid the political price and despite holding power, was publicly fired on CNN.

There's always a bigger bear!

The man who prosecuted criminals, from the mafia to Martha Stewart, is unrepentant:

It's a mistake to surrender moral authority to the group to still our own voices... ethical leaders choose a higher loyalty to core values over their own personal gain.[11]

Although he did the right thing, decisions carry a ripple effect in a broader ecosystem. Did it justify Trump's foreign policy reversal, kids in cages or Capitol Building attacks? Some argue not.

The world isn't necessarily fair, even if good people try to make it so. Bad people don't always get punished and good people aren't always rewarded. Busy people don't interpret signals in time.

The voice of righteousness sounds noble but doesn't always optimise outcomes.

Consider noxious mergers again. Keeping your head down helps duck the inevitable axe. Nevertheless, well-meaning employees often insist on advising new owners how things should be done – the old way. While this voice falls on deaf ears, powerholders hear one message. "Here's trouble!" I've seen many colleagues speak up only to become a cost saving. No one wants to be told they're wrong.

EVERYONE'S 'A GOOD PERSON'

As discussed earlier, the well-established *above-average effect* indicates most people think they're not just better drivers, dancers or decision-makers than others but more honest too. People are proud of their moral compass, nurturing a romantic image of who they want to be. Yet most exaggerate CVs, misrepresent facts and tell white lies to get ahead.

Every so often, values clash, even at the highest level.

In 2004, US Supreme Court justice Antonin Scalia refused to recuse himself in an energy policy case that involved his duck-hunting friend, Vice-President Dick Cheney. Scalia thought himself capable of presiding fairly. Despite the conflict, he told the *Los Angeles Times*, "I don't think my impartiality could reasonably be questioned." The mere suggestion offended his professional pride.

The third US president, Thomas Jefferson, spoke out against the domestic slave trade and trafficking to the colonies. While the 1776 Declaration of Independence signatories publicly supported gradual emancipation, privately, most owned African American slaves. Jefferson housed over 600 slaves at his Monticello plantation, including Sally Hemings, with whom it's said he fathered several children.[12]

What voice did Jefferson hear? Was it fairness and duty over bonds of affection? He likely justified a bifurcated existence with intellectual reasoning, resistant to cognitive dissonance.

People are more prone to misconduct when others bear the cost – and no victim is visible. It's why some conclude "let the fat cats pay." It's why scammers make false insurance claims every five minutes that cost £1.2bn annually. It's *moral hazard*. And it affects misjudgement in the workplace.

IT'S THE CULTURE, STUPID

In 2008, Société Générale was placed under a government and shareholder microscope. Over two years inexperienced trader Jérôme Kerviel cost the bank $7.2bn, six times the amount Nick Leeson lost at Barings.

Did Kerviel operate within a greedy culture or did an operating culture amplify Kerviel's greed? In my experience, investment banking is a toxic environment. Every conversation is about making, investing or hiding money. With risk-takers hired and rewarded, it's a fertile ground for dissatisfaction and dishonesty. Science finds proximity to money cues, like cash or screensavers that display dollar signs, primes selfish and uncaring behaviour.[13] It exacerbates the *moral climate*.

Son of a hairdresser and a teacher, 39-year-old Kerviel didn't attend the prestigious French elite schools like his colleagues. Was he desperate to fit in?[14] Governance loopholes provided the opportunity. Kerviel ignored the voice of regulatory compliance, breached risk limits, ignored policies and risked the bank's liquidity position. Like serial killer highs, the trading highs became ever more addictive.

In terms of context, Société Générale was growing fast. With 130,000 employees, it had under-invested in risk talent. Knowing the inherent failures and realising managers didn't catch or punish traders in breach, Kerviel balanced the low likelihood of capture against the high reward of peer recognition.

It's tempting to blame error on a single department or individual. It's also easier to explain. But behaviour is rarely so simple. Systems, context and co-workers contribute subliminally to judgement.

As most managers share corporate DNA with their recruited employees, it's unrealistic to think they would spot flaws in a doppelganger! It's partly why Société Générale management turned a deaf ear, ignored compliance warnings and didn't question a junior trader who suddenly accounted for 59% of desk earnings. Instead, they high-fived his outperformance.

As compliance didn't fully understand trading protocols, their knowledge gaps and outgroup status cemented a certain deference to traders. Information asymmetry is a trap that can derail judgement because we don't want to sound stupid in front of colleagues.

In 2014, Kerviel was sentenced to serve three years for forgery, breach of trust and unauthorised computer use. He subsequently countered that Société Générale was complicit and reached a settlement.

If you're like others, you probably don't pause to consider the effect of your workplace context on behaviour. In competitive ego-driven climates, misconduct can be due to a bad apple as much as a bad barrel.

It's no different in sport.

Medals, money or morals?

To date, 149 Olympic medals have been stripped from athletes in 36 countries for taking banned performance-enhancing drugs.[15] In 2023, the World Athletics Doping Agency (WADA) reported 1,560 findings among athletes. Arguably, this is a low percentage in relative terms but when so many competitors endure gruelling training and diet regimes for track and field success, unfairness destroys the integrity of sport.

While unethical behaviour will always be evident at an individual and organisational level, collusion doesn't often happen at a national level.

There are exceptions.

In the 2014 Sochi Olympics, scores of Russian athletes manipulated lab tests in a state-sponsored doping programme. Its brazenness rocked the industry. WADA imposed a four-year ban on Olympic games participation.

Having campaigned tirelessly for fairness in sport and overhauled the governing body's constitution since 2015, World Athletics President Seb Coe noted the shameful industry wake-up call. "The message could not be stronger... cheating at any level will not be tolerated."[16] It was a message of reform from which other sports could learn.

Coe predicted a landmark moment for clean sport to protect the integrity of athletics and ensure a level playing field.[17] A leader with self-belief in spades from the day he won a gold medal in Stuttgart's 1986 European Championships, he went on to reflect, "I'd done the last thing that they expected from me."

It's probably why he was chosen to represent Britain's bid for the 2012 Olympic Games and chair its organising committee. And why over 200 World Athletics member federations heard his voice and re-elected him for a third term. This was the first international sporting federation to achieve gender balance in 2023. A new world record!

This doping programme begs a bigger question. With so much to lose, why do athletes take such risks? Is it medals, money or both?

It's certainly medals. A study reveals 98% of US Olympic athletes reported a willingness to take performance-enhancing drugs if there was no chance of detection. One in two confirmed their willingness to take these if they could win every competition for five consecutive years.

What was more shocking was the athletes' level of desperation. They were willing to do so even if it meant dying from drug-related side effects.[18] For them, the reward justified the risk, as it did for Everest climber Doug Hansen and racer Ayrton Senna.

᛫ᛁ᛫ᛁ᛫ᛁ᛫ᛁ᛫

For some, cheating is justified. Shamed cyclist Lance Armstrong claims taking the drug erythropoietin was standard practice in 2000. There was no moral dilemma. Teams even administered blood bags in public. He openly states in *The Armstrong Lie* documentary, "I was very confident I would never be caught." He was wrong, thanks to the interpretative and investigative skills of dogged journalists.

That's not to say that money from sponsorships, books and appearances isn't a motivating factor, but in relative terms, athletics prize money is low. The 2023 World Championships in Budapest allocated $8.5m to the top eight finishers in each event. A gold medallist could expect $70,000 with $35,00 for silver and $22,000 for bronze. In comparison, tennis player Carlos Alcaraz collected $3.1m for winning Wimbledon a month before.

Athlete, trader or leader, most of us have good intentions. A toxic greedy context can tune out the right behaviours. A therapist might break client confidentiality – like Jerome Oziel who shared Erik Menéndez's confession with his girlfriend. A prosecutor might conceal exculpatory evidence or a medical manufacturer might increase the price of its medicine. For instance, in 2015, Turing Pharmaceuticals raised the cost of parasitic infection drug Daraprim stratospherically from $13.50 to $750 overnight. We make excuses to justify bad deeds from evidence tampering to price gouging.

Psychologists call this *moral disengagement.*

THE GREAT JUSTIFICATION

As discussed earlier, one character who both intrigues and disgusts people is the Angel of Death, Josef Mengele, who was on the run in South America for nearly four decades. According to Nazi journalist John Ware, Mengele's family thought their relative was "misunderstood."

After 21 years apart, Mengele's son Rolf wanted to understand his father. But Mengele warned him:

I do not have the minutest inner desire to justify, or even excuse, any decisions, actions or behaviour regarding my life. My tolerance has its limits.

In 1977, at a clandestine meeting facilitated by the Bosserts, Rolf met "a broken man" and "a scared creature." For two weeks, this 33-year-old lawyer cross-examined his father, hearing no voice of remorse, regret or self-recrimination.

Mengele had tuned out the *selektion* of thousands of Jews in cattle trucks, barbaric breeding experiments, infecting bodies, throwing babies from rooftops, stitching skin, injecting eye dye and endurance-testing electrocution. He disregarded telling Auschwitz prisoner A24840 "to strip and step inside a large vat with extremely hot water." Ninety-two-year-old survivor Cyrla Gerwertz recalled, "I said the water was too hot and he said if I didn't do what he ordered, he would kill me. After that I had to step into a vat with freezing water."[19]

Defending Hitler's intent to create the master race, Mengele justified how he "personally had never harmed anyone in his life." Denying responsibility, "I did not invent Auschwitz." Inattentionally deaf to depravity, he exhibited a rare fusion of bias blind spots, deaf spots and dumb spots.

Despite Mengele's self-pity, Rolf felt like he was with a stranger. What struck him was the deafness to truth and disregard for the voice of conscience. His father's moral perimeters stopped at the German border.

> I realised that this man, my father, was just too rigid. Despite his knowledge and intellect, he just did not want to see the basis and rules for the simplest humanity in Auschwitz. He didn't realise that his presence alone made him an accessory within the deepest meaning of inhumanity.

Nevertheless, like the Bosserts, Rolf wasn't prepared to turn his father over to authorities. Within 18 months, he didn't have to. The Angel of Death was dead, drowning after a suspected heart attack.

We're excellent at generating excuses such as "everyone's doing it" or "it's for the greater good." When behaviour conflicts with moral standards, we regulate thinking by distancing ourselves to avoid self-sanctions, according to psychology professor Albert Bandura.

When your inner voice justifies a misdeed, it facilitates subsequent misdeeds. Mengele "had to do his duty, to carry out orders." Jim Jones was saving followers, Simpson's lawyer was defending a client, Kerviel was enriching Société Générale and Holmes was pursuing pain-free testing.

It's easy to justify bad acts when you perform good acts.

Why good deeds justify bad deeds

Another way we justify behaviour is by balancing the moral scales. Every so often, when someone treats you badly, they try to compensate. Does an unfaithful partner give you flowers? Does a stingy boss placate you with plum projects? Compensation may alleviate guilt, but it doesn't correct the original wrongdoing.

Just as consumers balance purchasing choice, wrongdoers balance moral choice.[20] You might buy an expensive outfit with a cheaper accessory. If you perform an altruistic act, you might feel freer to perform a selfish act. This is *moral licensing*.

To illustrate how unbiased decisions legitimise biased decisions, Princeton researchers asked participants to make two consecutive hiring decisions.[21] Among equally qualified candidates, when male participants chose a female candidate (unbiased), researchers found participants were less concerned about appearing sexist (biased) in subsequent hiring decisions.

It's not just theory. Moral licensing plays out in practice. Jimmy Savile excused any hint of molesting teenage girls by highlighting his charity works. Rationalising that a good act cancels a bad act, he informed suspicious colleagues of his deal with "the man upstairs."[22]

It can work in reverse.

Companies like Warby Parker or L'Occitane en Provence donate to charity for each product sold. Studies find this giving-by-proxy strategy exerts a positive spillover effect on employees who feel encouraged to do good deeds in the future.[23]

Knowing how others tune in or tune out usefully informs the Decision Ninja's judgement capability.

The slippery slope

Imagine a legal assistant who completes their billing timecard every day and rounds up an extra ten minutes to make an hour. It seems harmless. But ten minutes becomes 30 minutes, then an hour and then a day. Each time, the legal assistant feels less discomfort and cognitive dissonance. That's how the *slippery slope* begins.

Tuning out of conscience starts with minor transgressions like rounding up fees, taking undue credit or telling white lies. Golfers move balls out of rough spots, thinking "Nobody will see it." Professional footballers feign injury to secure a penalty. Fraudulent accountants buy time to fix mistakes. Colonel Parker lied to enter the USA and continued this story for decades.

How far down the wrong path do people go before they reverse or find the right path?

"When we are busy focused on common organisational goals, like quarterly earnings or sales quotas, the ethical implications of important decisions can fade from our minds," Max Bazerman and Ann Tenbrunsel explain in *Blind Spots*.[24] They call this *ethical fading*.[25]

Individuals, organisations and governments are vulnerable to a combination of ethical fading and inattentional deafness, especially towards minority populations with little voice.

Out of sight usually means out of earshot.

Consider the plight of prisoners. The World Prison Brief estimates 11 million inmates exist globally. Many endure appalling conditions in flagrant abuse of human rights. Penal Reform International reports 102 countries with occupancy rates exceeding 110%.[26] Prison Centrale de Bukavu in the Democratic Republic of the Congo exceeds capacity by a phenomenal 528%. This chronic overcrowding leaves prisoners vulnerable to disease and malnutrition.

It's not just developing countries. The *New York Times* reports that US prisons operate at an average of 182% capacity. High-risk prisoners move dorms to escape violence. One prisoner was tied up and tortured by fellow inmates for two days in an Alabama prison.[27] Another was able to text his cellmate's mother indicating he would "chop her son into pieces and rape him" if she didn't send him $800. You may recall Jeffrey Dahmer's prison murder, or the prison attack on officer Derek Chauvin post-George Floyd. Countries as well as administrators tune out minorities in deaf ear syndrome.

IT'S NEVER AS BAD AS YOU THINK

Tenbrunsel and David Messick suggest that ethical fading is exacerbated by toned-down euphemistic language which normalises behaviour.[28] When Maradona illegally handled the ball in the 1986 World Cup against England, it was missed by referees but caught on camera. He referred to it as the "Hand of God."

Euphemisms dilute meaning, disguise or soften an act's severity.

Policyholders are fond of linguistic gymnastics. For example, the CIA applied 'enhanced intelligence techniques' rather than torture to Khalid Sheikh Mohammed. When initially found out, republican George Santos admitted embellishing his CV but not lying to secure votes. What we hear can't always be trusted.

Euphemisms are liberally used for sensitive topics. The Pentagon called nuclear radiation measures 'sunshine units' before changing this to strontium units. Pets are 'put to sleep,' fired employees 'pursue other interests' and dodgy managers 'cook the books.' Peng Shuai had a 'misunderstanding.'

Euphemisms assume inside knowledge like a special code; uninterpreted, they contribute to exclusion.

Prosecutors argue vicious child murders by parents or domestic abuse incidents are 'impulsive' or 'crimes of passion.' Usage is pervasive among conscience-free criminals. Ted Bundy references how he was controlled by a "disordered mind" rather than a deranged mind. Predatory Penn State coach Jerry Sandusky admitted "just horsing around in the shower" with young boys. "We were an extended family." Justifying bear hugs, showers and blowing on stomachs: "That was just me."[29]

Euphemistic labelling is one of multiple moral disengagement mechanisms that explain how people tolerate rather than terminate atrocities. I find these illuminating. For example, Jack the Ripper *diffused responsibility* to God's calling; Rwanda's Hutus *dehumanised* Tutsis as cockroaches; Kerviel *attributed blame* to compliance loopholes; Parnell *relabelled* fake safety certificates as the industry norm; the Catholic Church *displaced responsibility* by relocating errant priests from parish to parish. Many combine justifications, amplifying deaf spots. Once you know these, you can spot them every day.

Notwithstanding how these ethics-based derailers misguide judgement, role models exist.

TUNING IN: THE VOICE OF CONSCIENCE

In today's noisy world, people feel unheard. Shareholder, consumer and employee activism is rising, protesting against social injustice and human rights violations. Some organisations have actively embraced these human rights principles. One even adopted a legal stand against their parent.

Before Ben & Jerry's was acquired by Unilever for $326m, it had consistently used its voice to promote climate change, economic inequality and human rights. In a bold move post-acquisition, Ben & Jerry's sued Unilever for selling ice-cream in the Israeli-occupied West Bank. They settled the dispute, having made their point.

Numerous examples exist of firms genuinely using their voice for good. Outdoor clothing manufacturer Patagonia donates

1% of sales to environmental causes. Muhammad Yunus's microfinance entities lend to the world's poorest people and marginalised businesses, achieving a 98% loan-repayment rate. Many examples of genuine altruism exist in the corporate and charity sectors. It's important to distinguish between these cases and brands that virtue signal.

Moral positions also evolve: prisoners repent, policies get regulated, corrupt associations reform, executives refine their leadership style and individuals rediscover their humanity.

In contrast to Mengele, Catholic engineer and Nazi Oskar Schindler tuned in to his conscience. Initially profiting from plundering, in 1939 he bought a factory outside Krakow to support the army's revenue base. By 1942, it had expanded into an enamel and ammunitions plant with 800 employees, of whom half were Jews.[30] As depicted in the Oscar-winning *Schindler's List*, his hedonistic lifestyle was redirected to save 'essential' workers from the gas chambers. While he falsified records, Nazi comrades judged the right to life solely based on the Jewish faces they saw.

Penniless after the war, Schindler lived between Israel and Germany, supported by Jewish relief organisations. His grave is inscribed, "The unforgettable rescuer of 1,200 persecuted Jews." When I visited the enamel factory, I noticed a plaque now stands to the memory of one individual who listened to the voice of conscience.

One among many, Japanese diplomat Chiune Sugihara and his wife Yukiko also risked their lives to falsify 2,139 transit visas to save 6,000 Lithuanian Jews.[31]

Countless decent individuals tune into conscience every day and extend acts of kindness, making a real difference to others' lives, like the 12th juror. Nevertheless, we can't always decree what's ethical. Why?

There's no universal standard of ethicality.

◁◉▷

A global survey called The Moral Machine analysed 40 million decisions by 2.3 million people across 233 countries and territories.[32] Participants were given 13 hypothetical scenarios about the safety of self-driving cars.

In each case, the death of passengers and pedestrians was unavoidable. People had to choose between saving the lives of five different groups: the young, wealthy, homeless, elderly or women. Who would you have chosen?

Significant disagreement emerged across countries, indicating no consistent moral compass.

The ethics-based PERIMETERS traps dominate a noisy world where it's hard to hear the voice of conscience amid the daily din of data, disinformation and distraction. Nowadays, individual, corporate and national perpetrators are increasingly being held to account and brought to justice. But progress is slow, selective and the world isn't always fair. The worst offenders can escape justice.

Scores of inspirational voices take the right path and reinterpret motivations with a moral filter. Institutions play a role by dialling up rewards and punishments to stem the routinisation of deviance. Every effort makes a difference.

Human vulnerability to power, ego, risk, identity, memory and even ethical traps depends on a temporal mindset. Are you thinking ahead to the consequences? Are you wedded to past decisions and the voice of nostalgia? While seemingly irrelevant, these decision derailers impact the Time-based PERIMETERS traps, discussed next.

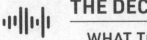

THE DECISION NINJA
WHAT TO REMEMBER

- Between ethical and unethical decisions lie a mere handful of judgement calls that determine whether you sail through life or spend your life in jail.
- People, not institutions, make unethical decisions. When powerholders are goal-obsessed, perimeters shrink and conscience and conflicts of interest get ignored.
- Society expects the modern leader to role model ethical judgement and set the moral tone. Increasingly, transgressions are punished and transgressors cancelled.
- Most people are proud of their moral identity but succumb to the opposing voices of pressure, temptation, relative comparison and competition.
- The slippery slope starts small with early warnings often heard in excuses, euphemisms, language, moral licensing and ideology.
- The complex process of moral disengagement allows people to tolerate and justify gross misconduct, preceded by a process of ethical fading.
- The world isn't always just or fair. What's best for the organisation isn't necessarily best for the individual. What's best for the individual isn't necessarily best for society.
- Extremes of evil are offset by extremes of goodness. Leaders have a moral responsibility to know the difference and rebalance what they see with what they hear.

CHAPTER 10

TIME-BASED TRAPS: HERE TODAY, WHAT TOMORROW?

"A true teacher is one who, keeping the past alive, is also able to understand the present."

Confucius

I T WAS A foggy Sunday afternoon in March 1977 when air traffic controllers and pilots grew frustrated with take-off delays. The Tenerife control tower was short-staffed, visibility was poor and the runway congested. Experienced Dutch pilot Jacob van Zanten sounded irritated but waited his turn. He discussed clearance for KLM flight 4895 with the Los Rodeos Spanish controllers. Co-pilot Meurs told the controller they were "now at take-off."

The controller replied, "Okay," adding "Stand by for take-off. I will call you."[1]

At the same time, a radio call from Pan Am flight 1736 caused a three-second frequency interference. Neither Meurs nor van Zanten heard the last sentence. They headed down runway 30 along with the Pan Am flight which was cleared for take-off. The planes collided at 160mph, resulting in 583 fatalities.

Desperate to make the take-off slot, van Zanten heard and anchored to a familiar message. It was what he expected and wanted to hear. Weather, mishearing and bad luck combined with human error in one of the worst disasters in aviation history. New standard language was subsequently introduced.

But misjudgement is attributable to more than language and process.

Time isn't something we think about as a decision influence. It's too abstract. Yet we unconsciously tune in and evaluate situations with a past, present or future orientation. Time-related factors such as impatience, nostalgia and procrastination curb reasoning, derailing the choices we make.

This chapter highlights how five temporal biases inadvertently distort what we hear. In a hurry, we use the gist of conversations rather than the detail to reach conclusions. Most people prefer to live in the permanent present with a short-term mindset, despite proven long-term benefits (present bias). Some fear change and stick with what's familiar rather than experiment or reinvent strategies (status quo). Others recast choices after the fact (hindsight bias), thinking "It worked before, it'll work again." The majority of us are awful at predicting how we'll feel in the future (affective forecasting error) and are inconsistent (noise) over time.

The world isn't binary. Extreme long-term or short-term thinking causes decision damage. Short-term thinking was illustrated by one of London's worst residential fires since World War II.

EXPERIENCE AND INTUITION

Just after midnight on 14 June 2017, a fridge-freezer caught fire on a fourth-floor flat in a 24-storey tower block. Within minutes, an inferno had spread up the tower, engulfing the exterior. Forty fire engines could barely contain it. London's Kensington and Chelsea emergency services advised residents to "stay put" in line with standard protocol. Some ignored this directive.

At 2:47am, residents were told to evacuate. Helpless onlookers watched as news channels live-streamed the inferno. Within four hours, 100 flats were engulfed in flames. Within 24 hours, the entire Grenfell Tower had burned out.[2] Seventy-two people lost their lives.

What happened? Structural and psychological factors combined, compounded by greed, incompetence and inertia. The 1970s building had been refurbished a few years earlier for £8.6m. To meet the available budget, the contractor swapped high-quality cladding for a combustible polyethylene filler material, boasting, "We will be quids in."[3] Documents "show the zinc cladding originally proposed was replaced with an aluminium type which was less fire resistant, saving nearly £300,000." However, "Both the cladding and exterior insulation failed all preliminary tests."

Management turned a deaf ear to safety and procured materials with a short-term mindset. Generating profit became more important than hearing the voice of probity. Corner-cutting and project overruns met deaf spots and disorganisation.

Experienced firefighters had little time for reflection while tackling the Grenfell blaze. They used experience-based intuition to predict the spread of the fire with incomplete and incorrect information. They didn't know the tower lacked sprinklers and a water system, that fire doors had failed safety standards, and emergency and police communication were uncoordinated.[4] In addition, the tower's lone central staircase provided insufficient means of escape.

The problem is this: perfectly informed judgement is a fallacy, but sometimes intuition is all we have under pressure in a 24/7 cost-conscious tuned-out world. So we rush to hasty judgement. Seasoned professionals use intuition to predict customer and patient responses. Lawyers anticipate reactions to a gallery of grief just as chess players and gamers anticipate an opponent's next move.

Best-selling author of *Blink* Malcolm Gladwell believes intuition serves us well but "can cause us to act on deep-seated bias, leading us disastrously astray."[5] When we thin-slice information, we rely on our gut. This supports System-1 thinking which can contravene good judgement. Growing up, it wasn't uncommon to hear "decide in haste, repent at leisure."

When making high-stakes decisions, you might find it useful to ask people to articulate why their intuition is right.

In a noisy world, tough decisions are made under time, financial, political and ethical pressure. Surgeons decide whether to operate on the elderly, generals decide when to invade territories and jurors decide whether to recommend the death penalty. Intuition and big data support rapid-fire judgement, but it's just that – judgement – which is compromised by short-term bias.

HERE TODAY, WHAT TOMORROW?

Nothing is as important as it feels when you're thinking about it – the next meal, game, project, payday, shareholder meeting or, in van Zanten's case, take-off slot. It's all about now – a modern emergency.

That's not new. Instant gratification is embedded in the fabric of business and our psyche. Consumers dash through express check-outs. Today, over 930 million LinkedIn users in 200+ countries crave instant feedback. It explains one-night stands and gambling addiction as much as the climate crisis or savings crisis. The brain responds to immediate rewards in *present bias*.

If you offered a child one marshmallow now or two if they waited 15 minutes, what do you think most would do?

This was tested in 1972. Only a third waited. A study 14 years later found a correlation between patience and higher adult confidence and IQ.[6]

It's not just marshmallows, it's money.

Most people choose a 10% pay rise today over 15% next year, favouring the certainty of today's reward over the uncertainty of future gains. We anchor to the current state when evaluating decisions. It's not logical, it's psychological.

We don't think far beyond today. Our minds fluctuate between tasks tonight and tasks tomorrow.

Short-term thinking starts young. Take the Catholic confirmation rite. When I was 12, nuns encouraged girls to pledge alcohol abstinence until age 21. Few took the pledge, and even fewer kept it. Catholic, Protestant Shaker and Orthodox churches also pledge vows of celibacy. These can backfire, as sexual abuse scandals prove.

Short-termism has material workplace implications. Overloaded teams demand swift solutions rather than sifting through data-dense spreadsheets. Companies reward short-term decisions even though their clients pay generously for well-considered solutions. In racing to the top, ambitious employees chase the fastest or most economical route. It's most likely why Grenfell leaders approved inferior materials.

We prefer immediate rewards. As a leader, when I distributed share options to high performers, some were oddly ungrateful. Would they have preferred Amazon vouchers, I wondered? With a typical five-year vesting cycle, the reward was too distant. A first-world problem!

You've probably heard the advice to "live for today." Of course, there's a certain wisdom in that – until tomorrow comes! Sometimes, later becomes never! This explains why we defer sensible decisions like saving, studying and succession planning. It explains why certain organisations traffic pangolins and hunt rare wildlife; and why the world simultaneously swelters, floods and catches fire as the climate crisis is passed from one generation to the next.

Moreover, it explains why we take unnecessary health risks.

LIVING IN THE PRESENT

For years, road maintenance workers were exposed to the blast of digger machines. In 2003, EU regulators issued a directive specifying the minimum requirements to protect workers from hearing loss. Despite this, some refused to wear protective earplugs. I asked one individual why. "Because nobody did back then." Peer pressure met present bias. Today, that individual is almost physically deaf. Short-term thinking derails our judgement and diminishes our welfare.

Organisations are equally guilty.

Consider exposure to asbestos. Corporate goliaths like Honeywell, Raybestos and General Motors use asbestos products to manufacture brakes, cement and valves even though it's a health hazard. The World Health Organization estimates that 90,000 people die globally from asbestos-related illnesses every year.

In Belgium, metal factory workers were found 87% more likely to die from mesothelioma, an asbestos-related cancer, than the general population.[7] Unprotected military personnel, plumbers, firefighters and workers in shipyards, steel mills, railroads and oil refineries unwittingly wear contaminated clothes home. Governments now subsidise medication for bronchial issues and lung-related cancer.

At a societal level, leaders neglect the multi-generational effects of conflict. The United Nations estimates 110 million mines are still active.[8] Land mines still explode in Sudan, Cambodia and Zimbabwe. Children of Chernobyl still bear the horrendous defects and deformities.

Powerholders are incentivised to prioritise short-term greed rather than long-term need. In doing so, unthinking organisations breach human rights when dumping chemical waste, trafficking human organs, exploiting labour in sweat shops, hunting elephant ivory or mining blood diamonds. Many knowingly pay below-minimum wages, fuelling long-term economic inequality.

There's no shortage of short-term thinking.

Remember Liz Truss's multiple moments of misjudgement? Former chancellor Kwasi Kwarteng urged her to "slow down" but she tuned out advice.[9] "My biggest regret is we weren't tactically astute and we were too impatient… the people in charge, myself included, blew it." Impatient to impress and conscious of 2024 re-election, Truss focused too much on today rather than tomorrow.

It's easy to lose perspective, even temporarily.

I witnessed loss of perspective during the 2017 British and Irish Lions tour. After 50,000 fans roared the Lions to a historic final draw against the All Blacks in Auckland's Eden Park, the mood in the changing rooms afterwards was heavy. While there was no winner, this was still the second Lions tour in history to end with a test series draw. It was also the first time the All Blacks didn't win in New Zealand.

It required a mental reset. Captain Sam Warburton and coach Warren Gatland valiantly tried to lift the team's spirits and broaden perspective beyond that moment. The reframe worked. The baritone sound of 'Fields of Athenry' soon bellowed from Johnny Sexton, Owen Farrell, Mari Itoje and Jonathan Davies to whom I awarded the Player of the Series accolade in a moment of grateful light relief.

Great leaders show that not winning doesn't necessarily mean losing.

Some individuals get it right. In tennis, I never fail to be impressed by Rafa Nadal's long-term thinking. A right-handed player, he trained with his left hand from childhood so he would not be disadvantaged on court. Today, he holds 92 ATP singles titles with career earnings of $135m.

The ambitious Decision Ninja plans long-term rather than settling for what's too easy or too familiar in the current state.

WHEN STATUS QUO ISN'T ROCK 'N' ROLL

I understand this. During my career, I was offered a better role externally. I had been miserable, and all signals pointed to a switch. I consulted risk-averse friends and recalculated pros and cons lists for the answer! I knew things wouldn't improve yet I succumbed to the comfort of familiarity and convenience in one of my biggest career regrets.

My perimeter view was bounded by today not by tomorrow.

Familiarity inhibits willingness to change. Despite better alternatives, we choose the *status quo* even though it can mean worse choices long-term. Two reasons explain why.

First, we think what we have is better than what we could have. It's why consumers watch the same movies, buy the same brands and re-elect the same politicians. I think of my mother-in-law. Married in 1959, her new husband complimented her signature bacon and cabbage dinner. Every day for the first year, she served the same meal. Only when he suggested an alternative did the menu change.

Second, the finality of high-stakes decisions such as divorce, surgery, moving house, merger or retirement feels disproportionately big. It's scary, especially when it's irreversible. Doing nothing avoids this trauma. When you see change as the enemy of certainty rather than the friend of opportunity, the PERIMETERS Effect is close by.

This orientation towards the status quo is evident at all levels. For instance, the Supreme Court considers verdicts by lower courts, yet only 0.5% are overturned. The 2022 landmark Roe vs Wade abortion amendment was only the 234th court ruling overturned in its 232-year history.[10]

The past and the present are handy heuristics until tomorrow arrives.

Unless the incentive to change is compelling, people stick to the default choice. Consumers tend not to change hairdressers or cancel subscriptions. My direct debit for a monthly charity donation lasted 24 years until the bank closed.

Naturally, embracing the status quo isn't universal or we would still be watching black-and-white TV and living like Fred Flintstone rather than investing in robotics, AI, 7G and the metaverse. Some get it right. In 1998, the International Space Station cost an estimated $150bn, built over a decade in partnership with 15 countries. That's future-focused!

Counterfactual thinking: playing with fire

Our risk aversion and unwillingness to disappoint others or ourselves maintains the status quo. Might we lose out on better choices? You don't know what you're missing until it arrives. I thought I didn't care what car I drove until I tried an automatic. I thought I'd be lost without a corporate role until I set up my own business. It's our risk preferences stopping us. What if the unknown is worse?

If immersed in status quo comfort, thinking outside the box isn't on your radar. Yet it can save lives.

A 1950s movie, *Red Skies of Montana*, tells the true story of 15 smokejumpers in the Mann Gulch mountains wrestling with a raging wildfire. Suddenly high winds cut off their escape route. Within ten minutes, the fire had spread 3,000 acres, threatening to engulf the smokejumpers. When the fire was just 100 yards from his feet, foreman Wagner Dodge made a decision that contravened perceived logic. He started another fire in front of him. Why?

Dodge hoped the wildfire would bypass this burned area.[11] It was an intuitive, experience-based gamble in a moment of panic. He crawled on his belly and prayed. Two men followed. Only these three smokejumpers survived. A counterfactual strategy was considered too radical.

Not wanting to change is a decision liability. Knowing why we don't change is an asset.

Ask yourself if the status quo is a useful barometer. What might you, your company, community or country lose? What opportunities might you be missing?

TICK TOCK: LOOK BACK TO MOVE FORWARD

Everything looks different in hindsight. Monday morning quarterbacks apparently saw 9/11, Covid, Brexit and crypto coming. Madoff explained his Ponzi scheme: "In hindsight, when I look back, it wasn't as if I couldn't have said no."[12] Former Yahoo CEO Marissa Mayer reflected on how paying $4bn for Netflix or $1.3bn for Hulu rather than $1.3bn for Tumblr would've been a much smarter 'transformative acquisition' choice.[13]

Few would disagree!

The past defines us. Elvis was haunted by the spectre of childhood poverty. It trapped him into limp movies and gratuitous overspending, afraid to break from a controlling agent.

"I've always done it like this." Is that good or bad? Unlike the old farmer's refrain, it's not hard to say. When executives simply rinse and repeat habits, strategies or routines that worked before rather than reengineer better solutions or processes, existing methods become institutionalised.

Processes look backwards but solutions look forwards.

Simply recalling yesterday's decisions influences today's choices.[14] Do you still think about your biggest mistake? How do the 15 publishers who rejected *Harry Potter* feel? Would a brave hedge fund manager who lost millions in GameStop's short squeeze reinvest? Errors etch in memory, yet recessions replicate and scandals proliferate.

History repeats itself, yet we believe this time it's different. This time, it usually isn't. Sir John Templeton was right when he said that "The four most dangerous words in investing are: it's different this time." A common refrain for relationships and diets!

The tuned-in Decision Ninja masters the best of what others have figured out. Some learn from past mistakes. Consider Dick Rowe, a talent-spotter for British music label Decca Records. In the 1960s, Rowe decided not to sign four Liverpudlians. He believed "guitar groups are on the way out," and they "have no future in show business."[15] Instead, he signed a local band, Brian Poole and the Tremeloes, rather than the soon-to-be-superstar Beatles. Colombia, HMV and Philips also followed suit. Like the Apple Watch and *Harry Potter*, once upon a time, they were too different.

Years later, when Decca negotiated the Rolling Stones deal, they wouldn't repeat history. Decca secured the Stones – at three times the typical royalty rates.

Past decisions are a liability if you're unaware of their present potency.

It's easy to recall our best decisions. They're as salient as our wittiest jokes. Next time we make a similar decision, we choose more quickly and confidently. It's a mental asset I've seen deployed in business and sport.

For example, at the point world number one tennis player Novak Djokovic played against unseeded Nick Kyrgios in the 2022 Wimbledon final, Djokovic had never won a set against his opponent. Pumped with this memory, Kyrgios won the first set. He wouldn't win any more. Djokovic tuned in to his experience memory of six grass-court wins to inspire a seventh Wimbledon and 21st Grand Slam title. Like Rowe or Kyrgios, we remember our mistakes more than our successes.

For some, judgement gets harder over time.

Experience as liability?

Time pays havoc with high-stakes decision-making. Salthouse's studies estimate the rate of dementia change doubles every five years.[16] The elderly navigate Netflix, yet characters and plots are forgotten within minutes. Harvard Kennedy School professor David Laibson once made a comment that struck a chord: "At a certain age, those with a lifetime of achievement risk a decade of embarrassment."

The problem is this: in many companies, powerholders are mature, boasting more experience than accurate recall. Their reliance on prior strategies, experiences or data can be seriously flawed yet unacknowledged or even unnoticed.

As previously discussed, these traps are closely inter-related. Memory-based error is an unspoken organisational liability rarely discussed or admitted. People fear accusations of ageism, but it's a reality – and a risk. When combined with power, it's toxic.

Time alters how we assess information. Take savings decisions. Research shows senior savers tend to avoid multi-choice options, seek fewer data sources and internalise fewer negative facts than younger savers.[17]

It's complicated because reasoning is individual-specific and there are many examples of individuals who continue to successfully hold office beyond their eighties. Nike's co-founder 85-year-old Phil Knight still chairs his sports empire. Australian media mogul Rupert Murdoch retired at 92. As I write, the Oracle of Omaha, Warren Buffett, is the oldest Fortune 500

CEO at 93. Queen Elizabeth II was the oldest monarch aged 96. Even Picasso painted until he was 91.

Whatever our age, we struggle to imagine future feelings, outcomes or situations.

TOMORROW? I CAN'T IMAGINE

When I worked in the City, I used to offer to dial into conference calls that were scheduled to take place during my holiday. Sad, I know! My enthusiasm rapidly evaporated when lying on a sandy beach.

We make decisions about tomorrow based on how we feel today.

In fact, we're terrible at predicting our emotions, in what scientists call *affective forecasting error*. It's hard to imagine outrage when relaxed or the joy of financial security when struggling to pay bills. It's hard to imagine being happy with a partner after 40 years but some are.

We struggle to envisage alternative scenarios or lifestyles to what we have today.

You might sympathise with the homeless but have no clue how they feel unless you sleep on the streets. As he grew up, it was probably hard for Carlos Alcaraz to imagine the euphoria of winning Wimbledon at age 20 until he actually won.

When companies are in the growth phase, executives struggle to imagine a future state. As head of international marketing for BlackRock which had just acquired Merrill Lynch Investment Managers, I remember presenting the strategic marketing plan at a townhall in 2006. As part of the long-term vision, I overlaid the logo on a Fortune 500 screenshot, suggesting that one day, BlackRock would be listed. I can still hear the sniggers! In 2009, BlackRock became the #1 asset manager globally, and by 2021, it ranked #192 in the Fortune 500.

It's hard to imagine a future that's far removed from today.

It's not just executives. A friend illustrated this in health-related circumstances. Days after her husband's admission to hospital for routine testing, Cindy was forced to make the agonising decision to turn off his life-support machine. By sheer coincidence, weeks before, Cindy's friend had made the same decision in similar circumstances. At the time, Cindy was surprised that such a gut-wrenching decision was possible at speed.

In a cold state, it's easy to falsely predict mindsets. We never know until the moment comes.

Do we overestimate how good or bad we'll feel about promotions, holidays or exams? As Stoic philosopher Seneca said, "We suffer more in imagination than in reality."[18]

It's hard to predict reactions to what we've never experienced. Yet we judge – and misjudge.

What are you wearing?

Psychologists Julie Woodzicka and Marianne LaFrance studied why people react differently in the moment from how they predict. In their experiment, over 200 women engaged in a hypothetical interview laden with sexually inappropriate questions, including "Do people find you desirable?", "Do you have a boyfriend?" and "Do you think it's important for women to wear bras to work?"

What do you think women said they would do?

About 90% predicted they would respond assertively or aggressively. Some predicted they would confront the inappropriateness, leave or even slap the interviewer; and 68% said they'd refuse to answer at least one question.

A follow-up experiment explored whether women would behave as predicted. Researchers recruited interviewees and videotaped their responses using the same questions.

What do you think happened?

It turns out 100% of the women answered every question.[19] Nobody stormed out, nobody reported wrongdoing and nobody slapped the interviewer.

We don't just have poor ability to predict emotions but poor ability to predict timescales.

Many organisations miscalculate the time required to complete projects, leading to extensive overruns, delays and wasted investment. It's the *planning fallacy*. For example, constructing the Sydney Opera House was estimated to cost $7m. It cost $102m and took 16 years. Conversely, planners took 11 years to plan the Golden Gate Bridge and just two years to build it.

Are planners inexperienced, over-optimistic or unprepared? Possibly none of these things. We use today's assumptions to predict tomorrow's possibilities.

While our temporal orientation derails judgement, it's also inconsistent over time.

THE INCONSISTENCY OF JUDGEMENT

In the 2004 presidential election, George W. Bush took out an advert themed "whichever way the wind blows." It lambasted Senator John Kerry for reversing his opinions about the Iraq War and terrorism.

In some circles, changing your mind is a social taboo. Of course, it's less material if it relates to a movie choice rather than a medical diagnosis, judicial sentence or house purchase.

Despite industry standards, judgement variance among and between experts is pervasive, whether it's in accounting, medicine, art, horse-racing or immigration. Kahneman, Sunstein and Sibony call it judgement "noise."[20] They argue variability is a neglected business risk because few managers compare outcomes over time or across groups. When so-called expert conclusions are inconsistent, it's a warning that something isn't right and more consideration is required.

As an example, Kahneman asked 50 underwriters to value a common risk. How much would you expect their estimates to differ? Executives guessed about 10%. A gross underestimation. Estimates varied by a staggering 50%.

Equally, when software developers estimated completion time for 60 tasks over three months, the estimated time varied by an average of 71%.[21]

If you ask people to describe 'culture' or define abstract terms like 'reasonable doubt,' 'fair' or 'cruel,' you'll find similar variance.

Variability is a function of subjectivity but also egotism, self-belief and confirmation bias where people seek supporting information for existing opinions.

Judgements also vary when the situation is complicated. Take sentencing. A dispassionate judge is obliged to compartmentalise emotion and discount aggravating factors. In 1974, Judge Marvin Frankel maintained sentencing is inconsistent across countries and crime. He found a heroin dealer might face from one to ten years in prison or a bank robber from five to 18 years, solely based on the judge.

Like the underwriters, professionals who analyse the same data frequently disagree. Do you disagree with colleagues? During Covid-19, countries differed radically about the right lockdown strategy and timing. Psychiatrists disagree about diagnoses. When evaluating the 1970s Hillside Strangler killer, experts fundamentally disagreed whether Ken Bianchi had multiple personality disorder or not.

When medical pathologists assessed 193 biopsy slides for Hodgkin's disease, their diagnoses were inconsistent.[22] Pathologists should have recognised its multidimensional characteristics, but each weighted different probabilities based on their respective education and school of thought.

Judgement varies in our homes, the pub and workplace. Inevitable disagreement happens around dinner tables, judges' benches, operating tables and board tables.

The savvy Decision Ninja expects this variability before rushing to judgement. They recognise it before others as a source of advantage and performance impact.

EVERY SECOND COUNTS

Better judgement can be attained with some effort, but it cannot be sustained without any effort. Taking time out for reflection requires such effort. Several studies illustrate how just a few seconds of incremental reflection improves most decision outcomes.

First, educator Mary Budd Rowe proved a three-second pause in answering questions generated between three and seven times more reflection. What's more, it led to higher willingness to think critically.[23]

Second, University of Rotterdam's Silvia Mamede tested whether doctors could improve diagnostic accuracy under pressure. She simply asked them to revisit their initial intuition. This improved diagnostic accuracy by 10%.

In a follow-up study, she asked doctors to write down their initial impressions and then check for supporting evidence. This two-step technique improved accuracy by a phenomenal 40%. Giving people time to revisit their intuition can boost judgement.[24]

In a third study, researchers asked two groups to guess how many of the world's airports were in the US. One group had to guess quickly, the other could revise estimates several weeks later. Those with time to reconsider evidenced higher-quality guesses.[25] Unsurprisingly, rushing to judgement produced worse decisions.

Our time is like gold dust. We're even willing to earn less money to get more – enter the four-day week. So why do we waste, abuse and lose time because we don't invest enough time to save time? Paying marginally more attention to interpretating what's said and not said neutralises the risk of decision error and inattentional deafness.

TUNING IN: THE VOICE OF PERSPECTIVE

A final quirk of time-based judgement is how we reward time spent. In the *labour illusion*, we reward effort over outcome. If a dinner-party host cooks a meal rather than orders take-away, you mentally reward the host, even if you dislike their chicken korma. It's the same for the hard-working underachiever who studies every day but always flunks the exam – we reward effort over results.

Influencers exploit this well. Host of the *Nudge* podcast, Phill Agnew explains why YouTube videos have earned influencer Mr Beast $54m and been viewed 26 billion times.[26] What does Mr Beast do? Well, not a lot. What he does is display effort. When he recited the longest word in the English language for over two hours, 30 million people viewed it. When he repeated the name "Logan Paul" 100,000 times over 40 hours, it attracted 26 million views. How exhausting!

If I told you this book took me 4,380 hours because I wrote for six hours a day every day for two years, it doesn't mean you'll enjoy it more, but science says you'll appreciate the effort more. It's why consultants distribute 100-page decks and plumbers leisurely fix your sink before producing the bill. We scorn low effort.

Most of us unconsciously decide with a past, present or future lens. No approach is risk-free. Too much living in the future leads to daydreaming and nothing gets done. Living in the past risks getting stuck in a rut, not letting go and sacrificing perspective. Living in the present stops us learning from history.

It's important to know the default mode of how your

stakeholders interpret the world. It's a source of power, as is rebalancing what you hear over what you see.

When you tune in to others, others tend to tune in to you. They listen more acutely to advice or instruction, saving everyone time, money and effort.

Temporal derailers will always challenge you to some extent but even a helicopter awareness can alleviate decision damage. It's a huge advantage for the Decision Ninja, especially when emotions ride high – perhaps the greatest set of PERIMETERS traps of all, explored next.

THE DECISION NINJA
WHAT TO REMEMBER

- Misjudgement amplifies under time pressure, accelerated by the voice of impatience, instant gratification and nostalgia.
- What we decide is influenced by whether we hear the voice of the past, present or future. Each temporal voice can create decision damage.
- When overweighting rewards closer to the present, people tend to procrastinate, delay and dither about future actions. This downgrades our decisions.
- Despite better alternatives, most people prefer the stability of the status quo over the novelty of change. It's a leader's responsibility to anticipate these mental handcuffs and psychological biases.
- Companies can leverage preferences and retain talent by creating strong cultures that provide valued stability.
- Rear-view mirrors over-romanticise past decisions, justified by hindsight. "I knew it all along" is a stale strategy. You can't look forward if you keep looking back.
- People are abysmal at forecasting preferences. We make decisions about tomorrow based on how we feel today. It's psychological not logical.
- Prior success or failure impacts objectivity. Apply a future lens. Ask "Will this matter in a day, week or year?" What's right today can be wrong tomorrow.
- We underweight the effect of expectations on interpretation and judgement. We hear what we expect to hear rather than what's necessary or true.
- Time invested is valued. Don't dismiss your effort, point to it.
- Too little reflection is a judgement liability, while every extra second of reflection is a judgement asset.

CHAPTER 11

EMOTION-BASED TRAPS: ROLLERCOASTER REASONING

"To hear with one's eyes and see with one's ears is the key to understanding."

Jiddu Krishnamurti

E VERY YEAR, NEARLY 500,000 children go missing in the US alone, with many more unreported globally. Even in a technology-driven world, many abduction, trafficking and murder cases remain unsolved, tormenting not just families but the professionals who spend years trying to locate them. One such seasoned FBI investigator with a distinguished 30-year career is Jeffrey Rinek.

On 24 July 1999, Rinek collected a witness in connection with the murder of naturalist Joie Armstrong. She was found brutally decapitated in a creek 100 yards from her rustic cabin in Yosemite National Park. The night before, she had written in her diary, "the monsters are gone." After all, the FBI had arrested two local criminals for the savage murder of three park tourists: Carole Sund, her teenage daughter Juli and friend Silvina Pelosso. The expert voice was trusted.

Coincidentally, the witness turned out to be Yosemite Cedar Lodge handyman Cary Stayner, older brother of abducted seven-year-old Stephen Stayner.

After Rinek took an alternative freeway exit due to road construction, the usual 45-minute journey lasted 90 minutes during which the pair developed an unlikely rapport. Rinek empathised with Stephen's case, criticising the abductor's unjust sentencing and enquiring about family support. Rinek admitted how unsolved children's cases deeply unsettled him, but gaining shreds of closure helped him move forward.[1]

At the station, Rinek skillfully conducted the interview, during which Stayner blurted out that he could give him closure. Rinek enquired about what. "On this… and more," Stayner muttered. It was a fragile moment.

In one of the most gripping books I've ever read, *In the Name of the Children*, Rinek recalls:

The push-pull process of obtaining a confession is full of minefields. It's a dance. Ask the wrong question, make an erroneous assumption, push too hard or too fast and a suspect may shut down forever.[2]

Empathetic Rinek tuned in and held his emotions in check, creating enough space to gain the trust that yielded an explosive murder confession. Over six hours, in graphic detail, a sobbing Stayner confessed not just to Armstrong's murder but also to the Sund-Pelosso murders.

Rinek told me he attributes this to "empathetic listening" as do his colleagues who heard the tape transcripts. The key was not to be judgemental when faced with sadistic killers recounting their horrors.

I've learned that nothing in life is as black and white as

we would like to believe, not even murder. The victims and killers I dealt with were by turns heroically brave and horrifically broken, vessels of innocence and volcanoes of rage. And to a greater or lesser degree, I empathised with them all.

Skilled interpretation and interest in human behaviour gives you the edge to hear what you don't expect, whether at an interrogation table, business table or breakfast table. As importantly, you have to deal with what you hear, however unsettling.

It is their voices that shake me to my core – the sheer incongruity between the sweet tones of youth and the words they spoke to me that no child should ever have to utter.

That's when real judgement is needed. It puts our mundane gripes into perspective.

This chapter doesn't tell you how to manage emotion. Lots of books do that. In fact, an estimated 23,000 books have 'happiness' in the title.[3] Every misjudgement in this book can be traced to one or more emotions. Between seven and 27 emotions exist on a spectrum of intensity and duration. I focus on six familiar emotion-led biases that trigger decision-makers. Anger, envy, regret and denial make us tune out just as hope and empathy lead us to tune in.

Sometimes, adrenalin-filled emotions like anger or envy destroy objectivity (hot/cold states). When we don't like what we hear, we panic or deny information (ostrich effect) to avoid doleful regret (regret aversion). Like Rinek, you hope what you hear isn't true (wishful hearing). Supporting the underdog may be kind (empathy) but it's prejudicial. Fortunately, emotional intelligence and self-regulation enables distancing for greater hearing and reasoned decisions.

FLEETING HOT AND COLD STATES

At the 2022 Oscar ceremony, Will Smith punched Chris Rock for an ill-timed joke. It was to have been the biggest night of Smith's career. He ruined it for himself, his family and the entire cast of *Richard Williams*. People respond emotionally in System-1 when they like or dislike what they hear. The illogical voice plays the drums in our head. In the moment, good judgement gets overridden.

The problem is our most important decisions are made through an affective lens.

Emotions constitute potent, pervasive, predictable, sometimes harmful and sometimes beneficial drivers of decision making.[4]

In a *hot state*, impulse accounts for a myriad of responses. A colleague may infuriate us, a lover disappoint us or a child worry us. Among other things, it partly explains road rage, domestic abuse, hate crimes and drunken texts. It explains why people resign on impulse. Footballer Kevin Keegan quit as England Manager in 2000, minutes after the team lost 1–0 to Germany and fans booed him off the Wembley pitch.[5]

The transition between hot and cold states happens fast. Tempers flare then flee, like a 200mph tornado. Singer Britney Spears married in Vegas then annulled the wedding 24 hours later.

It's hard to imagine a *cold state* when in a hot state. Economist George Loewenstein tried. In an experiment, he tested the effect of sexual arousal on male forcefulness, using date-rape scenarios.[6] One group of participants were aroused after viewing pictures of naked women. In this state, men admitted they would encourage a woman to drink more to increase her willingness for sex. Brave! They admitted willingness to slip drugs into a drink and being unlikely to take no for an answer.

The next day, the men returned to the lab. How did they feel?

In a cold state, they predicted being far more considerate of female consent.

Emotion is fleeting, triggering deaf ear syndrome when we tune out the voice of righteousness and even our values.

Hot and cold state transitions explain withdrawal of domestic abuse reports. Pre-Covid-19, UN Women estimated that 137 women were killed daily, 58% by an intimate partner or family member. Only 40% of abused women seek help like Nicole Brown Simpson. Victims who report in a hot state tend to drop claims in a cooler state. As a result, several US states now impose a 'no drop' policy mandating offender arrest. Although 140 countries outlaw domestic violence, regulations are only a partial deterrent.[7]

When consumed by any of the 27 different emotions, how can powerholders and policymakers tune in to voices that matter? In a hot state, outrage, envy, guilt or greed may spark bad judgement. For instance, anger is scientifically linked to misinformation and poor decisions. Conversely, awe, gratitude and pride might motivate winning decisions in business or sport.

Emotions are like a sword of Damocles. We can't control emotional thoughts, but we can control responses. Knowing which emotions help you on your way and which are in your way matter.

Hot states pass but feelings like revenge, hate, pride or disappointment fester – in some cases, for seven decades.

RAGE: THE RUNNING RIVALS

Cars don't experience road rage, drivers do. Nike's Vapofly running shoes don't win races, athletes do. And families don't feud, people do.

Before World War II, two brothers ran a very successful German athletic shoe business together. The 1936 Olympians won 12 medals wearing their trainers. A decade later, the business split. Adi and Rudi Dassler said they would never speak again. No one knew why.

Rumours suggest Rudi had an affair with his brother's wife. Others suggest a patent dispute or polarised Nazi sympathy. The *Daily Mail* suggests another reason.[8]

> During an Allied air raid on their hometown of Herzogenaurach in 1943, Rudolf and his family climbed into a bomb shelter that Adi and his wife were already in. "The dirty b******* are back again," Adi said, apparently referring to the Allied war planes. Rudolf was convinced his brother referred to him and his family. They divided the firm five years later.

What did Rudi hear? Did he mishear? What did he interpret? Adi relocated north of the river naming his business adidas. Rudi relocated south, calling his PUMA.[9] And so, two iconic brands were built. But the feud split the town – literally. Bars, hairdressers and grocery shops were polarised. While shareholders were rewarded, a family generation was destroyed. The brothers never spoke again.

Which emotions dominate any situation? Whereas outrage sparked sibling conflict, did pride or disappointment sustain it? When you next see adidas trainers, remember the price of amplifying the wrong voices and failing to adjust your mindset.

⫿⫿⫿⫿⫿

Deep-seated emotions trigger misjudgement every day, a dangerous career precipice, especially for aspiring and current powerholders.

Consider the hate crime against George Floyd. A history of white supremacy and unequal power enabled police officers to tune in to prejudiced voices and miscalculate low risk of punishment. Floyd's outgroup identity fused with black criminal stereotypes. With a sparse ethical compass, officers made an arbitrary arrest using excessive force based on hate-fuelled superiority. As Floyd's warning of "I can't breathe" was ignored, a black man's story sparked a global human rights movement.

This echoes the earlier findings that black drivers in Florida are more likely to be stopped than white drivers; and how white Jeffrey Dahmer's word was believed over black neighbour Glenda Cleveland.

Analysis of 57 studies show emotional attitudes predict racial discrimination.[10] At every level, emotion-based misjudgement pervaded this case as then-police officer Derek Chauvin tuned out conscience. Did he regret his actions? Did the Dassler brothers regret their feud?

Regret is crippling, but regret aversion is a powerful motivator that can help or harm decisions.

REGRET: IF I COULD TURN BACK TIME

What's your biggest mistake? You don't want to remember, right? It hurts. There's nothing worse than wishing you hadn't barked at someone, screwed up negotiations or fallen for a scam. Regret arises from thinking your position would have been better if you had done something differently. Very few people experience no regret like toddlers, some of the psychopaths you've met in this book and the cognitively impaired.

Too often, leaders regret not interpreting information differently. Consumers regret poor product selection. Investors regret not selling shares before a crash. Employees regret not moving jobs. Boards regret shoddy governance. Jes Staley and Ghislaine Maxwell regretted meeting Jeffrey Epstein. Juror Gary McClung regretted putting Brandon Bernard on death row. It's a long list.

At some stage, most of us regret not listening to advice or instruction. This debilitating state prompts regret aversion and can be useful to help us slow down decision-making and tune in to the right voices.

Those with no regrets are prone to boast about it. "*Je new regrette rien,*" as Edith Piaf famously sang. Such claims are understandable, especially if you've ever felt the agony of remorse. Actor Marlon Brando believed "to regret is useless in life. It belongs to the past."

Active choice hurts more than decisions mandated, imposed or defaulted. Why? Because you blame yourself for mistakes.[11] We minimise regret and self-blame in two ways: delegation and inoculation. Firstly, patients delegate decisions to doctors just as businesspeople delegate capital-intensive or market-sensitive decisions to consultants. Secondly, consumers inoculate through brand loyalty. Marketing professor Itamar Simonson primed consumers to think about regret before buying a smartphone.[12] The majority chose the safer but costlier Sony brand over a white-labelled product.

᭼᭼᭼᭼᭼

The voice of regret and your strength of *regret aversion* affects subsequent decisions. In 1994, Blackstone co-founder Stephen Schwarzman sold his company's stake in BlackRock's mortgage securities business to PNC Bank for $240m, a decision he openly regrets as a "heroic mistake." With $23bn in assets under management, this business rebranded to become the cornerstone for BlackRock, which now boasts $10trn in assets under management.[13] Schwarzman laments, "I should have been more wary of my emotions and more scrupulous with the facts."

He learned. "We all stumble on and have some success.

But it's a humbling experience to see what you don't do right." He believed in understanding behaviour. "Psychology would be one of my strengths as an investor."[14] It would be his superpower. Today, Blackstone is the world's largest alternative asset manager.

People regret everyday simple things like working too hard, eating too much or driving too fast. We also regret inaction rather than action. We might regret not partying enough, not visiting relatives enough, not moving jobs quicker, not ending relationships, not saving sooner or not reporting wrongdoing.

Even well-meaning parents experience high-grade regret. The father of JonBenet Ramsey regrets letting his six-year-old daughter enter beauty pageants. Her murder in Colorado is still unsolved.

Cary Stayner's mother regretted being emotionally withdrawn and begged the judge for her son's life, "Cary was the ideal son."[15] Cary himself wrote a letter of regret to brutalised Yosemite victim, 15-year-old Juli Sund, to try to gain closure. This letter was another data point to understand his perverse fantasies.

Madoff's son Mark desperately wanted his mother to cut her matrimonial ties. She didn't. Mark hanged himself two years to the day his father was arrested. Ruth Madoff bemoaned, "I just wish to my dying day that I had done what he wanted." These deep-seated regrets determine our wellbeing and future decisions.

◁|◁|◁|◁|◁|▷|▷|▷|▷

Daniel Pink collated 16,000 regrets in 105 countries and argues regret helps us live a better life. That's true if it stimulates greater retrospection and enables better decision-making. No one reflects more than the dying. Who wants to wish they lived a better life?

An Australian nurse recorded the regrets of dying patients. She heard little reference to Ferragamo handbags, Ferrari cars or Facebook followers. What was the most cited regret?

I wish I'd had the courage to live a life true to myself, not the life others expected.[16]

The second biggest regret was work/life imbalance. Guilty! Like many of us, astronaut Neil Armstrong regretted not prioritising family time. "My work required an enormous amount of my time, and a lot of travel."[17] In the moment, work commitment choices are justified with plausible explanations.

Other patient regrets included lacking "the courage to express my feelings" or not letting themselves "be happier." The common denominator is courage to be yourself rather than impress others.

A simple technique to calibrate pre-decision options is to apply the regret test, useful for ethical dilemmas. You can just ask "Might I regret this?" for an instant cooling effect.

How well you manage the PERIMETERS Effect determines whether your life is filled with regret or reward. While regret hurts, its cousins, envy and revenge, destroy lives.

ENVY AND REVENGE: DESCENT INTO DARKNESS

If you've ever experienced the ugliness of envy, you know it's toxic. I suspect it contributed to the most extreme conformity studies in psychology. Philip Zimbardo and Stanley Milgram sat together in the Bronx James Monroe High School. Zimbardo says, "He won all the medals at graduation, so obviously nobody liked him because we were all envious of him. But he was super smart and super serious."[18]

Professional envy operates on a spectrum of intensity. Envy can stimulate anger and revenge when resources and promotion prospects are scarce. It's more common than you think. In one study, 44% of employees admit seeking revenge on a co-worker.[19]

I know of one envious CEO who denied his popular direct report the rare opportunity to visit the Oval Office.

I've seen, heard and felt it myself. After a good performance run, a savvy chief investment officer once told me, "Be careful of success, now the real test begins." Success breeds envy in others. Planting false stories, undermining others, credit-taking and drip-feeding poison is the start. You're not always knifed in the back either. Sometimes enemies twist it in the front so slowly that the unwary Decision Ninja doesn't notice.

Like any dark sentiment, revenge festers as rejected Hunter Moore victims discovered with his revenge porn website. It's a judgement killer, literally and figuratively.

The silent killer

A related and disturbing phenomenon is family revenge. Following a sensationalist trial and a hung jury, in 1989, attractive brothers Erik and Lyle Menéndez were sentenced to life in prison for the premeditated, brutal murder of their parents in the front room of their $14m Beverley Hills mansion. The defence argued the brothers broke after years of sustained sexual and emotional abuse, while the prosecution argued it was greed.

Scorned Betty Broderick lived 100 miles from the Menéndez family. Ten weeks after the slaughter, this betrayed housewife was also driven to extreme revenge. Festering jealousy combined with misjudgement. After years of mental abuse and unrequited devotion, she snapped, shooting her ex-husband and his new wife at point blank range as they slept.

Emotions have opportunity costs. Every angry moment might mean fewer productive, reflective, intimate, connection, creative moments – or less freedom.

Revenge effects are severe. One defence mechanism is to tune out bad news completely.

DENIAL: OSTRICHES AND INCONVENIENT TRUTH

"All men by nature desire to know," said Aristotle, but do we? Like regret deniers, we avoid bad news that makes us mad, bad or sad. Does a manager really want to hear about grievances, micro-aggressions or complaints? When FBI leaders heard about Cary Stayner's surprise confession, they turned a deaf ear for three years and ignored the extensive proof, reluctant to expose their misguided rush to judgement. Excluded and sidelined, Rinek's contribution to justice was never recognised publicly or privately.

Similarly, Sam Bankman-Fried's parents, both Stanford lawyer professors, are convinced of his innocence. His mother claims, "Sam would never speak an untruth, it's just not in him."[20]

When we tune out warnings that are in our or others' best interests, it's known as the *ostrich effect* because we proverbially bury our heads in the sand.

Science says exposure to just three minutes of negative news leads to a 27% higher probability of a bad day.[21] No wonder avoidance occurs. The result? Unpaid household bills, deferred surgeries, shelved regulations – and avoidable accidents.

The market is littered with investors who tune out inconvenient or uncomfortable signals. George Loewenstein and colleagues tested account monitoring. He found investors mainly checked portfolios in rising markets rather than falling markets.[22] Why? Ignoring distressful news is easier.

Denial is a subtle but savage decision derailer.

Some privileged powerholders deny their contribution to error. Former chairman of the US Federal Reserve Alan Greenspan dismissed repeated subprime warnings and regulation appeals.[23] The result was one of the greatest financial crises in history and a decade of economic recession.

Greenspan had previously told a 1987 Senate Committee, "If

I seem unduly clear to you, you must have misunderstood what I said."[24] Even royalty demand answers from professional ostriches.

Two months into the 2008 crisis, the late Queen Elizabeth II opened a building at my alma mater, the London School of Economics. Her fortune had dropped £25m. When economists briefed her, she broke with protocol to ask, "If these things were so large, how come everyone missed them?"[25]

Four years later, she told Bank of England staff, "People got a bit lax... perhaps it is difficult to foresee."[26] She was right. Certainly, Elvis didn't foresee losing millions in revenue nor Jack Ma the repercussions of his Bund Summit speech! Why? It's easier to deny reality.

Tom Cruise played a lawyer in *A Few Good Men*, interrogating Jack Nicholson in the courtroom. "I want the truth!" he demanded, to which Nicholson coolly replied, "You can't handle the truth!"

Often, we can't handle the distress so choose deafness, our greatest liability.

Nevertheless, leaders have a moral responsibility to hear bad news. General Electric was notorious for delivering good news at staff townhalls in what were mockingly called "success theatres." The overly optimistic chief cheerleader remains a dangerous corporate species.

In *Homo Sapiens*, Yuval Noah Harari asserts humans are too emotional when communicating bad news anyway, suggesting robots will be better. He might be right.

·ıl|ı·|ıı|ı·|ı·

Roger this! You may have never heard of aerodynamic and mechanical engineer Roger Boisjoly. On 28 January 1986, millions of people witnessed the effect of his voice not being heard.

Boisjoly raised concerns about the Space Shuttle Challenger. For months, he predicted the rocket booster O-rings would fail in cold weather. The day before launch, a stressed Boisjoly recommended not to launch, but his red flags were ignored. He wasn't alone. Boisjoly testified how another dissenting Morton Thiokol engineer was told:

"Take off your engineering hat and put on your management hat."

Under pressure to satisfy NASA, their major client, management voted to launch. And NASA heard what they wanted to hear. With the world watching, the Space Shuttle STS-51L lost seven lives 73 seconds after take-off.

Boisjoly subsequently suffered a breakdown. Four decades later, he recalls the event on a televised documentary, his eyes watering, "I sat there, I was an emotional wreck."

Seventeen years later, history repeated itself. The Columbia space shuttle burst on re-entry into the earth's atmosphere after 16 days in orbit. Engineers didn't anticipate, appreciate or communicate the implications of foam insulation damage to the shuttle's wing. Again, seven crew died.

Over my career, I've witnessed too many organisations reject uncomfortable information. I've done it myself. We all have. What motivates this delusion? Three reasons explain it.

First, it's painful to think you're wrong, so it's easier to embrace excuses like market forces and timing. Second, bad news conflicts with lived experience, intuition or imagination. It's hard to adjust our mindset for events we've never experienced, like bankruptcy, redundancy, death or pandemics. And finally, we desperately hope bad news isn't true.

This leads to another judgement killer: the emotion-based deaf spot, *wishful hearing*.

HOPE: SOMEWHERE OVER THE RAINBOW

Have you ever applied for roles that you weren't quite qualified for, yet were surprised when the rejection came? Sometimes, we want something to be true so badly it deafens us to logic. That's wishful hearing. Fred Goodwin hoped the ABN Amro deal would boost earnings. Zobayan hoped fog would lift before his helicopter flight just as Jonestowners hoped for a better life.

What do you badly want to be true right now? Be careful, because wishful thinking supersedes reason, swayed by the promise and expectation of reward.

We hope for the best because we can't imagine the worst.

We need hope. It's motivational fuel – the skill is to calibrate it. Coaches use the lure of medals to inspire boxers, hurdlers, marathon runners and gymnasts to endure punishing schedules. In the four-year Olympics cycle, athletes sacrifice much yet few qualify. They neglect true probability in the hope of winning medals and representing their country.

In organisations, wishful thinking is a governance liability. If boards or committees hear excess optimism, it should sound an alarm. Whereas optimists engage and innovate, and are generally great fun to be around, they're also more likely to underweight risk. The bon viveur is rarely appointed to sense-check investments.

Organisations peddle hope to employees, tantalised with dreams of pay, promotion and prosperity. It's their carrot to ensure conformity. Then organisations peddle hope to consumers who fall for it every time. Estée Lauder sells beauty, the Maldives sells paradise, Harley Davidson sells cool and Tinder sells romance.

Hope also infects the entrepreneur who naively tunes out the average 95% failure rate. You can't underestimate the power of FOMO. Venture capitalists and private equity firms aren't immune. They dream of the next unicorn, sometimes prematurely elevating superstars, seduced by overconfident personalities. Naturally, some unicorns deliver. Bloomberg estimates 1,000 start-ups like ByteDance, SpaceX and Stripe are valued at over \$1bn. [27]

Nevertheless, hope is a momentum trap.

As British writer G.K. Chesterton wrote: "Hope is the power of being cheerful in circumstances that we know to be desperate." The skill is to use it responsibly.

You may recall the pandemic mantra, "Wearing masks saves lives." Neuroscientist Tali Sharot finds that hope-based messages typically have longer-lasting effects on behaviour than fear-based messages.[28] Compare "Wear your seatbelt and live longer" to "Don't wear your seatbelt and risk dying." Framing matters.

The power of hope can delude the dreamer or sustain the struggler.

The next emotion for the Decision Ninja to consider is one exploited by spin doctors and media: empathy. While empathetic connection worked in Jeff Rinek's favour, like ego-based self-belief, it can be a double-edged sword.

EMPATHY: CHEERING FOR THE UNDERDOG

Most people have inbuilt empathy for victims, the abused and the underdog. We celebrate when the underdog triumphs against the odds. It's why the world united to help Ukraine. It's why movie producers trigger audiences to fist-pump for Rocky Balboa and Slumdog Millionaire's Jamal Malik. Fans want the #2 team to get to #1. Consumers want John Leonard to get the advertised Pepsi jet.

Nowhere was this more evident than in the 1988 Winter Olympics. The first British downhill ski jumper to compete was an outlier underperformer. Eddie 'The Eagle' had broken more bones than records yet his talentless perseverance captured the euphoric crowd. They roared him forward in the 70- and 90-metres events.

Even though he came last in both, media celebrated like he had won gold.

We want the underdog to succeed against the odds. Why? We see ourselves in that underdog, facing challenges rather than getting chances.

Here's a thought: can empathy prejudice companies, candidates and competitors? Should the judge, umpire, art critic or talent scout award the underdog higher points than a more qualified competitor? Should the disadvantaged student be given the last place on the course?

While this emanates from kindness and feels intrinsically good, it's still a form of positive discrimination.

Being the underdog has advantages. Any perceived disadvantage can be converted into advantage. During my sponsorship of the 2012 Ryder Cup, former European captain Paul McGinley changed my perspective. Defying conventional wisdom, master strategist McGinley shared how being #2 was underestimated. The defending champions usually fail to perceive the underdog as a threat yet face the suffocating weight of expectations. In contrast, the underdog enjoys freedom to experiment with alternative strategies.

In Gleneagles Scotland, the world watched as the Europeans triumphed over the formidable Americans, securing an unexpected victory of 16.5–11.5 points. The European underdog had risen, claiming its rightful place in history.

Whether in sports, business or the dance of daily life, smart leaders tune in to the underdog mindset. Everyone loves a comeback story, whether it's Tiger Woods' 2019 US Masters victory or Leicester City's 2016 Premier League win despite astonishing odds of 5000 to 1.

TUNING IN: THE VOICE OF COMPASSION

One thing is for sure. Using emotion strategically can boost your career trajectory. Staying with golf, José María Olazábal won two Augusta Masters and captained the winning 2010 Ryder Cup team in Medina. With millions at stake, Olazábal knows how to perform under pressure. I asked how he handled nerves at critical moments. He said the body freezes, but you become familiar with the sensation, expect it and learn to tolerate it. Your inner voice calms you to reframe the moment of fear to one of expectation. I found this insight really useful when making presentations.

However, not everyone prioritises emotion over logic, even in business. Ogilvy vice-chairman Rory Sutherland criticises businesses for valuing rational thinking more than instinctive thinking. He argues that simply wearing a suit doesn't make you more logical and less emotional. Arguing for the psychological over the logical, he maintains overweighting logic destroys the essence of inspiration.[29] The impact is forsaken opportunity, me-too products and corporate stagnation.

Just as successful communicators, negotiators, actors, entertainers and producers use emotion to reorient audiences, charities use it to garner support and raise funds.

In 1984, the BBC reported "a biblical famine in the 20th century" that claimed a million Ethiopian lives. The world had tuned out, desensitised to a distant crisis. As images of 85,000 starving children went viral, the voice of this underfunded plight was heard.

Boomtown Rats singer and political activist Sir Bob Geldof was inspired to form Band Aid, uniting a stable of 75 global superstars to help alleviate poverty. The hit single 'We Are the World' generated $60m in sales from seven million records.[30] Thanks to his attuned leadership, nearly 40% of the world's population in 110 countries tuned in to a star-studded live concert to support famine relief. With 40 telethons raising funds, the single and Live Aid concert combined raised over £150m and saved two million African lives.[31]

We took an issue that was nowhere on the political agenda… were able to address the intellectual absurdity and the moral repulsion of people dying of want in a world of surplus.

However, everything comes at a price. Ironically, through his altruism, Geldof lost his identity as a musician. He was now "the saviour of the poor." Thirty years later, he recalls how it destroyed his passion.

No one was interested. Saint Bob, which I was called, wasn't allowed to do this anymore because it's so petty and so meaningless. So, I was lost.[32]

This loss of identity was an unintended consequence of doing what was morally right, and another example of how the PERIMETERS traps fuse together.

No situation or decision is devoid of emotion, it's a complex web.

The phrase "emotion decides and reason justifies" is so cliché it's ignored, like the drone of airline safety instructions. But it has merit. In its vice-like grip, we're more likely to flip out or freeze, mishear and tune out reason than we realise.

The successful Decision Ninja learns to regulate emotions and manage leakage in daily conversations. To gain perspective and reduce intensity, some employ self-distancing techniques. At its core is *situational reappraisal*, the ability to identify and label the vagabond bias-inducing emotion.

Interpreting communication means deciphering implicit messages. It requires your willingness to pause long enough to gain a better understanding of what's really meant or what people are trying to say.

That's exactly what Jeff Rinek did. He allowed himself to

be vulnerable enough to invest himself in missing children and understand human behaviour well enough to connect with depraved perpetrators. But emotional connection incurs an emotional price. He openly references his battle to regain equilibrium following PTSD events. "I can't let go of those I couldn't find and couldn't help."

I think this committed federal agent gave more comfort and closure to more people than he realises. Today, as a 71-year-old retiree, Rinek still accompanies victims' families to stressful parole hearings, such is the enduring value of his voice to others.

I've often found that professionals making routine decisions rarely realise how much their voice, advice and words mean. While Rinek listened to abused children and their abusers all his life, now the most important voice in his life is his devoted wife, Lori.

Awareness of the power of pausing and the PERIMETERS traps is a significant step forward and a source of relative influence and peace of mind. Ask yourself who else might suffer if you don't pause and reflect?

This is particularly the case when it comes to the effect of collective others on our decisions – the Relationship-based traps, discussed next.

THE DECISION NINJA

WHAT TO REMEMBER

- Emotion dictates who you hear, what you hear and when you hear it.
- All decisions contain emotion. Sharpening your emotional weathervane anticipates these traps. What matters is not the emotion but your response to it.
- Emotion is transient. The hotter the decision temperature, the more likely reason will be drowned out, leading to lost time, wasted money, cratered relationships and diminished influence.
- Science shows responding emotionally to visual cues predicts greater discriminatory judgement.
- Emotions are multifaceted. While empathy can evoke confessions and save lives, it can also wreak unintended repercussions.
- Good judgement stems from consciously interpreting emotions rather than unconsciously suppressing them.
- As emotion is multidimensional, consider the communication frame to check if you're being triggered.
- Emotional intelligence boosts judgement; an extension of emotional intelligence is sonic intelligence, or what we hear with a calm, noise-free mind.
- All emotions can be useful. Even guilt, pride, worry, awe, envy, embarrassment or shame can change behaviour when effectively and ethically deployed.
- Mitigate future error by applying the regret test.
- Reframing can accelerate desirable results and mediate moments of misjudgement.

CHAPTER 12

RELATIONSHIP-BASED TRAPS: CROWD CONTAGION

"A misconception remains a misconception even when it is shared by the majority of people."

Leo Tolstoy

PHILLIP WAS LIKE any ordinary employee. Except his story wasn't any ordinary story. After three decades on the corporate treadmill, 54-year-old Philip swapped his dealership job for a second career as a British postmaster. He wanted an easier life. In 1999, the government rolled out a £1bn Fujitsu-designed state-of-the-art accounting system to 11,500 Post Office branches and 70,000 employees.

Phillip's coastal post office thrived. However, unexplained discrepancies began to emerge and the accounts wouldn't balance. This continued month after month. Phillip's pleas fell on deaf ears. "It's only your branch," he was told. A 40-page contract obligated all employees to settle shortfalls.

Over nine months, Philip depleted his savings and mortgaged his house, even borrowing £20,833 from his 92-year-old mother.

Broke, he fiddled the books to buy time. In a Kafkaesque nightmare, the Post Office duly charged him with false accounting. Despite the situation, Phillip pleaded guilty. "It was the only way to avoid prison," he told me. Publicly shamed, he was reduced to living on welfare, his family ostracised.

With thousands of Phillips accused of wrongdoing, over 700 were prosecuted. Over 20 years, the Post Office prosecuted, coerced and convicted innocent employees of fraud, false accounting and theft. Individuals lost their homes, children, marriages and dignity. At least four individuals took their own lives.

The accounting discrepancies didn't result from a sudden outbreak of mass employee dishonesty but flaws in the new IT system. Any sensible reinterpretation would have deduced that. A chorus of innocence went unheard. Instead, the Post Office enriched itself in one of the greatest miscarriages of justice in British legal history.

In 2014, the Post Office HQ persisted in its ostrich-like denial. "There is absolutely no evidence of any systemic issues with the computer system."[1] Not so. By 2019, the High Court ruled leadership was aware of system flaws but failed to disclose them. Almost 100 convictions have since been overturned and, according to *The Guardian*, over £120m paid to 2,600 affected individuals. Each will receive £600,000 compensation.

However, the cover-up continues. Marina Hyde of *The Guardian* reports 60 people died without finding justice or retribution. Supporting Jeffrey Pfeffer's theory, the presiding CEO departed "£5 million richer" and no executive has been prosecuted. Meanwhile, scars linger in every affected village, and Phillip still awaits compensation.

What happened? Truth was obscured amid a crowd-based rush to misjudgement. Fujitsu and Post Office leadership were tone-deaf. Collective groupthink was underpinned by motivated hearing and deaf ear syndrome. Executives made snap judgements and overweighted improbable patterns of fraud. They tuned out.

This chapter highlights six distorting influence of group relationships (i.e., the crowd) on who we hear. When do we tune in? When should we tune out? Rather than address the abyss of 1:1 relationships, I explain how the collective voice can deafen decision-makers when it matters most.

Derailment starts with the need for belonging (conformity bias). We obsess about what others think, comparing ourselves to strangers and affiliates. We act as 'they' do (mimicry). We overweight difference (social comparison) and our relative ranking. Ironically, if unsure, we elevate crowd opinion. Assuming the crowd is correct, we imitate its behaviour (bandwagon effect) as it's easier to go along with the group (groupthink). The problem is we can lose our voice in the crowd and contradict private views (preference falsification) to fit in.

Notwithstanding the crowd's power to inspire order, stimulate reform, boost social cohesion and sometimes promote justice, we tune out the voice of objectivity when it matters – even if we know better.

THE SILENT ROAR OF THE CROWD

Belief in personal agency makes it easy to underestimate the shadow of strangers. We think we decide autonomously yet *mimic* behaviour whether in the office, gym, church, pub, club or restaurant.

Here's a surprising example of the subliminal effects of Thaler's seemingly irrelevant influences on judgement. With whom you eat, where you eat and how many people you're with dictate your choices.[2] Science finds the average person consumes 96% more in groups of seven compared to eating alone.[3] People also tend to make unhealthier choices with overweight companions.[4] Moreover, where you sit in a restaurant influences how much food is eaten. People typically consume less in dark corners.[5] Even plate size matters. When hotels or canteens provide smaller plates, consumption reduces. This demonstrates how supposedly irrelevant factors influences our choices and voices.

The effect of larger crowds may feel more obvious. Consider a football referee who hears background crowd noise. Will cheering or booing really shape an official's decision? Researchers checked it out.[6] Forty qualified referees evaluated incidents during a 1989 Liverpool vs Leicester City match. It turns out crowd noise correlated significantly with favourable referee decisions. Those who heard crowd noise awarded 15% fewer fouls against the home team compared to those who didn't.

What you hear is as important as who and what you see.

It's not just referees who are affected by noise but also fans. While sporting events or concerts create safe spaces for disinhibited emotional release, crowds alter individual psychological states. Identities blur as individuals fuse with groups.[7] Sometimes, this triggers fan chanting and hooliganism.

The crowd isn't all bad. Its roar can spur wannabe athletes like Eddie the Eagle or Ryder Cup players on the first tee. At the 2012 London Olympic Games, I roared Kenyan David Rudisha to break the 800 metres world record. A cheering crowd motivates runners, football teams and tennis players. John McEnroe often talks about how the crowd didn't need him to win, but he needed the crowd to win.

For sure, the voice of the crowd influences behaviour. It sells records, sways juries, mobilises armies and sparks riots. As importantly, where you fit in this crowd matters to your choices.

Social comparison as misinformation

We're fixated by others, individually and collectively. From the school egg-and-spoon race, we're programmed to impress and compete. It's why we try to keep up with our equivalent corporate or community Kardashians.

What do you drive? Mini, moped or Mercedes? It's a signalling device. The more you compare salary, TikTok followers or cars, the worse you feel, and the more you spend. Frequent comparers feel envy and tend to be more dissatisfied, especially following a downwards rather than upwards *social comparison*.[8]

If you're changing your car, you trade off the cost, quality and aesthetics. Right? Or in the moment, is it more likely that you're unconsciously swayed by the brand symbolism, bragging rights and neighbours' anticipated response? Most people are.

Then there's the neighbourhood effect. The weekly Dutch Postcode Lottery randomly selects a postal code to win cash and a new BMW. Economist Peter Kuhn and colleagues studied the effects of lottery wins on neighbours' consumption and found non-Lottery participants who live next door to winners tended to buy more cars.[9]

"Care about what others think and you will always be their prisoner," ancient Chinese philosopher Lao Tzu reminds us.

This notion foreshadows the PERIMETERS Effect. When we obsess about relative titles, rankings and status, we lose our identity quicker and squander our happiness.

It's interesting to consider who you want approval from too. While others are a barometer of our success, it's peers who provide unexpected reinforcement.

From athletes to astronauts, we crave approval from peers more than bosses. In 2011, I was fortunate to sit beside Neil Armstrong at a corporate dinner in the Palace of Versailles. My investment colleagues wanted to know how a seven-million-part machine that weighed 40 Boeing 747s propelled Apollo 11. As neither an engineer nor a space buff, I wanted to understand this enigmatic personality.

If you landed on the moon and received the Congressional

Gold Medal of Honour or Presidential Medal of Freedom, might these rank among your proudest achievements? I'm guessing they would. Among all the accolades, Armstrong told me he felt proudest of his early industry awards. Why? He identified primarily as an engineer, which is probably why he reverted to lecturing in engineering post-Apollo.

Similarly, at 77, Michael Collins valued his 1956 silver Luvin cup prize from test pilots "more than later distinctions." Even Carl Icahn is proudest of his prize-winning thesis, perhaps more than a billion-dollar empire.

Remember how badass John McEnroe lost the 1980 Wimbledon five-setter against Bjorn Borg, yet he valued more that Nelson Mandela enjoyed listening to it?

Being heard by your peers and admired others matters more than we think.

THE CROWD AS ORACLE OR FOOL?

Does crowd size matter? The crowd can be a handful of colleagues or a country. Is the crowd wise or stupid? It depends.

According to James Surowiecki in *The Wisdom of Crowds*, it's smart to listen. "Under the right circumstances, groups are intelligent, and are often smarter than the smartest people in them."[10]

During Covid-19, the world went crazy for exercise bikes and toilet-rolls. Today, it's solar panels, pickleball and lip fillers. The *bandwagon effect* triggers consumers to follow the crowd. Did thousands of mourners queue for hours to see Queen Elizabeth II, Pope John Paul II, Martin Luther King and footballer Edson Pelé lie in state partly because others did? Sometimes herding is irrational, sometimes not.

We think the crowd knows best. "If everyone else is doing it, it must be good," explains Robert Cialdini. It reduces the need to think, shorthand for what's popular – not necessarily what's right or what's best for you."

Knowing what others are watching, downloading, driving, eating or doing simplifies life. Few want to get it wrong. It's why 70 million Instagram users signed up to Meta's Threads platform within 48 hours of launch, overtaking ChatGPT to become the fastest-growing consumer app in history. It's why crowdsourcing and hackathons are popular idea-generation techniques. It's why consumers tune in to the voice of strangers before purchasing, as Amazon's five-star ratings for diamonds, dumpsters or drills become the swing factor.

Moreover, it explains why analysis of Hungarian elections over four years showed voters switching to the winning side once cognisant of which candidate was ahead.[12] Science shows if our view differs from the majority, we tend to move towards the mean.

We learn greatness from others, yet our greatest errors are taught by others.

History has proven the stupidity of crowds too. Hype doesn't always deliver expected outcomes.

Buzzkillers: following the buzz

In 2017, entrepreneur Billy McFarland announced a high-end luxury party in the Bahamas for 5,000 revellers at $100,000 a ticket. But A-listers never showed, and revellers were greeted with rain-soaked mattresses and cheese sandwiches.[13] The over-hyped Fyre Festival was a damp squib. Investors lost $26m and islanders lost their life savings. Uninsured McFarland didn't cancel, afraid of "letting everybody down."[14] Herding rarely ends well.

In volatile markets, nervous investors dash to withdraw funds, activating bank runs. Think Silicon Valley Bank, Countrywide Financial, Northern Rock and Toyokawa Shinkin Bank. Hysteria has crashed markets throughout history from the dot-com boom to Tulipmania. During the 1600s, a Dutch *Semper Augustus* bulb cost the same as 12 acres of land.[15] The 1700s spawned the South Sea Bubble, revolutionaries defined the 1800s while hippy flower power marked the 1900s followed by 1980s shoulder pads, girl power and boy bands.

Today's tulip equivalent is cryptocurrency. Many hopefuls piled into now-bankrupt FTX. Former SoftBank COO Marcelo Claure said of his $100m investment, "We should NEVER invest because of FOMO and we should always 100% understand what we are investing in. I totally failed here on both." Like investors, we jump on the bandwagon at a whim. It's a judgement killer.

With brands and artists, too many follow the buzz rather than being their own buzz. It's a mistake. Professor Elizabeth Moss Kantar argues brands that chase trends tend to miss significant differentiation opportunities. Companies declare they want more innovation and then ask, "Who else is doing it?" This type of me-too thinking characterises industries that have been disrupted by computing, mobile, AI, robotics or 3D printing. In an era of hyper-connectivity and viral communication, fast followers can be too slow.

Like Post Office leadership, busy decision-makers and problem-solvers elevate the voice of the crowd and follow its assumed wisdom. While conformity simplifies decisions, the crowd's momentum-driven voice is often ill-informed.

The skill is to know which crowd is right.

CONFORMING TO BE HEARD BY THE HERD

The desire for acceptance by the crowd is universal. Kerviel felt estranged from fellow traders just as Madoff felt like "an outsider" in finance establishments.[16] Elvis stood out in high school, felt unaccepted in New York and like a trespasser in Hollywood. And Prince Harry felt like a "spare."

Not doing as others expect carries a social cost but doing as others expect carries a greater cost.

We people-please and conform to avoid social ridicule and exclusion. More than anything, the 'unheard' want to be heard. Ironically, in a crowd, nobody gets heard, except the crowd.

Conformity is socially ingrained. When someone tells a joke, is the joke funnier if you're alone on your sofa or with a crowd? Of course, it's no funnier in either context. Yet a study showed 21% of viewers rated an advert funnier when in groups of three than when alone. One unintended social consequence is the average joke-teller thinks they're Charlie Chaplin!

Do you laugh at the unfunny boss? It's *conformity bias*.

It's easy to lose your voice as a compliant employee. Among others, the Memphis Mafia bewailed losing their identity. Like swarming CEO acolytes, when the King slept, they slept, when he partied, they partied.

Professional advisers aren't immune from conformity. Some pander to the voice of the fee-paying client, breaching codes of conduct. Historically, some facilitated excessive drug use and patients died prematurely. Elvis's doctor allegedly prescribed 10,000 doses of stimulants and narcotics in 1977. The doctor claimed these covered the 150-person entourage. "I cared too much" about a sick client with high blood pressure, obesity, colon and liver damage.[7]

Another Dr Feelgood, Conrad Murray contravened his professional oath by administering Michael Jackson acute levels of propofol and benzodiazepine before his 2009 tour, inducing fatal levels of intoxication. Murray was sentenced to four years for involuntary manslaughter.

Wanting to please is understandable. Overprescribing drugs, falsifying accounts, trafficking, cheating, smuggling or overbilling is justified with "If it's not me, it would be someone else." However, the world demands a higher standard from professionals than mindlessly obeying the voice of the paymaster.

Nowadays, consultants are increasingly held to account. Construction multinational Carillion collapsed with $7bn debt in 2018 after distributing £234m in dividends, assuming they had a healthy balance sheet.[18] British members of parliament accused auditors KPMG of complicity by "failing to exercise and voice professional scepticism." They were fined a record £21m by regulators. Similarly, Bain & Co. was banned from South African government contracts for three years after leaders "brazenly assisted" corruption when providing tax and revenue services.[19]

When unsure, rather than independent thinking, people look to predecessors.

"What did they do?"

Just as often, they look to the sentiment of the group.

THINKING IN GROUPS AND UNTHINKING GROUPS

It's not just spouses, employees or doctors who conform, it's groups. When we conform to the wisdom of the collective team, club or social network, that's *groupthink*.

Take juries. As we saw in Chapter 2, research finds only a quarter of jurors change their mind from initial conclusions formed during trials. In analysis of nearly 400 criminal trials, votes of dissenting jurors were compared with votes of conforming jurors.[20] Thousands of jurors listed both their private verdict and final verdict. It turns out a third secretly disagreed with the final verdict.

When it mattered, they conformed to the crowd. Sometimes, we would rather be wrong collectively than wrong individually. Hiding behind the herd feels safe. But it isn't smart.

What if you're the 12th juror deciding beyond a reasonable doubt? Today, it's recognised that one in 25 Americans sentenced to death have been wrongly convicted, condemned by jurors who tune in to the crowd.

Groupthink is amplified in every competitive workplace. If your manager values teamwork, rest assured your promotion, pay and popularity depend on how collegiate you sound. That sparks conformity!

Disagreeing with bosses affects your likability, despite the vacuous invitation to "challenge me" or "feel free to disagree." They tune out the voice of dissenters, ignoring those with whom they disagree or dislike. A lesson I learned late! Science proves it.

In an experiment, psychologist Julia Minsen split participants into pairs and recorded their views. First, each member of the pair read their partner's answers to controversial questions about the death penalty, marijuana or trade unions. Then each was asked to consider all available participants and choose who they wanted on their team, who they would approach for advice or select to represent the company.

Did they favour their partner? Only if they shared the same views.

Simply knowing whether someone else thinks the same as you is enough to influence whether you rate them or like them. Welcome to politics! No wonder information goes unspoken.

Judgement isn't always rational. As shown previously, science shows we form tribal affiliations with strangers. This can be based on random preferences or tangential links such as eye-colour, height or shoe size – anything that creates a them'n'us distinction.

Groupthink is inevitable if advisers, boards, committees and thinktanks don't address it. *Nudge* co-author and former White House adviser Cass Sunstein advocates the 'Delphi method.' It's simple. Team members just write down their idea anonymously before exchanging them. It avoids the group nucleating around one idea and reduces corporate brown-nosing.

Nobody wants to be alone. Yet much as we value others, others lead us astray.

Another form of conformity is *preference falsification*. The problem is truth is hidden so hard to hear.

FALSIFYING PRIVATE PREFERENCES IN PUBLIC

How often do you hide what you really mean for social, political or professional survival? Or because you just want to fit in and belong? You're portraying someone else to be like everyone else. Who wants to be fired, jeered or ostracised? When private information differs from what's publicly expressed, it's a source of misinformation communicated to yourself and others.

With fake personas and opinions punctuating our daily lives, no wonder Elizabeth Kendall and Trevor Birdsall were stunned when their friends Bundy and Sutcliffe were exposed as serial killers.

Under pressure, citizens obey rulers and feign ideological support for the incumbent political regime. This is preference falsification, coined by economist Timur Kuran.[21] When the Berlin Wall fell, leading journalists apparently struggled to find communists to interview. Some call suppression of private views living a lie. Kuran argues private views become public lies as honest preferences are misrepresented and this lip service contributes to intellectual impoverishment.

That's why it's important to decode preferences stated by politicians, advisors or leaders. Always apply the filters, "Is this what they really mean?" and "Are there alternative interpretations?" How can you know anyone's true preferences without consciously rebalancing what you see with what you hear?

Data scientist Seth Stephens-Davidowitz argues our Google searches are the ultimate confessional that reveal our deepest concerns. We type in our secrets. "Am I being brainwashed?", "Am I a bully?" or "How do I hide an affair?"

Falsifying preferences not only contorts your true identity, it preserves suboptimal structures. For example, imagine you agree with your boss that hybrid working is unproductive yet secretly think that's bonkers. Now your colleagues do the exact same. What happens? Your boss is none the wiser. Tied to your office desk, you all fume five days a week, costing millions in resentment. It's a subtle source of misinformation.

Watch for inconsistency between what you think privately and what you say publicly. It's a warning you're being triggered and good judgement is threatened.

Falsifying preferences not only wastes time and money, it damages reputations and lives.

TUNING IN: THE VOICE OF CONSENSUS

No PERIMETERS trap is all bad news. The crowd often remains a prevailing force for good.

At a societal level, activism can change laws, reform countries and bring attention to neglected voices. Pre-social media, 1970s environmental activists lobbied public bodies arguing that propellants such as hairsprays were creating a hole in the ozone layer. By 1987, an international agreement called the Montreal Protocol was established to phase out production and consumption of chlorofluorocarbons.

In the wake of Black Lives Matter, major diversity initiatives were announced by megabrands including Estée Lauder, Reebok, Apple and Google. Some pledged millions to black communities in an effort to uphold solidarity. The bandwagon rolled. Ethnically diverse appointments, TV anchors and judicial panels suddenly appeared everywhere.

Modern crowds appoint themselves as judge and jury, cancelling inappropriate voices. And it's getting stronger. When Ye, formerly Kanye West, made anti-Semitic comments, adidas cut sponsorship ties and reportedly lost $441m in sales. The crowd followed. A week later, Nike cut Brooklyn Nets' Kyrie Irving. "At Nike, we believe there is no place for hate speech and we condemn any form of antisemitism." However, months later, Yeezy shoes were back on sale with a proportion of profits donated to charity![22] Sometimes, principles move like candles in the wind.

Social norms reflect how people construct and interpret the world. Cialdini's lifetime research validates the power of *social proof* to improve behaviour. Making people aware of what others do motivates mimicry in simple ways. In one experiment, he placed signs in a hospital emergency room to encourage patients to take pain medication. Signs with the highest compliance rate read, "95% of patients who took this medication had relief within 15 minutes." Similarly, when McDonalds labelled the McFlurry the most popular desert, sales increased by 55%. It reduced buyer uncertainty.

Social proof is not just about the power of many people but many people like us!

The more similar the group, the more likely you'll conform. When charity campaigners knock on your door, smart ones tell you which neighbours donated. Why? They know you're more likely to follow the trend of people like you. You probably noticed this with mask-wearing messages. To maximise influence, announce how many similar people do whatever it is you want done.

Governments have used social proof to improve seatbelt adoption, recycling, water conservation, organ donation and charitable giving. It has also successfully reduced drink-driving, litter and tax evasion.

In 2016, drink-driving accounted for 38% of fatal Irish crashes. Governments rolled out a "Don't Drink and Drive" campaign, supplemented by Coca-Cola's decade-long campaign, the #Holidays-Are-Coming. This campaign represented an ambitious change in attitudes and behaviour.

Coca-Cola rewarded designated drivers with two free Cokes using the taglines "Cheers for being a hero" and the "Gift of a lift."[23] Designated driving became normalised. By 2019, there were 70% fewer fatalities compared to a decade earlier.

Your relationship with the crowd changes perspective. Knowing which crowd to tune in to is easier than you may think. That said, one factor will determine whether you tune in or out of the crowd: the lure of the narrative it tells.

At this stage, you're familiar with the characters in this book who listened to the wrong or right voices. Story-based derailers are discussed next.

THE DECISION NINJA
WHAT TO REMEMBER

- More is not always merrier. The voice of the crowd can puncture or propel judgement. Differentiate the crowd you see from the message you hear.
- Relative comparison unsettles critical thinking and triggers conformity. We misjudge our success by what others say, do and have – not by who we are.
- Collective conformity steers decisions in uncertainty yet is a crippling source of misinformation and misfortune. Society demands a higher standard of judgement from paid experts, advisors and leaders.
- Crowning the crowd as Oracle risks not hearing contrary voices and stifling independent thought.
- The ripple effect sparks conformity, herding and groupthink. Play your own tune not someone else's.
- Excessive desire for acceptance stops us from tuning in. Red flags include falsifying private opinions and dread of discommoding others.
- You can't stand apart from the crowd if you're busy following it. To really stand out, pick the right crowd.
- Don't underestimate the crowd's power to cancel virtue-signallers or wrongdoers.
- Beware social proof about how you 'should' behave or what 'most people' like, buy or want.
- Praise peers as it's valued more than you think. But never forget that bosses dislike disagreement!
- History has proven the wisdom, stupidity and power of collective relationships. The skill is knowing when to listen to their counsel and when to use your own.

CHAPTER 13

STORY-BASED TRAPS: GREAT EXPLANATIONS

"If you judge a fish by its ability to climb a tree, it will live its whole life believing it is stupid."

Albert Einstein

THE DAY AFTER Rwandan President Juvénal Habyarimana was assassinated in 1994, a 100-day genocide began. Against a polarised narrative and social class divide, an estimated 700,000 soil-tilling Tutsi were savagely slaughtered by a Hutu cattle herding majority. In mixed settlements, neighbours murdered neighbours with machetes while militia raped village women. Yet UN peacekeepers stood by.

Vitriolic messages of Rwanda's 'Hate Radio' were broadcast to seven million people. One study calculated that these broadcasts influenced an additional 50,000 people to murder their friends. US Agency for International Development Administrator Samantha Power encapsulates it well, suggesting killers "carried a machete in one hand and a radio in the other."[1]

A rare recording sourced by NPR captures the Hutu hatred of the Tutsis.

Rwanda belongs to those who truly defend it. And you, the cockroaches, are not Rwandans. The cockroaches will not escape... If we completely exterminate the cockroaches, nobody in the world will judge us.[2]

When the genocide ended, the Rwandan government began reconciliation. They consulted University of Massachusetts professor Ervin Staub. A Hungarian Jew, Staub believed in humanity yet understood dehumanisation was a stepping stone to depravity.[3] Years before, a friend had saved Staub from the concentration camps by hiding him in their basement.

Staub trained conflict-resolution experts and conducted information programmes across the community. He used something else, the power of narrative. Just as radio was used to spread hatred, radio was used to spread peace.

A soap opera storyline called 'Musekeweya' was developed, translated as 'new dawn.' It was directed by machete attack survivor Andrew Musagara who once avowed, "I don't want to remember."[4] The story told of tribal village members who united to overcome oppression. Normative messages around peace and interracial marriage were planted to heal wounds and stem lingering prejudice.

The voice of reconciliation was successful.

Rwanda's Love Radio became a national chart-topper for 16 years. Rwandans tuned in to the message and started to treat neighbours differently. Today, there are only Rwandans, not tribes.

The aural medium was successfully used to change lives.

The final PERIMETERS chapter addresses how five story-based decision traps increase vulnerability to misjudgement when we pay too much attention to social, political and organisational narratives. These traps amplify deaf spot risks and encompass elements of ego, power, time, ethics and crowd relationships.

Regardless of the message, the storytelling authority figure, idol, expert or underdog disproportionately influences who you tune in to (messenger effect). Of course, appearance plays a role, underscoring visual dominance (beauty bias). Pattern seekers fill in knowledge gaps about people, riddles, black swans and unsolved mysteries (associative thinking). The problem is narratives get accepted as fact (illusory truth effect) rather than explored as fiction or assumed as fabrication. Incorrectly, we judge success or failure by how the story ends (outcome bias) rather than how the end was reached.

Story-based decision biases have one thing in common: they feed mishearing, misinformation and misjudgement. Instead of seeking truth, we're swept up in Spielberg momentum and become inattentionally deaf. It's the fodder of fake news. No one is immune from mass delusional beliefs including government leaders, academics and policyholders,

It's human nature to weight stories over scientific data. It's why fake news and conspiracy theories spread. It's why smart people believe in mystical seances, fairies, Santa and the paranormal. Conversely, it's why positive narratives boost well-being, resolve conflict and inspire innovation. Hope reigns eternal.

The Decision Ninja skill is to discern the message from the messenger.

YOU'RE THE ONE THAT I WANT

"Friends, Romans, Countrymen, lend me your ears," said Mark Antony in Shakespeare's Julius Caesar. Well, we lend our ears to selected messengers. Two types of messengers are go-to sources of information – ourselves and others.

When we trust others, it stops us from asking questions, like Thierry de La Villehuchet or the Jonestowners. People believe in phantom promises, corporate myths and tales of salvation. The problem is what you hear is never all there is – and you can't trust everything you hear.

It's why, every year, people are defrauded out of millions by con artists, romantic playboys and financial scammers. It's why spies and serial killers are successful. We shouldn't trust what we hear but it's easier in a noisy world.

What we hear is based on how we feel about the storyteller. Have you ever noticed how your social media post gets 50 likes but someone else's with the exact same content get 50,000? It happens in meetings when someone repeats your idea only to get a round of applause. That's the *messenger effect*.

When Elon Musk changed his Twitter bio to #bitcoin on 29 January 2021, bitcoin's value jumped 20% to $38,566.[5] When Carl Icahn announced a $500m investment in Apple in 2013, its stock rose $17bn. That's the messenger effect.

Steve Martin and Joseph Marks argue we hear the messenger before the message, influencing "who we listen to and what we believe."[6] In other words, the messenger becomes the message. Moreover, we *see* the messenger before we *hear* them.

Why do we hear certain voices over others? Is it their words, images, slides or videos? Analysis of 166 healthcare interventions found it's none of these – the most influential messenger fulfils three conditions:[7]

1. Likability
2. Similarity
3. Credibility

First, as discussed earlier, we tune in to the voices of admired heroes, favourite co-workers or close friends more than someone we dislike. What if a critical message comes from a vicious competitor or patronising neighbour? We reactively devalue the message. It's a deaf spot. What's more, we label the disliked as stupid or narcissistic.

While awaiting sentencing, Madoff called Markopolos "a

joke in the industry." The disliked tend to become the outgroup. It's a mistake. By tuning in to the maverick or misaligned voice, you gain unexpected insight, advantage and perspective.

Second, messenger similarity determines what and who you hear, like the door to-door salesperson or affable politician. Throughout history, outgroup truth-tellers have been disbelieved. Think Roger Boisjoly, Glenda Cleveland and Fred Clay. Tribal influence occurs because you identify with "someone like me." It dictates who hears your message just as much as whose message you hear.

The *messenger effect* impacts decisions from healthcare to finance. Studies show microloan borrowers are more likely to take credit from social groups who are perceived as similar.[8] It turns out that lower-status groups tend to be more sensitive to messenger familiarity.

This insight was used to help prevent HIV/AIDS transmission. Over two years, Philippines male taxi and tricycle drivers were selected to communicate condom-use messages to passengers.[9] It worked. Well-constructed peer-mediated interventions are generally successful in changing attitudes.

Third, credibility is essential to be heard. We don't listen to dopes! Trained recruiters believe exaggerated CVs from experts, but as previously discussed, overreliance on expertise is a derailer. Recall how boards at Theranos and RBS accepted the projections and promises of leaders dripping in degrees.

People love a story from credible messengers. Professor Amy Cuddy's TED talk on the power pose was based on research with just 42 subjects yet to date, 43 million people have watched it.[10]

All voices are not equal in every situation, hence the need for selective filtering. Credibility, familiarity and similarity decree whose voice we tune in to and out of.

THE BEAUTY BONUS

I've argued throughout how we trust, rate and believe who we see more than what we hear. Irrationally, what looks good is also deemed good. It's the *beauty bias*.

Tons of research finds that attractive men and women are perceived as stronger, more sensitive, intelligent and modest than unattractive people. When participants evaluated essay quality and writer's appearance, attractive writers got higher grades, despite identical content.[11]

Every day, messenger credibility is enhanced or undermined by appearance. Financial whizzkids Harry Markopolos and Michael Burry were not considered Hollywood glitz – people judged who they saw not what they heard.

Non-airbrushed British chief medical officer Dr Chris Whitty was cruelly mocked by social media. The *New Statesman* reported how Whitty was the "subject of countless memes, mainly down to his calming, nerdy presence."[12]

Is this really surprising in an Instagram visual world?

It's unfair but appearances drive candidate selection, pay and promotion. Attractive students get better grades. Attractive employees get better pay.[13] Not only are the Brad Pitts and Naomi Campbells of the world privileged, but they're more trusted and associated with higher social skills and competence.[14] It's why the good-lookers are hired by airlines, broadcasters, cosmetic and glamour industries.

Gravitating towards good-looking messengers is human, albeit a major commercial and legal risk. This well-known trap has landed powerholders, regulators and investors in trouble.

Ultimately, the storyteller we see affects the story we hear – and don't hear.

·ı|l|·|ıı|l·|ıı|l·

Remember WeWork CEO Adam Neumann? When he peddled the story of the world's first physical social network, he stood out at six feet with long dark hair. Attractive to some! His combination of credibility, similarity and likability helped him raise billions from founder-friendly capitalists.

He could spin a story, telling conference attendees, "Together, we can build a community that can change the world." Investors fell under his spell. One investor told *New Yorker*'s Charles Duhigg, "He was the most charismatic pitchman I ever saw." Duhigg describes him somewhat differently, "A hype artist... like the cocaine that Silicon Valley venture capitalists were just waiting to snort."[15]

Attractive and well-groomed professionals are rarely suspected of misconduct. Did Ghislaine Maxwell look the type to lure teenagers to a sexual predator? Attorney Simona Suh believed suit-clad Madoff "didn't fit the profile of a Ponzi schemer." Police didn't initially suspect attractive charmer Ted Bundy, the Menéndez brothers, Cary Stayner or smooth John Wayne Gacy. Forensic psychologist Ciara Staunton explains, "We tend to make the mistake of associating grim murders with ugliness."[16]

Good-looking politicians get paid more and win more elections.[17] It's not just looks. Even tall people get hired more, earn more and secure more elections, gaining additional podium opportunities to be heard. Since 1776, the taller US presidential candidate has consistently won.[18] It's a vicious cycle.

This beauty bias is easy to spot in the workplace. Just glance at departments around you. Companies like Virgin, Vogue or Fox News have a distinct look. You can spot when visuals are prioritised in recruitment.

That said, attractiveness can be judged by the oddest things. Pittsburgh professor Richard Moreland analysed class attendance and found that frequent attendees were considered more attractive than infrequent attendees.[19]

For the beneficiary, this bias is an asset. For organisations, it's a liability because it reinforces the discriminatory tendency to judge what we see over what we hear.

This discrimination derailer extends to courtrooms. A jury pays more attention to what's seen than heard. For the same crime, attractive defendants typically receive more lenient sentences than unattractive ones.[20] They're also twice as likely to be acquitted. That's the beauty premium.

Some jurors consciously fight bias, like Hazel Thornton who sat on Erik Menéndez's first trial for seven months: "Just because you're looking at someone you wouldn't trust... doesn't mean they're not telling the truth all or part of the time on the stand."[21]

As a group, social norms influence decisions. Like in any group, tempers frayed, rivalries formed and fellow jurors with contrary positions became "ignorant asses." There was no 12th juror willing to shift position. The jury were evenly deadlocked, resulting in a hung jury.

To be heard, attractive messengers still need a credible story.

IT'S THE EXPLANATION THAT COUNTS

Decision-makers prefer pitches, presentations and strategies with logical arguments. The need for certainty drives us to rationalise a chaotic world and attribute meaning where there may be none. The most difficult questions remain unanswered – dilemmas, black swans or unsolved cases.

What explains over 70 ships and planes allegedly disappearing in the Bermuda Triangle? Where is Madeleine McCann or 1930s Atlantic aviator Amelia Earhart? Is the Loch Ness Monster real? What happened to Malaysian Airlines flight MH370 which disappeared over the Indian Ocean with 269 passengers on board?

People search for motives or explanations in *associative thinking*.

'Whydunit' preoccupies us just as much as 'whodunnit.' We want to know why Michael Peterson and Jérôme Kerviel committed their crimes. Our brains are pattern-recognition machines that compulsively fill in blanks to autofill a story that's congruent with those beliefs. When Kenneth Parnell convinced Stephen Stayner that his parents approved his legal adoption, it made sense. They were poor with five children after all.

When explaining decisions, we collate reasons based on available facts rather than accurate facts.

To illustrate, in 1977, psychologists Richard Nisbett and Timothy Wilson asked female consumers to choose between four pairs of stockings. Consumers explained their choices, referring to style, colour or texture – but the stockings were identical. Laden with justifications, we concoct an acceptable answer from narrow reasoning to fulfil our explanation-seeking gaps. When learning of their error, their pride insisted on detecting differences. They entrenched further. The justifying reasons after the fact may or may not be true but we defend our errors.

Clients and customers love explanations and to hear chief explainers.

The most successful fund managers I've worked with are master storytellers. They promise clients stellar returns and eloquently justify their stock selection and asset allocation strategies. The result is loyal clients who stick during underperformance. In these periods of underperformance, I've noticed how the more fragile rock stars lose confidence. Not only do they need reassurance from their colleagues about the return of their investment crown, their clients need reassurance, desperate for an anxiety-reducing story.

Wishful thinking takes over. And any half-decent explanation will often suffice.

When explaining these outcomes, one word is critical: "because." Funds underperform "because markets are due a correction" or "because we bet on Iceland not Iran." The reason almost doesn't matter. What matters is you give one. Without a strategic compass, decision-makers are situationally deaf. Cialdini's research found when a reason was provided for a request, compliance increased by over 300% compared to when no reason was given.[22]

Always give a reason! It connects dots even if the connection is spurious.

Another story-based challenge is believing what we hear repeated, no matter how ludicrous.

THE ILLUSION OF REPETITION

In Chapter 8, Zajonc's mere exposure effect showed how catchy phrases, favourite tunes or slogans stick. Think "Crooked Hillary," "Location, Location, Location" or "Have a break, have a Kit-Kat." The problem is the more you hear the message, the more you think it's true. It's the *illusory truth effect*.

The repetition of stories, slogans and mantras underpins organisation and political power. Without oversimplifying complex events, the repeated articulation of *Mein Kampf* and other works supported Hitler's dominance. Modern leaders now utilise social media as a repetition and reputation medium.

Called the "Trump of the Tropics," Brazil's former president Jair Bolsonaro tapped into an anti-establishment zeitgeist and achieved mass following. His bigoted campaign promised a licence for violence. His polarising hate speech echoed that of Rwanda. He told a Congresswoman she wasn't "good enough to be raped," that poor Brazilian blacks "are not even good for procreation" and that black activists "should go back to the zoo." He even told *Playboy*, "I would rather my son die in an accident than be gay."[23]

His shocking messages garnered attention and penetrated the noise as 212 million citizens tuned in to his voice.

How repetition fuels breaking news

Another attention-grabbing narrative that affects our vulnerability to decision damage is breaking news. While the search for truth is the lifeblood of journalists, sometimes the hunt stretches acceptability. In 1996, at Centennial Olympic Park, Atlanta, security guard Richard Jewell spotted a suspicious package. Jewell successfully vacated the 25-foot-square area that contained a bomb. He was declared a national hero.

Days later, following an unsubstantiated tip, *Atlanta Journal-Constitution* reporter Kathy Scruggs listed Jewell as the FBI's prime suspect. Jewell went from hero to zero overnight, described as "a hapless dummy, plodding misfit, Forrest Gump."[24] Introverted Jewell was hounded, recalling, "They had people over there who could read lips. They had a sound dish. They could hear everything that we said."

No one heard his voice, drowned out by sensationalist outrage. False data encoding superseded accurate data decoding.

Eventually, Jewell was cleared but not before his self-esteem and reputation were destroyed. "I hope and pray that no one else is ever subjected to the pain and the ordeal that I have gone through." Ironically, the only newspaper that didn't settle was the *Atlanta Journal-Constitution*.

Vanity Fair reports, "The phrase 'the Jewell syndrome,' a rush to judgement, has entered the language of newsrooms and First Amendment forums."[25] Blame-seeking and desire for single-point accountability frequently combine.

In reality, the truth gradually dilutes as stories pass through generations. In 1994, psychologists Gordon Allport and Joseph Postman found accuracy decreased 70% by the fifth or sixth storyteller.[26] That's how propaganda lives on. You can't trust all you hear because what you hear is not all there is.

Of course, how the story ends determines whether you applaud or castigate the outcome.

WHAT HAPPENED IN THE END?

If you speed through a red light and nobody gets hurt, was it a good decision? What if the Theranos blood-testing system had worked? If Apollo 11 had missed orbital rendezvous, would launching still have been a good decision?

Winners are never judged by how they win! They're judged by what they win.

The societal voice of censure or approval is driven by consequences. As Société Générale, Wells Fargo and the British Post Office showed, leaders and the market judge by results. Rwanda may applaud a united country today but that doesn't excuse yesterday's brutal butchering. You judge others, and they judge you.

No one wants to think they made a bad decision. Even using the best information, facts later emerge.

The decision only appears wrong if the outcome feels worse than the alternative. It's *outcome bias* and a product of the *rear-view mirror syndrome* which influences decision assessment.

Whereas some outcomes are discernible, evaluation isn't always clear.

Consider armed bank robber Walter Miller who escaped from a North Carolina prison in 1977. Much like Ross McCarty, he was on the run for 40 years. By the end of this time, Miller was married with four children and known as 'Bobby Love.' When finally captured, he felt relief rather than regret, "I feel like a big burden has been lifted off my shoulders."[27]

Even when outcomes are clear, interpretation can be delusional. Following WeWork's IPO failure, Neumann cried, "What's really painful is, I made so many good decisions."[28]

I think he told so many good stories rather than made so many good decisions!

Another human quirk affecting situation evaluation is the

tendency to overlook near misses, like the goal almost scored, the car almost crashed or the flight almost missed.

Organisational catastrophe expert Catherine Tinsley agrees, "People are hardwired to misinterpret or ignore the warnings embedded in these failures, and so they often go unexamined or, perversely, are seen as signs that systems are resilient and things are going well."[29] It's a missed opportunity.

What dictates judgement is how you frame the outcome. Zimbardo claims, "He who makes the frame becomes the artist or the con artist." Framing is a powerful technique that affects what you hear.

REFRAMING NARRATIVES: THE COURTROOM STORYTELLER

Did you run a half-marathon or quit halfway? Did you rise at 3am or sleep from 9pm? Are you 'out of stock' or 'sold out'? Is your missed flight a disaster or a funny story to tell others?

Every time you spot a self-sabotaging bias, are you failing or growing? It's the latter!

Imagine a surgeon advises you about a heart operation, stating the survival expectancy as either "95% of patients live" or "5% of patients die." It's the same probability, yet remember how loss-framing influences choice. Framing determines how we interpret problems – as a gain or loss, good or bad, urgent or not. Knowing that humans are binary and loss-averse, retailers use framing to dip into your wallet.

Storytellers rely on reframing to persuade patients, customers, employees, voters and investors. Just like the storytelling fund managers, criminal trial outcomes depend on which side tells the better story. It's legal *Jackanory*. Jurors hunt coherent arguments to formulate verdicts while defence attorneys use emotional arguments to eke out juror sympathy.

In the TV series *The People vs OJ Simpson* prosecutor Marcia Clark advises Chris Darden, "The defence has been obsessed with telling stories. Lawyers resort to stories to distract from the facts." Darden, who led the glove fiasco, responds, "People like stories. It helps them make sense of things."[30]

He wasn't wrong. Johnny Cochrane won the Simpson case by framing it about racial injustice, three years after the Rodney King riots. Bloody images of Nicole Brown and Ron Goldman were replaced by riot images of injustice. The jurors repeatedly heard the rhyming refrain, "If the glove doesn't fit, you must acquit." On 3 October 1995, 150 million viewers tuned in to hear the outcome. I was one of them.

Who doesn't want the right ending? A new chapter was written in 2007 when Simpson was convicted of armed robbery and served a nine-year sentence.[31]

᛫ı̣ı̣|ı̣|ı̣|ı̣|ı̣|ı̣ı̣᛫

Influential courtroom storytelling dates back decades. In 1924, Clarence Darrow defended two privileged homosexual teenagers, Nathan Leopold Jr. and Richard Loeb in the wanton kidnapping and murder of Leopold's cousin, 14-year-old Bobby Franks. Driven by intellectual curiosity to commit the perfect crime, Leopold was caught as he accidentally dropped his custom-made eyeglasses. He confessed his motive as "a sort of pure love of excitement… the satisfaction and the ego of putting something over." Darrow reframed the story around insanity.

The result? Two murderers escaped the death penalty.

Similarly, Todd Spodek defended heiress Anna Sorokin, reframing fraud as the act of an immigrant who fooled greedy bankers – she escaped grand larceny. In the 1990s, Leslie Abrahamson framed Erik Menéndez's double murder as parental abuse, resulting in a hung jury.

We accept the story we want to hear and turn a deaf ear to the rest. Or we don't rewrite the story. Stephen Stayner saw himself as more victim than hero while Buzz Aldrin likely saw himself as more hero than victim.

The Atlanta citizens absorbed media headlines about an alleged hero-turned-bomber. Loyalists in Russia, Northern Ireland and Jonestown accepted narratives grounded in cultural identity. Victims of the depraved heard the charismatic chorus of Cary Stayner, Kenneth Parnell, Phillip Garrido, Ted Bundy and John Wayne Gacy. All misjudged.

Often, we're so gripped in Oscar-worthy drama, we don't question compelling or awe-inspiring stories. Even toddlers frame stories for parental favours. It's what cements myths, conspiracies and folklore.

I too swallowed the corporate line over 30 years. It was easier but fundamentally misjudged. Internal communications and human resource departments masterfully curate stories to motivate performance and retain staff. Jeffrey Pfeffer urges employees to be circumspect and look past uplifting stories with "modest amounts of validity." It's the best advice you'll get as an aspiring ladder-climber.

Great storytellers can reframe any message to change perception and behaviour.

TUNING IN: THE VOICE OF TRUTH

Storytelling is a gift. The Tinder raconteur gets the date, the defendant goes home, the politician gets elected and the candidate gets the job – only if they tell a better story than everyone else.

Meet Ozan Varol.

A nervous 22-year-old interviewed for the 2003 Mars Exploration Rover's operations team. A once-in-a-lifetime role, the candidate was both underdog and NASA outgroup member. Asked by the interviewer what made him different, the candidate replied.

There lived two men in rural Turkey who spent much of their lives in poverty: Osman the bus driver and Şakir the shepherd. Their grandson grew up in a family with no English speakers and didn't know anyone who had achieved anything extraordinary. He is now sitting here interviewing for a position to serve on a Mars mission.

I never forgot this. And neither did the interviewer! When the candidate got the call, he "felt like Muhammad Ali had called him for boxing tips." Today, Ozan Varol is a former law professor at Stanford, rocket scientist and best-selling author.

The story of your life is not your life, it's just a story – but how you tell it can change your life.

Stories are powerful mediums to make smarter judgements. The noble cause can work for rebels, Russian Bolsheviks, French Revolutionaries and suicide bombers just as much as it can inspire courageous civil rights and human rights movements. Throughout history, stories have transformed behaviour and attitudes, pointing to past victories, present suffering and future triumph. I think of the great Martin Luther King as I recently stood in the Lorraine Motel just feet from Room 306 where he was assassinated.

Psychologist Dan McAdams agrees, "We are all storytellers, and we are the stories we tell."

You have a personal and professional narrative even if it's hard to articulate. If you don't control your narrative, your narrative will control your judgement as well as your reputation. Like the 12th juror, when you make any decision, you have the power to change other people's lives. It's a huge responsibility that should be used wisely and with the utmost of respect.

You've met the villains: Madoff, Mengele, Bundy, Simpson, Lombard, Stayner, Kerviel and the British Post Office.

But you've also met exceptional heroes: Jeff Rinek, Oskar Schindler, Harry Markopolos and Roger Boisjoly. And those who used their voice for good: Bill Clinton, Tina Turner and Bob Geldof. There are too many more to mention.

Hearing what matters helps hone a next-generation skill. That's the focus of Part Three.

THE DECISION NINJA

WHAT TO REMEMBER

- Stories are all-encompassing, seductive and emotion-triggering machines which spark System-1 thinking. When absorbed in their movie momentum, we fail to pause, slow down and discern rhetoric from reality.
- Understanding how the mind responds to stories helps resist the PERIMETERS Effect.
- Every story, pitch, newsfeed or presentation contains misinformation risk and adds to the reservoir of conflicting and competing voices in our heads.
- Information veracity can be distorted by similarity, credibility and likability. These are both sources of misinformation and hidden tools of persuasion.
- The best storyteller wins when people tune in. We believe repeated stories with congruent explanations, salience and resonance – it's a source of misinformation.
- If you want to be heard, consistently use the word "because" in communication.
- We rank decision quality based on how the story ends not by how the outcome was achieved. Always consider the means as much as the end to sharpen your judgement quotient.
- Storytelling is a gift, as you can reframe any situation to suit your agenda and boost influence.
- Stories can derail us but also be used responsibly for prosocial purposes that improve the planet and inspire generations.

PART THREE

TUNING IN: JUST-IN-TIME JUDGEMENT

"When you talk, you are only repeating what you already know. But if you listen, you may learn something new."

Dalai Lama

THE PERIMETERS TRAPS and associated biases have just revealed how much we can't trust what we hear. What you hear isn't all there is, and what you say isn't necessarily what people hear.

In a noisy, full-on, tuned-out world, well-intended decision-makers typically rely on first impressions and don't slow down long enough to probe contradictions, coincidences or inconsistencies. We haven't time. The result is a Molotov cocktail of misinformation that fuels predictable human error, collateral damage and avoidable regret.

If you don't slow down, you can't selectively filter the voices you hear. If you don't reinterpret filtered voices, you can't get judgement right. If you can't get judgement right, you can't get decisions right.

Better judgement saves time, money, relationships and reputation. It only takes a reasonable commitment to temper the adrenalin rush and selectively tune in to voices that matter in a given situation and discard the rest.

The benefits of tuning are apparent at the individual, organisational and societal level. Tuned-in individuals will be more persuasive, differentiated and even popular, while organisations become more trusted, sustainable and productive. A tuned-in society can hope for more tolerance, equity and harmony.

Predictable damage can be avoided with greater preparedness.

This path to power, performance and prosperity is encapsulated below:

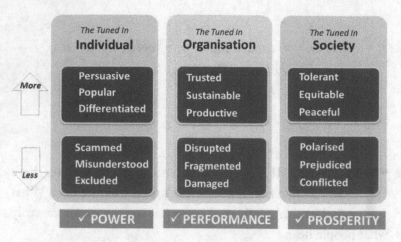

While the human condition is bias-prone, that's different to being bias-destined. When you see, hear and speak the truth, you multiply your performance impact and connection with others.

In this final part, I provide a roadmap for the tuned-in Decision Ninja to counteract the biases delineated in the PERIMETERS traps.

As a problem-solver, embracing what I call *decision friction* empowers you to step back and reinterpret information with a 3D lens – considering the psychological blind spots, dumb spots and deaf spots. This will rebalance what you see with what you hear.

It's a fast track to being a happiness superspreader and a wiser 12th juror. For leaders, influencers and powerholders, it's both a fiduciary and a moral obligation.

CHAPTER 14

HEARING WHAT MATTERS: SONIC STRATEGIES

"Everything can be taken from a man but one thing... to choose one's attitude in any given set of circumstances, to choose one's own way."
Viktor Frankl

THINK ABOUT AN important decision you're about to make. In this chapter, I present a bundle of science-based strategies that deliberately interrupt your thinking to help you optimise that decision. When thinking about a past mistake, you will learn how you might have approached things differently.

Listening interpretatively, intentionally and selectively is a choice. If you decide you want to be a successful Decision Ninja, you first adopt the right frame of mind, treating judgement as a controllable factor before consciously assessing any unconscious decision risk and selecting a counter strategy.

Great judgement is a choice. For you, that choice becomes either an asset or a liability, depending on whether you intentionally decide or default to error.

Your regret or reward quotient depends on how much attention you pay to the PERIMETERS traps. It's a simple equation:

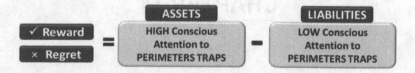

The more conscious attention paid to potential error, the more likely regret is avoided and reward gained.

THE AAA MINDSET: ASSETS AND LIABILITIES

We don't control circumstances, but we do control our greatest asset – our minds. Chesley Sullenberger couldn't prevent low-flying Canadian geese from obstructing his aircraft engines. Yet he trusted his inner voice well enough to land a plane on the Hudson River, saving 155 lives. In the critical moment, sound judgement is possible, courtesy of our inbuilt cognitive instrumentation. It conquers any defects in our mental malware.

The trick is to slow down System-1 impulses long enough by deliberately interrupting your thought process.

Think of all the excellent decisions you've made in your life. In relative terms, not so many disasters, right? Sometimes society sensationalises errors which activates a tendency to catastrophise our own errors.

Your mind minimises liabilities when you control three factors: outcome anticipation, outcome attitude and outcome acceptance. It's a triple A or AAA mindset.

Decision Stage:	ANTICIPATION (Pre)	ATTITUDE (Pre/Post)	ACCEPTANCE (Post)

Let's consider each in turn:

Anticipation of outcome: This is the first step. By anticipating the best and worst-case scenario, you're better prepared to limit emotional overreactions. If Purdue Pharma had put lives before profits, the opioid crisis might have been contained. If Hillary Clinton had anticipated the private server media frenzy, she may have been the 45th US President. If Alec Baldwin, Mark Stanley and Juan Rodriguez hadn't been tired or distracted, lives would have been saved. Life is full of regrets, what-ifs and maybes. Anticipatory regret creates a sense of imagined loss which we're motivated to prevent.

Attitude to outcome: The next step in cultivating an AAA mindset is pre-determining your attitude to unknown outcomes. It's an underestimated mental asset. Accused of murder, Michael Peterson pre-selected his attitude to conviction when he accepted an Alford Plea. Magician Harry Houdini accepted mortality risk in the Chinese water torture trick. In *Alchemy*, Rory Sutherland suggests we create attitude. "Give people a reason and they may not supply the behaviour; but give people a behaviour and they'll have no problem supplying the reason themselves."[1] You can nudge yourself to shrewd judgement when your goal is to become a great decision-maker, connector, problem-solver or influencer.

Acceptance of outcome: We don't choose misjudgement; we just don't always control judgement. When you can't reverse a decision, acceptance of outcomes is a powerful asset. Accepting consequences as the best decision at the time limits blame. There's no magic bullet and you're not going to hit the bullseye each time. Alcoholics Anonymous urges members to accept what cannot be changed. It's the same with irreversible misjudgement.

Wear the AAA crown! Consciously managing outcome anticipation, attitude and acceptance better prepares you to rebalance those decision inputs and contain vulnerability to risk of error in a noisy, visual, polarised and high-speed world.

INTRODUCING 'DECISION FRICTION' – A MENTAL SPEED BUMP

Decoding bias isn't a question of intelligence or personality. That said, conscientious people typically find bias-busting easier than if you operate frantically with your hair on fire!

Becoming a Decision Ninja only relies on being intentional, noticing what's said and what's not said. It's how journalists interrogate sources, analysts scrutinise earnings, investigators crack cases and negotiators win deals.

By interrupting your own thought patterns, you slow down the reasoning process and broaden your intentional interpretation to hear the right voices at the right time, as Jeff Rinek did. As Mary Budd Rowe found, every second of reflection counts towards improving your judgement.

In the digital world, the term 'friction' has negative connotations. It describes an unwieldy energy-depleting process that prevents a seamless customer experience – like hard-to-cancel subscriptions or completing lengthy application forms. It's what smart companies avoid.

But a problem in one domain can be a solution in another.

If you deliberately interrupt your thoughts before forming a judgement, you gain those valuable seconds of reflection. This is what I call decision friction.

What is it? It's simply a series of conscious prompts, rules, nudges, questions or mechanisms that jolt you out of impulsive System-1 thinking towards more deliberative System-2 thinking. This friction allows you to pause.

While online friction is unwelcome, decision friction is welcome in this case as it prevents misjudgement before it happens. Think of it like a speed bump for your mind. It slows you down long enough to overcome the PERIMETERS traps.

Making this even easier to implement in the decision moment, decision friction is only needed temporarily, just long enough to filter derailing voices during hot states.

Across five categories, I've identified 18 science-based strategies to help decision-makers to reflect, reinterpret and reappraise more. These are encapsulated in the mnemonic **SONIC**.

Slow down
Organise your attention
Navigate novel perspectives
Interrupt mindsets
Calibrate situations, strangers and strategies

Each contains a handful of bespoke tools for smart decision-maker to deploy to counteract default biases. Every incremental second of recalibration aids judgement.

S	O	N	I	C
Slow down	**Organise your attention**	**Navigate novel perspectives**	**Interrupt mindsets**	**Calibrate situations, strangers & strategies**
The 'five whys'	The decision environment redesign	Always consult before deciding (ACBD)	Interrupt yourself: default to error	The PERIMETERS bias checklist
Argue against the argument	The digital distraction detox	de Bono's thinking hats 2.0	Interrupt others: decision diagnostic	The interpretation habit
Time out tools	4x BIAS screen	Zoom out for independence	Adopt a third ear	Implementation intentions
	The Pomodoro method	The Janus option	Embrace U-turns	

With 80-hour working weeks standard in some industries, individual decision-makers and groups need pausing instruments and easy-to-use hacks to slow down. No single solution can neutralise liability. Each should be tailored to the time available, the particular decision type, its severity and approximate consequentiality.

Choose whichever solution you find easiest, based on your confidence and experience making similar decisions. No solution is right for all situations or individuals but having a suite to choose from alleviates decision anxiety and stress.

IMPLEMENTING SONIC JUDGEMENT STRATEGIES

Pythagoras once said, "A fool is known by his speech, and a wise man by his silence."[2] Let's start with the first set of 'S' strategies and explore ways to slow us down long enough to recalibrate and reinterpret what we hear – or don't.

S: SLOW DOWN

I find three effective techniques are *the 'five whys'*, *argue against the argument* and *time out tools*.

The 'five whys'

In the 1970s, Japanese car manufacturer Toyota developed a simple approach to solving complex problems that is now used in Six Sigma processes by manufacturers, consultants and start-ups globally. It rightly assumes most organisations' technical problems conceal human problems.

As the name suggests, when a decision problem arises, executives ask "Why?" five times to ascertain its underlying causes. This technique is useful for probing false reasoning and diagnosing assumptions. Moreover, it mitigates biases such as probability neglect, loss aversion and commitment escalation.

You might use this technique when feeling vulnerable or uncertain about what to do. For example, Tim Stoen at Jonestown might have asked: Why does God only speak to one man? Why have guns if we're free? Why do we need protection? Why does salvation involve cyanide? And why can't children be saved?

Any question combination is possible. And it's simple to remember.

When you hear something that doesn't make sense, pause, then probe and ponder, just as Officer Jacobs did after meeting Garrido's children. Do it five times. This technique slows you down. Your perspective broadens as you go deeper, analysing and filtering the voices that are most important. In addition, intentional questioning becomes a habit.

Argue against the argument

Another slowing-down technique is using counterfactuals. Sometimes, it's called *take the opposite view*. If you're unsure about choosing engineering in college, counterfactuals help you imagine a future in journalism or horticulture. Or if you believe euthanasia prevents distress, research whether euthanasia causes distress.

Policy adviser and commander-in-chief Sandy Berger told the Presidential Oral History Program how Bill Clinton does it.

Clinton would reach a conclusion and would subject that conclusion to the counterargument. When we prepared for a press conference, Clinton would give an answer and we'd critique it... He'd tear that answer to shreds. He'd be the most devastating counter-questioner you could possibly imagine.

Research shows how disconfirming data and generating alternatives improves accuracy and insulates against overconfidence.[3] Some decision-makers also stress-test assumptions and validate reference points.

You can simulate better or worse scenarios.[4] Thierry de La Villehuchet could have tested a better scenario, "If I listen to Markopolos, my clients will be more financially secure."

Or a worse scenario, "If I listen to Madoff, more of my clients will be ruined."

Counterfactuals can be effective against dogmatism, polarisation, and the discrimination experienced by Termaine Hicks, Fred Clay and George Floyd.

Time out tools

The World Health Organization recommends a National 'Time Out' Day as a universal protocol to boost patient benefits. It's pretty simple: medical staff take a day to take time out to reflect on critical decisions.

This enables procedure checking and communication exchanges.[5] The *New England Journal of Medicine* reports this has reduced adverse events by 35.2% and site infections by 16.7%.[6] By definition, enhanced safety also lowers malpractice and mortality rates. It's a solution patients encourage to mitigate delayed or erroneous diagnostics.

While Time Out is used to improve patient safety in medical settings, the concept can be applied in any industry. For some companies, the equivalent is 'email free' Friday, sabbaticals, volunteering days or regular offsites. For some, remote working makes taking mental reflection time easier.

Pick the schedule and practice that works best for you and your team.

The well-established theory of *cognitive load* assumes that a strategic pause improves the ability to think under pressure.[7] It's true. Although reflective reasoning increases mental effort, it's a small price to pay for smarter reasoning and hearing what really matters.

As a fast talker myself, the power of the strategic pause is somewhat alien so when I heard about a 'pause button' tool, I was curious. It's a technology hack that self-regulates impulse. It acts like a nudge. Just as you count steps with Fitbit, you use a credit card style wristband containing three buttons: Pause/Play/Rewind. You activate these when you need time to adjust behaviour, like an alarm reset.

Many argue that pausing to reflect is disguised procrastination. For some, it may be but even strategic procrastination can help you slow down to reconsider what you hear rather than what you see.

It's still a fundamental way to deescalate tensions, preserve relationships and prevent crises caused by mishearing or misinformation.

These slowing-down techniques neutralise potential misjudgement through deliberate decision friction. Of course, you can always take a walk too! What matters is not which method you use but the attention you pay to problem-solving during Time Out. If you commit your attention to finding the right voice, everyone wins.

O: ORGANISE YOUR ATTENTION

"What you give your attention to, you become," Stoic philosopher Epictetus once wrote.

Does your big decision have some, all or none of your

attention? Unconsciously, you might magnify the dilemma disproportionately, which thwarts rational judgement, or deny reality in the ostrich effect.

You pay attention to what you want – an art my husband has mastered! Some might prioritise watching Saturday sport over clearing the shed. Hard to fathom, I know. Of course, you'll only master judgement if the incentives are self-serving enough.[8] That's our friend, motivated reasoning.

Let's explore four hacks that counteract data overload and support decision focus: *the decision environment redesign*, *digital distraction detox*, the *4x BIAS screen* and the *Pomodoro method*.

Decision environment redesign

When a supermarket designs its aisles, their product placement designers determine whether you buy fruit or fruit pastilles, apples or apple cider. Choice architecture is the bedrock of behavioural scientists and marketers who define how online and offline options are served to you.

The principle can be used by you as a decision architect.

Think about where you go to reflect and make high-stakes decisions. Perhaps your office, kitchen, garden or bedroom?

Does it resemble an ad for Extreme Hoarding or for House of the Year?

You control that environment. Changing the physical design facilitates a cognitive refresh. It's not rocket science. Just as if you want to lose weight, you might serve dinner on breakfast plates. Or if you want to stop smoking, you purge your cigarette stash. To consciously reflect and declutter your mind, you declutter and architect your decision space.

Some organisations facilitate employee reflection. For example, Marc Benioff installed a mindfulness zone in many offices. "Innovation is a core value at Salesforce. It is deeply embedded in our culture."[9]

Mindfulness is on-trend, although it dates back 2,500 years to the Buddhist philosophy of 'a beginner's mind.' It advocates more reservation of judgement as expertise grows.

Organisations must do more than provide reflection rooms. They can mitigate the pressure that depletes performance and amplifies both first-order and second-hand employee stress.

Consider the fast-paced climate at investment banks, newsrooms, hospitals and rescue organisations. We've seen what happens when organisation culture prioritises and rewards quick decisions. Of course, redesigning your decision context complements the effect of the time out strategy.

It's a personal choice how and where you reorient. You can do it anywhere. If your context is distracting, organising your attention is the first step.

The next step is managing those deafening rings, pings and dings.

Digital distraction detox

Is your phone beside you as you read this? How many computer tabs do you typically have open? Shamefully, I've just counted 63!

Are you getting constant interruptions, alerts and notifications? Can you hear dogs barking, cars whizzing by or toddlers crying?

What's crazy is that people interrupt themselves 44% of the time.[10] No wonder there's an attention crisis!

What's distracting you, and from what? Multitasking stops us tuning in to the right voice – or any voice! In *Indistractable*, Nir Eyal suggests our technological distraction comes from boredom, anxiety or insecurity. Compulsive checking, skimming, scrolling and scanning is a vicious cycle. Tools designed to serve us become our masters.

How much interference will you tolerate before limiting your distractions?

Ironically, to reduce the tsunami of digital algorithms that pump out all day long, Eyal suggests we manually remove notifications, ban phones or adopt various technology-based app solutions that hide feeds, remove clickbait or block internet access at set times. As a serial multitasker, I use the *time boxing* technique which allocates every hour to a calendar schedule. It's also apparently used by former US secretary of state Condoleezza Rice. I find it works more often than it doesn't.

These are temporary fixes to the technology platforms that kill our attention and judgement. But when these hacks become ingrained habits, they become effective longer-term solutions that help avoid judgement killers.

4x BIAS screen

An easier way to free up attention is to double-check critical information. It saves you time, money and reputation, something the Mars Climate Orbiter team appreciates.

Fact-checking is just a discipline, as is bias-checking. When I work with organisation leaders, I advise them to use four filter questions when evaluating an important pitch, presentation or proposal. It's a set of checkpoints they go through in decision-making Olympics! The questions spell out BIAS.

Bias: what biases might hinder interpretation?
Intuition: what did I hear that sounded odd or wrong?
Authenticity: what aspects should I probe further?
Signal: what did I *not* hear that I should have?

This 4x BIAS screen is a heuristic anyone can apply. Some clients convert it into posters, laminates or mugs. Those who introduce it into the decision process automatically incorporate decision friction and reduce the odds of human error.

The Pomodoro method

Another straightforward time management technique that carves out reflection time is the *Pomodoro method*. First used by Dr Francesco Cirillo, it takes its name from the Italian word for 'tomato' and in fact was inspired by the tomato-shaped kitchen timer – you'll never see a tomato the same way! There are five steps:

1. Select the topic of focus.
2. Set a timer for 25 minutes.
3. Work on the task.
4. Take a five-minute break.
5. Repeat Steps 2–4 until the issue is resolved.

For the distraction-prone, it slows down the mind and limits unwelcome interference.

These four strategies help redirect attention to filtering the voices that matter. It doesn't matter which strategy you choose. What matters is that you choose one.

Now you've got the tools to slow down and organise your environment, the next step is to select the precise strategies that generate more perspective and neutralise the trilogy of error.

N: NAVIGATE NOVEL PERSPECTIVES

Listening may be perfunctory in polite social circles and occasionally a drag, but it's not listening that drags you down. We know we love the sound of our own voice. Remember Dick Bass's mountain monologue?

We care too much about being heard and not enough about hearing others.

Being a successful Decision Ninja demands navigating alternative perspectives. As Aristotle says, "It's the mark of an educated mind to entertain a thought without accepting it."

You only need to listen and consider the thought. Like a parachute, the mind must remain open. It is this openness that blasts through decision derailers such as narrow thinking, polarisation, impression management and ingroup bias. And therefore, it's a fast track to greater social tolerance, fairness and understanding.

In this category, I recommend four techniques: *always consult before deciding (ACBD)*, *de Bono's six thinking hats 2.0*, *zoom out for independence* and *the Janus option*.

Always consult before deciding (ACBD)

I became aware of this technique in a negotiation class with Harvard Law School's Dan Shapiro. He calls it *always consult before deciding* or ACBD. Like buffalo stampeding through the Serengeti, overconfident leaders sometimes move forward without consulting or considering consequences.

When you consult before deciding, there's no guarantee you'll take the advice as *psychological reactance* can set in. You don't have to give others a veto or a vote, just enable their voice. It's a sensible start.

Soliciting external opinion is hard.

Influence guru Robert Cialdini recommends an effective technique. "If you simply change the word 'opinion' to 'advice,' research shows you'll get significantly more favourable responses." People "take a half step towards you."[11] Again, it mitigates hostility and promotes harmony.

Why? Because people feel like you're in it together.

If Liz Truss had tuned in to her party rather than herself, she may have lasted longer in office! As Elvis and Fred Goodwin exhibited, pride can stop us revealing inherent weakness or asking for help when it matters.

de Bono's thinking hats 2.0

Developed by psychologist Edward de Bono, the *six thinking hats* technique is excellent for lateral decision-making. It helps an individual working through a decision dilemma or mitigating groupthink in an organisational setting. Each conceptual hat has a colour that symbolises how you might interpret a given situation. It's designed to broaden idea generation in a brainstorm. For example:

- Blue: strategic (planning, forecasting)
- Yellow: optimistic (benefits, rewards)
- Black: pessimistic (risks, weaknesses)
- White: factual (neutral data, statistics)
- Red: emotional (intuition, instinct)
- Green: creative (new ideas, alternatives)

Different colours allow you to hear and respect multiple perspectives. You can tailor these to any scenario, from sourcing innovative ideas to predicting stakeholder responses. For example, when working with clients, I consider both problem and solution from six perspectives: clients, shareholders, media, government, employees and regulators. Each can be considered a listening hat.

Not only do de Bono's thinking hats slow down the decision process and introduce decision friction, but they trigger supplementary routes to investigate problems and hear alternative options. For instance, Theranos could have tried this technique to create alternative solutions for the Edison technology.

By navigating new perspectives, creative judgement – and better judgement – is possible!

Zoom out for independence

It's hard to be objective when you're morally conflicted, overwhelmed or under pressure. Even the popular pros and cons list is laden with inherent bias.

Zooming out and soliciting third-party advice can short-circuit the PERIMETERS Effect. Social psychologist Scott Plous agrees. "The most effective techniques involve consideration of alternative perspectives." It's why boards appoint independent directors to kill conflicts of interest, ethical fading and groupthink.

New voices can resonate with us more than familiar voices. Do you find your colleague or partner sometimes tunes in admiringly to someone else's voice more than yours? "But I told you the same thing last week," you bemoan. It's the novelty factor. It boils down to the fact that strangers' voices can boom louder than familiar voices as they're more salient. Although it's annoying, it's also useful.

Professor Max Bazerman has conducted extensive behavioural research into commercial negotiations. When he applied independent perspective-taking to the negotiation process – in other words, considered external advice – he found it vastly improved the probability of a successful final offer.[12] Who doesn't want a better deal?

To promote lateral thinking and broaden our mental perimeters, many companies introduce secondments, transfers, shadowing and regional exchange programmes. This technique also promotes inclusive decision-making.

Another common perspective-taking technique is to ask yourself "What would a friend do in the same situation?" By visualising another's situation, especially someone you care about, you create emotional distance and negate the tendency towards herding and confirmation bias. Moreover, your instinctive response accelerates a prompt conclusion.

Perspective-taking remains an underused tool, especially when we are prone to ego-based biases.

The Janus option

The dual-headed Roman God Janus suggests it's possible to look forward and back simultaneously, gaining the fullest perspective. It reminds me of Standard Life's motto to "Look forward, look back, look all around."

It's worth being a Janus at times!

As discussed in Chapter 1, we unconsciously simplify dilemmas in narrow thinking through binary 'A or B' options. Authors Chip and Dan Heath warn that these dichotomous dilemmas are "a classic warning sign you haven't explored all your options."[13] There's always another choice.

For every decision, whether buying a house or breaking into a house, you entertain six alternative options:

1. Do nothing.
2. Reframe the decision.
3. Defer the decision.
4. Ask for help.
5. Follow the crowd.
6. Make the decision.

Contemplating a broader spectrum of options always reduces decision anxiety and bias-induced error. If you think broadly like Julius Caesar, you can cross your own Rubicon and rewrite your story.

Ironically, the 'vanishing options' technique helps to generate more options. As the name suggests, the existing options vanish.[14] You imagine being unable to choose any option under consideration to force creativity. This works when the situation feels complex, like devising military strategy, managing underperformance or breaking up. It's less useful for picking toothpaste. Of course, you must manage the risk of generating choice proliferation too!

If you're still feeling stuck in a polarised mindset, consider two questions: Which option will I regret more? And what else could I do with the time, money or resources?

Moreover, when paralysed by indecision, as I share in my TEDx talk, I apply what I call the 'Probability Test':

- What is the worst thing that can happen?
- What is the probability of this happening?
- If it happens, what will I do about it?

All of these techniques help navigate novel perspectives and gain reflection time by interrupting yourself, explored next.

I: INTERRUPT MINDSETS

Every smartphone buzz or blink interrupts your headspace and creative flow when you're writing, speaking or strategising. According to *The Great Acceleration* author Robert Colvile, the average Fortune 500 CEO enjoys only 28 uninterrupted minutes per day.[15] The interrupted then work faster and experience greater stress. The University of California Irvine estimates it takes 23 minutes to revert to a pre-interrupted state! That's a lot of lost time and a guaranteed judgement killer.

Interrupting your train of thought has rarely been welcomed, until now. Like decision friction, deliberate interruption can be useful for the Decision Ninja and the teams, direct reports or stakeholders whose minds you want to influence.

Conscious strategic interruption can be achieved in several ways to mitigate the PERIMETERS traps: *interrupt yourself by defaulting to error, interrupt others in a decision diagnostic, adopt a third ear and embrace U-turns.*

Interrupt yourself: default to error

Remember how Alan Greenspan and the SEC dismissed financial warnings and the devastating consequences of turning a deaf ear? Before assuming your counterpart is wrong in a pre-programmed Pavlovian reaction, assume you're wrong rather than right.

Deliberately defaulting to error saves time, money and angst. But becoming a more human-centric intentional leader requires self-control and some humility.

We should accept decision error as a sign of humanity rather than a sign of deficient intellect.[16] Nudging helps. On *The Brainy Business* podcast, host and author Melina Palmer explores the practical aspects of nudging. She suggests we build predictable error into habits that serve as reminders to perform certain actions. For instance, car manufacturers build in "dings" to remind drivers to wear seatbelts and incorporate flashing warning lights to remind drivers to change oil.[17]

Assuming others' error means being selectively cynical. If you ask a shop assistant the price of a game console, you expect them to mention tomorrow's sale. You don't assume they will lie by omission, but people do.

An inbuilt default to error is a smart insurance policy against misjudgement risk.

Always ask yourself: Does this information make sense? Which PERIMETERS traps are most relevant? Which biases are most likely to trigger me?

This healthy paranoia increases decision friction. Hot-shot detectives, journalists, therapists and investigators instinctively do this by tuning in to what matters, what's said and what's not said. As management guru Peter Drucker states, "The most important thing in communication is hearing what isn't said."

In addition to proactively self-interrupting, you may occasionally need to interrupt the mindset of wavering investors, procrastinating clients, troubled teens, difficult employees, and so on.

Interrupt others: decision diagnostic

To avoid being duped by others' storytelling, another option you have is to introduce a *decision diagnostic*. Giving others additional time can clarify disturbing data, vague instructions, conflicting orders, mandates or briefings. What if the FBI had paused to reinterpret Kenneth Williams's memo or the SEC had analysed Harry Markopolos's 29 red flags? Every second of reflection counts.

If Jeff Rinek hadn't empathetically listened to Cary Stayner, two more innocent individuals would have been wrongfully convicted and families never at peace. If an abused Tina Turner hadn't left Ike, you wouldn't be reading about her here.

Co-founder of Harvard's Program on Negotiation, William Ury advocates "giving others the benefit of the doubt until you check out the facts yourself by asking clarifying questions." Clarifying questions can be open or closed. Open questions allow you to hear more and might include, "Can you help me understand this better?" or "What did you mean by that?" Closed questions confirm what you heard.

To interrupt mindsets, you can tailor questions about the messenger and the message, summarised below.

The receiver (you)	The message	The messenger (others)
Does this information make intuitive sense? Do I need help? Will I still agree tomorrow?	Is this a fact, opinion, assertion, inference, hypothesis or claim?	What is their decision context? Are they relaxed? Are they under time, social or financial pressure?
Which traps are most relevant to this situation?	Is the argument consistent, reasonable and verified?	Do you like, admire, envy or respect the messenger? Are they credible, familiar or similar to you?
What biases are most likely to trigger an adverse response?	What are the known risks and outcomes? What is unknown?	What biases might they be subject to? Are they in the ingroup or the outgroup?

By interrupting a colleague, patient, investor or customer, you have more time to reflect. Unless, of course, they interrupt you first! Decision friction significantly augments the probability of a U-turn.

Embrace U-turns

Wharton professor Adam Grant rightly argues it's shrewd to rethink existing ideas.[18] That often means going against the crowd – and possibly, yourself. This tactic might feel obvious, yet we don't always do what's obvious. If British rail companies and United Auto Workers had listened to employees or Hollywood had heard screenwriters' concerns, strikes could have been avoided.

In effect, Grant advocates a mind-flip about mind-flipping.

Instead of stigmatising opinion reversal, rethinking should be applauded. Grant recommends building a challenger network, described as "a group of disagreeable people we trust to point out our blind spots." For some, that's your partner, husband or wife. "They give the critical feedback we might not want to hear but need to hear." Their role is to prompt doubt and bend beliefs like a pliable paper clip.

Take a moment. Write down the names of two or three experienced leaders in your challenger network to appoint as allies.

Adopt a third ear

Freud's student Theodor Reik advocates we listen with a third ear – metaphorically speaking.[19] Rather than accepting the idol, boss or expert's voice as gospel, you can pose an open-ended query with one word: "Really?"

That single word communicates being curious but not convinced. And it's non-confrontational so elicits what others don't know as much as what they do.

This judgement-enhancing method was available to employees at WeWork, FTX, Wells Fargo, RBS and Theranos. Unfortunately, many chose not to utilise it. This simple word is an invitation to hear new data while respecting others' positions and guarding against a hostile response.

These various interruption-based strategies lay the foundation for the Decision Ninja to filter and recalibrate situations, strangers, stories and strategies.

C: CALIBRATE SITUATIONS, STRANGERS AND STRATEGIES

When tuning in to messages in a chatter-filled world, recalibration of what you hear can be achieved with three behaviourally informed tools: the *PERIMETERS bias checklist*, the *interpretation habit* and *implementation intentions*.

The PERIMETERS bias checklist

As thinking is exhausting, consulting the ready-made PERIMETERS bias checklist will simplify decisions at vulnerable moments. This look-up list is available on the website www.nualagwalsh.com and synthesises the 75+ biases, fallacies and effects covered in this book. It's a go-to reference for any situation and assumes a default to error.

Complementing the SONIC interruption questions, ask yourself which category of PERIMETERS trap and associated bias is guiding the voices you selectively hear – conscience, criticism or the crowd; hope, hype or history? Maybe it's idols, braggers or experts? Remember the spectrum of voices heard and unheard?

Checklists are used in complex environments when processes are repetitive or multi-stage. Creating these lists requires collaboration which, in turn, fosters shared responsibility. Investor Charlie Munger believed checklists protect revenue, accountability and productivity.

> I'm a great believer in solving hard problems by using a checklist. You need to get all the likely and unlikely answers before you; otherwise, it's easy to miss something important.[20]

Behaviour is too complex for simple or single solutions. Checklists are valuable, but mistakes happen when people don't follow them, like at Zeebrugge, Tenerife, Chernobyl and multiple manufacturing plants.

Checklists are more risk-reduction than cast-iron guarantee. This makes bias-checking a sensible habit for the aspiring Decision Ninja who is keen to preserve reputation, side-track error and boost performance.

The interpretation habit

When facing a high-stakes scenario, you can introduce decision friction by simply hesitating. It's the mental speed bump. Best-selling *Atomic Habits* author James Clear recommends tiny habitual changes to produce big results.[21]

For maximum decision effectiveness, practise pausing, probing, reflecting or fact-checking. Covid-19 taught us how quickly new habits form. Think pandemic-inspired shopping consumption, fitness tracking, content streaming and remote working.

We are already familiar with automated habits and know they simplify life in everything from online grocery orders to direct debits.

Then create rules like "I'll always consult the checklist" noting the relevant conditions for your situation. For example, you might consult it in certain scenarios:

- "when a decision affects me financially."
- "when a decision affects another's welfare or happiness."
- "when my reputation, or that of my organisation, is at stake."
- "when I'm stressed, pressured, panicked or unsure what to do."

You decide your rules and conditions. When bias-checking and interpretation is habitualised, inattentional deafness and error risks dissipate. You're more likely to redefine the rat race on your own terms.

Timing also matters.

In *How to Change*, Katy Milkman suggests capitalising on key life moments like births, deaths, anniversaries or new seasons. This mental reset triggers new habits that motivate us, like New Year's resolutions. She coins it the *fresh start effect*.[22]

Once you make the commitment to be a Decision Ninja and think like a 12th juror, managing new habit creation in bite-sized chunks with concrete plans makes the change feel feasible and less daunting. You feel more confident and in control.

Implementation intentions

The final tool in this arsenal to avoid judgement killers is an *implementation intention*, an established psychological technique to overcome low willpower. It's an 'if–then' plan that addresses those stubborn *behaviour-intention gaps* from dieting to shed clearing. You want to be successful as a Decision Ninja but, like most people, you're too busy to start.

Peter Gollwitzer and Paschal Sheeran found that certain hacks turn goals into action, from appointment-keeping to voting.[23] Voting is as much about habit as civic duty and precedent. When voters were asked if they expected to vote, the specific prompt "When will you vote?" rather than "Will you vote?" increased probability by 25%.[24] In the 2008 US presidential elections, planning questions increased voting likelihood by 4.1%.[25]

Pre-planning has been shown to improve smoking cessation, exercise, recycling and appointment-keeping.[26] Pre-commitment works because it triggers consistency bias. It also avoids explicit instruction which often causes unwanted psychological reactance.

We can apply implementation intentions to bias-checking in four steps. Initially, articulate your intention to develop a bias-checking habit or become a Decision Ninja then develop a plan of what, when, where and how:

What: confirm intention: "Consult the PERIMETERS checklist in high-stakes situations."
When: "I'm unsure about a decision."
Where: "In my office, garden or car."
How: "I'll print it, post it and reference favourite chapters."

Bonus insight! If you add the word "because" to your plan, commitment strengthens further.[27]

Why: "Because I want to live my best life and avoid regret."

For overwhelmed and flustered decision-makers, it's not enough to remind them about the need for reflection. That's why implementation intentions make the action feel real and current. They reduce stress and bring the future closer to today, addressing present bias and status quo bias. It's how I finally got my shed cleared!

All of these SONIC recalibration strategies assume a commitment to think deliberatively and prevent predictable error. That commitment marks the transformation to Decision Ninja.

AMPLIFYING YOUR SONIC INTELLIGENCE

Again, neuroplasticity, or the brain's ability to rewire, gives us hope. Expectations are self-fulfilling – that's great news for the Decision Ninja!

If you expect great outcomes, you increase the probability of delivery.

In *The Expectation Effect*, David Robson powerfully underscores the power of expectations. "There is very little reason to be pessimistic about our capacity for self-transformation."[28]

If you can prime yourself to think better, you can prime others to do better.

If you tell yourself you're a smart listener, interpreter, problem-solver or great judge of character, we know from the power of suggestion and mere repetition effect that you'll believe it – and become it!

If you tell yourself you're like a 12th juror, you'll feel more social and moral responsibility to slow down a premature rush to judgement.

Listening selectively means dialling into the most relevant radio station. You can't hear all voices at the same time. Listening and interpreting communications intentionally is a 21st century skill. The SONIC strategies menu can be applied individually or in a bundle, as it suits the situation.

There's no silver bullet or perfect judgement, but decisions can always be better. Even mild effort will pay off and boost sonic intelligence. The trick is to start small. Even a 1% differential would save time, effort and money.

Throughout this book, many characters have faced high-stakes judgement calls. Long-distance runners make critical judgements under pressure – when to break away, what is the precise moment on the track, how to outpace rivals. Hundredths of seconds make the difference between Olympic gold or bronze.

Business leaders, surgeons, therapists, lawyers, military generals, child protection services, police, pilots and astronauts must cope in the moment – and make the right call.

On the Gemini 10 flight, Michael Collins and the crew faced unchartered challenges in the command module. Collins struggled to distinguish where exactly the perimeter of the Earth was delineated from the stars. In order to navigate safe re-entry to Earth, accurate geo-coordinates were crucial. As well as affecting lives, his decision affected future space travel.

Co-pilot John Young simply said, "Just do your best."

That's all anyone can do as we try to make a difference, not just for ourselves but for those in our care.

It's enough.

CHAPTER 15

IN TUNE: THE DECISION NINJA

> *"If you know the enemy and know yourself, you need not fear the result of a hundred battles.*
>
> *If you know yourself but not the enemy, for every victory gained you will also suffer a defeat.*
>
> *If you know neither the enemy nor yourself, you will succumb in every battle."*
>
> **Sun Tzu**

SEVERAL YEARS AGO, Irish TV networks released a mini-series called *Amber* about a schoolgirl who went missing. Viewers recognised the familiar Dublin streets on her last-known journey, from Dundrum to Dun Laoghaire. She never returned home. Amber's grief-stricken parents were filled with self-reproach and frustration. What could they have done differently? And what happened?

The final scene depicts Amber walking down a lonely road followed by a white van. Finally, the answer, viewers thought.

No. That was the end.

Outrage lit up switchboards and social media. Aghast viewers were left hanging. Yet I think the ending was brilliant. Each explanation-hunting viewer could identify with the parents' agony. For a moment, we were every tortured parent, relative and frustrated investigator of a missing child – Stephen Stayner, Jaycee Lee Dugard and Madeleine McCann.

What happened?

Every day, policymakers, politicians, prisoners, plumbers and parents seek explanations for life's decisions and unexpected events. We want happy endings. It's why the comeback kid is romanticised in comics, sports and movies. It's why we cheer Eddie the Eagle to success against the odds.

We want to know that Termaine Hicks secured his place at Yale, that Elizabeth Kendall found a loving relationship and Adi Dassler reconciled with brother Rudi on his deathbed. We want to be a life-changing 12th juror.

Now you can.

I hope this book has shown you how.

᛫᛫᛫|᛫|᛫|᛫|᛫|᛫

The examples in this book remind us that not all decisions have *Pollyanna* endings. Some remain unknown, like those of Amber, Jon Benet Ramsey and flight MH370.

Sometimes, well-meaning parents tune in to the wrong voices, like the Stayners, Felicity Huffman or Juan Rodriguez. Some take depravity to extremes, like Josef Mengele and Jerry Sandusky.

We know how innocent children pay the price like Jaycee Lee Dugard, Stephen Stayner and Holly Ramona. As did the victims of Cary Stayner, Ted Bundy, John Wayne Gacy, Jimmy Savile and Jim Jones.

Context drives some children to succumb to evil. The Menéndez brothers slaughtered their wealthy parents. Jaylen Fryberg shot his classmates over lunch. British teenagers left two-year-old James Bulger to die on a train track. I use outliers to make a point. Clearly, the majority of parents make healthy decisions and raise well-functioning children.

Ambitious ladder-climbers, Anna Sorokin and rogue trader Jérôme Kerviel made choices in a noxious climate that amplified the wrong voices. These traps play out every day.

When romantic partners feel jealous, most sulk. Others wreak revenge like OJ Simpson or Betty Broderick.

Even A-listers like Elvis Presley and Michael Jackson tuned out reality when it mattered. Just like millions of ordinary individuals, risk-averse Hollywood actors overpay insurance premiums for low-risk probabilities.

Why? Context and cognition lethally combine in the PERIMETERS Effect.

When policymakers tune out, human error produces needless fatalities and damage at scale. The second-order leadership repercussions of Elf Aquitaine, Société Générale, RBS, WeWork, BP and Yahoo translate into mass redundancy, less disposable income and permanent psychological effects. Recall the victims of Grenfell, Theranos, the British Post Office, the Catholic Church, Madoff, Purdue Pharma, FTX and many more.

At a national level, economies have been destroyed in Germany, Northern Ireland, Rwanda and elsewhere. Tuning out critical voices continues in the Middle East, China and Russia. Although uncomfortable, we must focus on the destructive impact of tuning out to appreciate the power of tuning in.

THE 12TH JUROR AS HAPPINESS SUPERSPREADER

Unmanaged, the trilogy of error can become a trilogy of terror.

Each unmanaged PERIMETERS trap sends decision-makers astray.

Although we can no longer hear the voices of Derek Bentley, Alex Kearns or Kobe Bryant, we can take inspiration from the courage of whistleblowers and the wrongfully convicted voices of Fred Clay, Julia Rea, and many others. Moreover, we can learn from each.

Let's revisit how the PERIMETERS Effect pervades the wrongfully convicted. Each stood against a *powerful* justice system, their *ego* shattered, facing the *risk* of the death penalty.

Each earned a criminal *identity* as cruel *memory* burnished, wronged by the *unethical* behaviour of self-interested wrongdoers.

Serving *time*, each learned patience, managing *emotional* rage and accepting injustice which resulted from a collective crowd and condemned *relationships*. These victims tell their *story*. The difference is, now they're heard.

To survive, some tuned in to the voice of religion, Lady Justice or themselves. Living their best life is now about making every second count. They chose resolution over retribution in toxic circumstances.

Julia Rea puts it well:

When I was in solitary confinement, I was captivated by a stem of clover that looked like a bouquet of cala lilies. I learned how important gratitude is to joy. I lost everything I own more than once. I have a quiet joy now that gives me strength. In our current culture, we need this – it's the gift of grace that I cherish.[1]

Learning from history neutralises error. First German chancellor Otto Von Bismarck said, "Only a fool learns from his own mistakes. The wise man learns from the mistakes of others." Investment titan Warren Buffett agrees. He kept a checklist of others' mistakes and is now worth $106.2bn. That's learning!

In the words of Richard Feynman: "You keep on learning and learning, and pretty soon you learn something no one has learned before."

In a noisy world, biased judgement can be detected with conscious effort and marginal deliberation. Being more sensitised to reinterpreting what's said differentiates powerholders from non-powerholders.

You can even learn from nature. While we share an evolutionary history with the animal kingdom, different species communicate at different frequencies to humans, and many hear better. For example, a household kitten can detect a pitch up to 64,000hz while human hearing ranges from 20hz to 20,000hz, and a bat hears ten times more than you!

Naturally, humans have the intellectual capacity to convert their capabilities!

What's more, an aural revolution has begun that upgrades this listening skillset. Noise-cancelling headphones marked the start, literally shutting out the daily din. Audio-based social network Clubhouse exploded during the pandemic, with ten million weekly listeners, each reflecting a human need to be heard. Listening devices and smart speakers like Alexa, Siri, audiobooks, Apple HomePod and Spotify are integrated into our daily lives, representing multi-million-dollar industries.

And podcasts are de rigueur. People now listen to over two million podcasts in 100+ languages – 68% tune in to the whole episode. It's a medium that facilitates concentration and connection. Most tune in very selectively, specifically to learn.

It's no coincidence that, as stakeholders feel less heard and activism is rising, government, media and business became less trusted. But opportunity exists to be a happiness superspreader through good judgement, combining sonic intelligence with emotional intelligence

IN TUNE: THE SOUND OF SUCCESS

The benefits of tuning in appropriate voices aren't in doubt. Some examples in this book will always be a source of inspiration, others a cautionary tale.

Whereas journalists Veronica Guerin, Kathy Scruggs and Jamal Khashoggi miscalculated their decision context, John Ware, John Carreyrou and Charles Duhigg dug up every buried assumption to disclose the truth.

Whereas law enforcement didn't listen to George Floyd, Ally Jacobs listened to doubt, freeing an abducted child after 18 years' captivity.

Whereas pilots Ara Zobayan and Jacob van Zanten misheard or miscommunicated instructions, Chesley Sullenberger relied on the voice of experience to save 155 lives.

Whereas business and political leaders like David Coulter, Tony Hayward, Liz Truss, Tony Blair and Alan Greenspan tuned out uncomfortable truth when it mattered, others did the opposite. James Comey, Marcus Rashford, Bob Geldof and Ervin Staub tuned into the voice of conscience to improve lives for millions of underprivileged people.

Larry Fink, Vera Wang and John McEnroe tuned into their inner voices to reinvent a better future.

In contrast to self-silencing jurors, we saw how whistleblowers Harry Markopolos, Tyler Shultz, Roger Boisjoly, Ed Pierson, and Peng Shuai spoke up when it mattered.

We witnessed how Ren Zhiqiang, Judge Hiller Zobel and Sinéad O'Connor used their voices to try to right wrongdoing. And Elizabeth Kendall, Ann Rule and Trevor Birdsall made the tortured decision to report friends and family to police.

Whereas FBI agents missed signals for Waco, 9/11 and numerous school shootings, negotiators like Chris Voss talked hostage-takers off the ledge. Jeff Rinek devoted his professional career to finding murdered and missing children like Stephen Stayner or Jaycee Lee Duggard and fictional Amber. The echoes of those they saved – and those they couldn't – never go away.

Many used their voice to improve the hand dealt. Is a situation good or bad? The old farmer thinks it's hard to say! But people find a way. As McEnroe says, life is like a game of tennis, sometimes you win and sometimes you lose.

Take your best shot and keep finding the courage to step on the court… The questions you have to answer are: 'Am I getting better as a person?' and 'Is what I'm doing bringing me and the ones around me happiness?' The answers will tell you whether or not you're really winning.[2]

You can change how you think to live your best life. We learn from those who tuned in only to tune out and turn situations around. Oskar Schindler profiteered then saved hundreds from the gas chamber. Tim Stoen tuned in to Jones's promises before reappraising them. Tina Turner tuned in to an abusive husband before finding her power, as did Priscilla Presley in leaving hers.

Not all won.

Sinéad O'Connor was trapped by the voice of an abusive past and spent a lifetime wanting to be heard. At one stage, she even released a poignant track called 'Thank you for hearing me.' Today, she is buried in the same cemetery close to my grandmother, an influential voice in my own life.

Recall the wonders of focused listening or Kim Peek's remarkable memory. Applaud the Chilean rescuers who listened to save trapped miners.

Those who stand out professionally use behavioural insight as a route to exceptional judgement. The intelligent decision-maker understands themselves better than they understand their products, patients, clients or markets.

Most people want to do the right thing, preventing mistakes to reward those they care about, and those in their care. Understanding how misinformation becomes a judgement killer reduces this risk.

Without realising it, you're already a 12th juror who makes a difference to others' lives. Unconsciously, you prevent predictable error every day.

Now it's about doing it consciously.

It's easy to be the boiling frog that doesn't notice incremental danger.

Good judgement is unlikely if you speed through red lights in the fast lane. The best drivers follow green lights, balancing speed with alertness, scouting for risk yet processing the sound of trucks, horns and lashing rain. They regard the SONIC strategies as speed bumps of the mind.

The good news is decision reward is yours to attain with enhanced cue detection, intentional interpretation and intelligent listening.

If you routinely embrace decision friction, you'll secure those extra seconds of reflection to choose the *right* voice, not the first voice, the loudest voice, the most convenient, senior, famous or familiar voice.

You'll neutralise the judgement killers that needlessly wreak havoc, squandering time, money and lives. You'll be more likely to optimise your personal influence and professional impact, more likely to make smarter choices and be a happiness superspreader.

Ultimately, when you tune in, you win. Moreover, tuning in means you stand out rather than miss out, lose out or get left out.

A FINAL THOUGHT: PERIMETER PERSPECTIVES

The Apollo 11 crew were fortunate to experience a truly lateral perspective. At 240,000 miles from Earth, they had the broadest possible view of mankind. And yet their visual senses could still be distorted by lunar cycles and sun shadows.

On the moon, their auditory senses were heightened in atmospheric silence. Knowing delusions and illusions were possible, they relied on science and their senses; they relied on what they saw, what they heard and what they spoke. Their ability to interpret and decipher Houston's instructions was paramount. To get home safely, they relied not just on their judgement but on the voices of their distant colleagues.

Neil Armstrong inspired generations, not just because of the lunar landing but because of his humility in appreciating that it took a village to accomplish it – with thousands in a supporting cast.

Countless leaps are possible by understanding human behaviour. One small step on this path can translate into a giant leap towards better lives for individuals, organisations and society.

From the moon, astronauts visualised the impression of everything terrestrial, from the Jonestown jungle to the gates of Graceland.

What if the Graceland residents had glanced at the moon a little more often? What if they had stretched their perspective beyond the perimeters? Might outcomes have been different? I think so.

Elvis Presley inspired millions of people yet short-changed his life. Every time you hear his haunting voice, I hope you might remember the risks and rewards, regret and relief of the decisions we make – or don't make.

As a Decision Ninja, in your personal and professional

context, you have the power to write your own story and construct the best possible ending. It's free, and sometimes, takes only seconds.

By hearing others, those who hold power and influence have the opportunity to heal a divided world, calm conflict and alleviate senseless violence. Those who tune in consciously and strategically will literally make the world a better place.

I hope the perimeters of your worldview are broadened a little more with this book. I hope you next tune in to what matters and hear things that others don't.

Above all, I hope that others hear your voice and you achieve what matters most to you.

Thank you for tuning in.

ACKNOWLEDGEMENTS

A s WRITING IS a solitary sport, I was only able to write this book with the invaluable support and encouragement of others.

With deep gratitude to my tuned-in husband for a list of plaudits too numerous to mention. Similarly, my warrior mother was on every step of this journey – and every other. I hope I have done her proud. The voices of my beloved grandparents were silent, but their echoes ever present. To Jacqueline Walsh, Louise O'Reilly, Joan Fitzpatrick, and Emma Hinchey, we are different voices but always in tune. Thank you for everything.

In a ruthless industry, my highly talented editors Craig Pearce and Nick Fletcher are a rare professional delight, supported by the excellent Harriman House team, notably Elena Jones and Chris Parker. Nothing was too much trouble, even when it was!

At Jericho Writers, Sharon Zink and Diana Collis provided invaluable comments and encouragement on early manuscripts.

I am hugely grateful to those who supported this book. Each will be immortalised as part of its fabric: Dr Robert Cialdini, Lord Sebastian Coe, Dr Daniel Crosby, Tracy Davidson, Victoria Degtar, Adam Grant, Debbie Hewitt MBE, Dr Dario Krpan, Steve Martin, Paul McGinley, Melina Palmer, Jeffrey Rinek, Dame Robina Shah DBE, Allyson Stewart-Allen and Rory Sutherland.

The foundations of *Tune In* lie with Harvard's Professor Jennifer Lerner and the London School of Economics' renowned Department of Psychology and Behavioural Science.

I am indebted to each, especially the class of 2020. Moreover, I fully acknowledge the 500+ experts whose lifetime's works are referenced here.

To the individuals whose judgements are explored, no one stands on any moral pulpit as one day, it could be any of us – and likely will be. Your stories matter.

The decades of professional experiences shared with former colleagues and friends at PA Consulting, Merrill Lynch, BlackRock and Standard Life Investments contributed in no small way. Current MindEquity clients, board members and colleagues at The British & Irish Lions, Football Association, GAABS, World Athletics, Innocence Project, Basketball Ireland, CISI, Diversifi, UN Women and the Harvard Club of Ireland; you remind me about the decisions that matter – and the power of those who make them.

To those who tuned in at crucible life moments, thank you Quentin Price, Corinne Wiltshire, Paul Elliott, William Devine, Ralph Egan, Gerard Doyle, Willie and Emma O'Connor, and Baroness Margaret McDonogh.

Ger, Phillip, Sean, Phil, Breffni, Niamh, Nate, Ann, Rob, Marie, Paula and Martin – your voices reverberate far longer than you may think.

To Daire, Ciaran, Lauren, Shannon, Myles, Grace, Niall, Emily, Hannah, Evan, Rory, Fiona and Ciara, consider this my most valuable legacy to each of you. If you don't hear me, now you can read me! To all the younger clan, may this direct your path.

To Lisa Greene, thank you for decades of friendship. Elaine Connolly, Aedin Cooke, Brian Egan, Justin Edge and Vanessa Griffin, thank you for the voice of perspective when it mattered.

During this process, I learned that being an author isn't easy. I acquired a profound respect for anyone holding that title. To my sister who asked how I would define success, the answer is simple. Firstly, it's completion of a book that tells the stories that moved me, knowing some warranted entire books of their own. Secondly, it's acceptance that nothing is perfect, but it's as perfect as you can make it – and that's enough. Thirdly, it's the hope that those closest to me avoid each of these predictable errors.

And especially thanks to you the reader. No one has the monopoly on sound judgement. I would very much like to hear your voice and can be reached at nuala.g.walsh@gmail.com.

·ıı||ı·|ıı|ı·||ı·

As any errors are entirely mine, please reach out for correction in future editions.

If you're interested in more resources on this topic, visit www. nualagwalsh.com where you can:

- download the *PERIMETERS* Checklist and other tools
- take the *'PERIMETERS traps'* test
- find 100+ of my published articles.

Thank you for tuning in.

NOTES

Preface

1 Hemingway, E. (1998). *Across the River and Into the Trees* (Vol. 2425). Simon and Schuster.

Introduction

1 Clarke Keogh, P. (2004). *Elvis Presley: The Man, the Life, the Legend.* Simon & Schuster.

2 Ibid.

3 All Top Everything (2019). "The Best-Selling Solo Music Artists of All Time."

4 Guralnick, P. (2014). *Careless Love: The Unmaking of Elvis Presley.* Little, Brown and Company.

5 Connolly, R. (2017). *Being Elvis: A Lonely Life.* Liveright Publishing.

6 Elvis Presley News. Quotes from Elvis Presley. www.elvispresleynews.com/quotes-from-elvis/

7 Connolly, R. (2017). *Being Elvis: A Lonely Life.* Liveright Publishing.

8 Clarke Keogh, P. (2004). *Elvis Presley: The Man, the Life, the Legend.* Simon & Schuster.

9 Ibid.

10 *Elvis by the Presleys.* (2005). Edited by David Ritz, Random House.

11 O'Connor, S. (2021). *Rememberings.* Houghton Mifflin.

12 McEnroe, J. (2023). Stanford Commencement Speech, www.youtube.com/watch?v=wzhsT3ojyz0

13 Ibid.

14 Union Avenue 706 (2012). "Elvis Is Everywhere: Springsteen's

Darkness on the Edge of Town and The Promise." 12 August, unionavenue706.com/2012/08/12/springsteens-darkness-and-the-promise-elvis-everywhere

15 Schilling, J. & Crisafulli, C. (2007). *Me and a Guy Named Elvis: My Lifelong Friendship with Elvis Presley.* Penguin.

16 Ibid.

17 National Highway Traffic Safety Administration (2015). "Critical Reasons for Crashes Investigated in the National Motor Vehicle Crash Causation Survey," US Data, February, crashstats.nhtsa.dot.gov/Api/Public/ViewPublication/812115

18 Rankin, W. (2007). "MEDA Investigation Process." Boeing.com magazine, Issue Q2, www.boeing.com/commercial/aeromagazine/articles/qtr_2_07/AERO_Q207_article3.pdf

19 Mortality in the US (2021). www.cdc.gov/nchs/products/databriefs/db456.htm

20 McKinsey (2019). "Decision making in the age of urgency." 30 April.

21 Botelho, E. L., Powell, K. R., Kincaid, S. & Wang, D. (2017). "What sets successful CEOs apart." *Harvard Business Review*, 95(3), 70–77.

Chapter 1: Mishearing, Misinformation & Misjudgement

1 Cited in Conan Doyle, A. (2020). *The Boscombe Valley Mystery.* Lindhardt og Ringhof.

2 Association of Certified Fraud Examiners (2022). "Occupational Fraud 2022: A Report to the Nations," legacy.acfe.com/report-to-the-nations/2022.

3 Lynch, D. (2023). "In 2005 I woke to a flurry of texts from Sinéad asking me to follow her to Jamaica... What followed was part odyssey, part superfan lottery win." *Irish Independent*, 30 July.

4 Carluccio, J., Eizenman, O. & Rothschild, P. (2021). "Next in loyalty: Eight levers to turn customers into fans." McKinsey, 12 October.

5 Fitzgerald, M. (2021). "Robinhood sued by family of 20-year-old trader who killed himself after believing he racked up huge losses." CNBC.com, 8 February.

6 Klebnikov, S. (2020). "20-year-old Robinhood Customer Dies by Suicide After Seeing a $730,000 Negative Balance." *Forbes*, 17 June.

7 Farnham Street (2023). "The OODA Loop: How Fighter Pilots Make Fast and Accurate Decisions." www.fs.blog.com

8 Botelho, E. L., Powell, K. R., Kincaid, S. & Wang, D. (2017). "What sets successful CEOs apart." *Harvard Business Review*, 95(3), 70–77.

9 Kahneman, D. (2011). *Thinking, Fast and Slow*. Macmillan.

10 Lee, D., Barak, A. & Uhlemann, M. (1999). Forming clinical impressions during the first five minutes of the counselling interview. *Psychological Reports*, 85(3), 835–844.

11 Myers, S. (2014). "The Shortening of Movies." *Medium*, 14 October.

12 Wordsrated (2022). "Bestselling books have never been shorter." 20 June.

13 Davies, N. (1981). "The Wasted Suspicions of Sutcliffe's Friends." *The Guardian*, 8 May.

14 Evans, R. & Campbell, D. (2006). "Ripper Guilty of Additional Crimes, Says Secret Report." *The Guardian*, 2 June.

15 The Byford Report (1981). www.gov.uk/government/publications/ sir-lawrence-byford-report-into-the-police-handling-of-the-yorkshire-ripper-case

16 Microsoft (2023). "Work Trend Index Annual Report. Will AI Fix Work?" 9 May, www.microsoft.com/en-us/worklab/work-trend-index/will-ai-fix-work

17 Sullivan, B. & Thompson, H. (2013). "Brain, Interrupted." *New York Times*, 3 May.

18 Silver, N. (2012). *The Signal and The Noise: The Art and Science of Prediction*. Penguin.

19 Slovic, P. (1973). Behavioral problems of adhering to a decision policy. Paper presented at the Institute for Quantitative Research in Finance, Napa, California, 1 May.

20 Tsai, C, Klayman, J. & Hastie, R. (2008). Effects of amount of information on judgment accuracy and confidence. *Organizational Behavior and Human Decision Processes*, 107(2), 97–105.

21 Kato, H., Jena, A. B. & Tsugawa, Y. (2020). Patient mortality after surgery on the surgeon's birthday: observational study, *BMJ*, 371(m4381).

22 Yousif, N. & Halpert, M. (2023). "Alec Baldwin Charged with Involuntary Manslaughter in Rust Shooting." BBC News, 31 January.

23 King's College London (2022). "Do we have your attention? How people focus and live in the modern information environment." The Policy Institute, February Issue.

24 Lehmann, S. (2017). The dynamics of attention networks in social media. *Journal of Complex Networks*, 5(1), 96–123.

25 Hunt, E. (2023). "Is Modern Life Ruing Our Powers of Concentration." *The Guardian*, 1 January.

26 Ibid.

27 Hari, J. (2022). *Stolen Focus: Why You Can't Pay Attention*. Bloomsbury Publishing.

28 Weingarten, G. (2007). "Pearls Before Breakfast: Can one of the nation's great musicians cut through the fog of a D.C. rush hour? Let's find out." *Washington Post*, 8 April.

29 Vedantam, S. & Mesler, B. (2021). *Useful Delusions: The Power and Paradox of the Self-Deceiving Brain*. Norton & Company.

30 Keller, E. & Fay, B. (2012). *The Face-to-Face Book: Why Real Relationships Rule in a Digital Marketplace*. Simon and Schuster. Detailed further in "Comparing Online and Offline Word of Mouth."

31 Harford, T. (2013). "Lies, Damned Lies and Greek Statistics." *Financial Times*, 25 January.

32 Aggarwal, P., Brandon, A., Goldszmidt, A., Holz, J., List, J. A., Muir, I., Sun, G. & Yu, T. (2022). High-frequency location data shows that race affects the likelihood of being stopped and fined for speeding. University of Chicago, Becker Friedman Institute for Economics Working Paper.

33 Collins, M. (2001). *Carrying the Fire: An Astronaut's Journey*. Rowman & Littlefield.

34 Levie, W. H. & Lentz, R. (1982). Effects of text illustrations: A review of research. *ECTJ*, 30(4), 195–232.

35 Potter, M. (2014). Detecting and remembering briefly presented pictures. In K. Kveraga & M. Bar (Eds.), *Scene Vision* (pp. 177–197). MIT Press, Cambridge, MA.

36 CBS News (2022). "Liz Truss gives first speech as Britain's prime minister." 6 September, www.youtube.com/watch?v=_KlyCeVIlYw

37 Taylor, H. (2022). "Kwasi Kwarteng says he and Liz Truss 'got carried away' writing mini-budget and 'blew it'." *Irish Times*, 12 October.

38 Parker, G., Payne, S. & Hughes, L. (2022), "The Inside Story of Liz Truss's Disastrous 44 Days in Office." *Financial Times*, 9 December.

39 Hunt, E. (2023). "Is Modern Life Ruining Our Powers of Concentration." *The Guardian*, 1 January.

40 Shotton, R. (2014). "Fast and Slow Lessons." *The Guardian*, 7 April.

41 Wilson, T. D., Reinhard, D. A., Westgate, E. C., Gilbert, D. T., Ellerbeck, N., Hahn, C., Brown, C. & Shaked, A. (2014). Just think: The challenges of the disengaged mind. *Science*, 345(6192), 75–77.

42 Killingsworth, M. & Gilbert, D. (2010). A wandering mind is an unhappy mind. *Science*, 330(6006), 932–932.

43 Husman, R. C., Lahiff, J. M. & Penrose, J. M. (1988). *Business Communication: Strategies and Skills*. Dryden Press, Chicago.

44 Rowe, M. B. (1986). Wait time: Slowing down may be a way of speeding up! *Journal of Teacher Education*, 37(1), 43–50.

Chapter 2: Judgement Killers

1 Markopolos Testimony (2009). Public Documents. *Wall Street Journal*, 3 February. www.wsj.com/public/resources/documents/MarkopolosTestimony20090203.pdf

2 Clark, A. (2010). "The Man Who Blew the Whistle on Bernard Madoff." *The Guardian*, 24 March.

3 Lovitt, B. (2006). "Beyond Gypsy Blancharde: When Mothers Harm Their Kids for Attention." *Rolling Stone*, 25 February.

4 Markopolos Testimony (2009). Public Documents. *Wall Street Journal*, 3 February. www.wsj.com/public/resources/documents/MarkopolosTestimony20090203.pdf

5 Pernar, M. (2019). "Lecture: Ethics: mine, ours, theirs." *Group Analytic Contexts*, Winter Issue.

6 Finn, N (2019). "Inside the Short, Tragic Life of Nicole Brown Simpson and Her Hopeful Final Days." ENews, 12 June, https://www.eonline.com/news/1048564/inside-the-short-tragic-life-of-nicole-brown-simpson-and-her-hopeful-final-days

7 Frammolino, R. & Newton, J. (1995). "Details Emerge of Close LAPD Ties to Simpson." *Los Angeles Times*, 2 February.

8   American Psychological Association (2023). Dictionary, dictionary. apa.org/blind-spot

9   Shepherd, K. (2020). "Philadelphia police shot a man and accused him of rape. After 19 years in prison, he's been found innocent." *Washington Post*, 17 December.

10 Pronin, E. (2008). How we see ourselves and how we see others. *Science*, 320(5880): 1177–1180.

11 Thaler, R. H. (2015). *Misbehaving: The Making of Behavioural Economics*. Norton & Company.

12 Pronin, E., Lin, D. Y. & Ross, L. (2002). The bias blind spot: Perceptions of bias in self versus others. *Personality and Social Psychology Bulletin*, 28(3), 369–381.

13 Kukucka, J., Kassin, S. M., Zapf, P. A. & Dror, I. E. (2017). Cognitive bias and blindness: A global survey of forensic science examiners. *Journal of Applied Research in Memory and Cognition*, 6(4), 452.

14 Marriage, M. (2021). "KPMG UK Chairman Told Staff to 'Stop Moaning' About Work Conditions." *Financial Times*, 9 February.

15 Kahneman, D. (2011). *Thinking, Fast and Slow*. Macmillan.

16 Simons, D. & Chabris, C. (1999). Gorillas in our midst: Sustained inattentional blindness for dynamic events. *Perception*, 28(9), 1059–1074.

17 Kaponya, P. (1991). *The Human Resource Professional: Tactics and Strategies for Career Success*. Greenwood Publishing Group.

18 Merckelbach, H. & van de Ven, V. (2001). Another White Christmas: fantasy proneness and reports of 'hallucinatory experiences' in undergraduate students. *Journal of Behaviour Therapy and Experimental Psychiatry*, 32(3), 137–144.

19 Scheer M., Bülthoff H. & Chuang L. (2018). Auditory task irrelevance: a basis for inattentional deafness. *Human Factors*, 60(3), 428–440.

20 University College London (2015). "Why focusing on a visual task will make us deaf to our surroundings." 9 December, www.ucl.ac.uk/news/2015/dec/why-focusing-visual-task-will-make-us-deaf-our-surroundings

21 Singleton, G. (2016). "Akrasia: Why Do We Act Against Our Better Judgement?" *Philosophy Now*.

22 Dobbs, M. (1984). "Publication of French Scandal Report Grips Nation." *Washington Post*, 7 January.

23 Ariely, D. & Jones, S. (2012). *The Honest Truth About Dishonesty*, New York: Harper Collins.

24 Cohn, S. (2009). "Madoff: All SEC Did Before 2006 a 'Waste of Time'." CNBC, 2 November.

25 Restle, H. & Smith, J. (2015). "17 successful executives who have lied on their résumés." *Business Insider*, 15 July.

26 Rodrigues, J. (2016). "The 'Fake Sheikh's' top scoops: from Sophie Wessex to Sven's sexploits." *The Guardian*, 5 October.

27 Sawchuck, S. (2019). "Most School Shooters Showed Many Warning Signs, Secret Service Report Finds." *Education Week*, 7 November.

28 Kutner, M. (2015). "What Led Jaylen Fryberg to Commit the Deadliest High School Shooting in a Decade?" *Newsweek*, 16 September.

29 John Wayne Gacy: Devil in Disguise. (2021). A televised documentary.

30 Bond, C. & DePaulo, B. (2006). Accuracy of deception judgments. *Personality and Social Psychology Review*, 10(3), 214–234.

31 Death on The Staircase. (2004). A televised documentary.

32 Pietrantoni, G. (2017). Jury Deliberation. *The Review: A Journal of Undergraduate Student Research*, 18(1), 7.

33 Maloney, A. & Zeltmann, B. (2022). "Deep Regrets." *The Irish Sun*, 9 January.

34 Chen, L. (2016). "Mayer's role in Yahoo's decline." CEIBS, 10 October.

35 Mason R., Asthana A. & Stewart, H. (2006). "Tony Blair: 'I Express More Sorrow, Regret and Apology Than You Can Ever Believe.'" *The Guardian*, 6 July.

36 Hari, J. (2022). *Stolen Focus: Why You Can't Pay Attention*. Bloomsbury Publishing.

37 Evans, G. (2022). "Alex Jones Told to Pay $965m Damages to Sandy Hook Victims' Families." BBC News, 13 October.

38 Kramer, R. (1997). Leading by listening: An empirical test of Carl Rogers's theory of human relationship using interpersonal assessments of leaders by followers. Doctoral dissertation, George Washington University.

39 Dowd, M. (2013). "Why Did Pope Benedict XVI Resign?" BBC News, 28 November, www.bbc.com/news/magazine-25121121

40 McCarthy, C. (2023). "Lily Allen blasts 'spineless' tributes to Sinead O'Connor in furious social media posts." *Irish Mirror*, 31 July.

41 Walsh, N. (2021). "How to Encourage Employees to Speak Up When They See Wrongdoing." *Harvard Business Review*.

42 Moberly, R. E. (2007). Unfulfilled expectations: An empirical analysis of why Sarbanes-Oxley whistleblowers rarely win. *William & Mary Law Review*, 49(1).

43 Sinzdak, G. (2008). An analysis of current whistleblower laws: Defending a more flexible approach to reporting requirements. *California Law Review*, 96(6), 1633.

44 Witz, B. (2019). "Judge Overturns Conviction of Ex-Penn State President in Sandusky Case." *New York Times*, 30 April.

45 Douglass, F. (2019). "Frederick Douglass plea for freedom-of-speech in Boston." *Law & Liberty*, 21 August.

46 Mitchell, T. (2020). "Xi Jinping Critic Sentenced to 18 Years in Prison." *Financial Times*, 22 September.

47 Blake, H. (2023). "The Fugitive Princesses of Dubai." *The New Yorker*, 8 May.

48 Marsh, R. & Wallace, G. (2019). "Whistleblower testifies that Boeing ignored pleas to shut down 737 MAX production." CNN Politics, 11 December, https://edition.cnn.com/2019/12/11/politics/fatally-flawed-737-max-had-significantly-higher-crash-risk-faa-concluded/index.html

49 Varol, O. (2023). *Awaken Your Genius: Escape Conformity, Ignite Creativity, and Become Extraordinary*. PublicAffairs.

50 Williams, J. (2017). "Harvey Weinstein Accusers: Over 80 Women Now Claim Producer Sexually Assaulted or Harassed Them." *Newsweek*, 2 November.

51 BBC News. (2012). "Savile Abuse Part of Operation Yewtree Probe 'Complete'." 11 December.

Chapter 3: You Can't Trust All You Hear

1 Bogue, T. (2013). "'I want to go with you but they won't let me': Memories of My Friend Brian Davis." 14 November, https://jonestown.sdsu.edu/?page_id=34231

2   Bellefountaine, M. (2014). "Christine Miller: A Voice of Independence." 12 March, jonestown.sdsu.edu/?page_id=32381

3   Cited in Stoen, T. O. (2016). *Love Them to Death: At War with the Devil at Jonestown.*

4   Lord, C. G., Ross, L. & Lepper, M. R. (1979). Biased assimilation and attitude polarization: The effects of prior theories on subsequently considered evidence. *Journal of Personality and Social Psychology*, 37(11), 2098.

5   First appeared in Olson, M. (1965). *The Logic of Collective Action.* Harvard University Press.

6   Kunda, Z. (1990). The case for motivated reasoning. *Psychological Bulletin*, 108(3), 480.

7   Civelek, M. E., Aşçı, M. S. & Çemberci, M. (2015). Identifying silence climate in organizations in the framework of contemporary management approaches. *International Journal of Research in Business and Social Science*, 4(4).

8   Wiedeman, R. (2019). "The I in We." *New York Magazine*, Intelligencer, 10 June.

9   Ibid.

10 Brown, E. (2019). "How Adam Neumann's Over-the-Top Style Built WeWork. 'This Is Not the Way Everybody Behaves'." *Wall Street Journal*, 18 September.

11 Duhigg, C. (2020). "How Venture Capitalists are Deforming Capitalism." *The New Yorker*, 23 November.

12 Edgecliffe-Johnson, A. (2022). "WeWork's Adam Neumann on Investing, Startups, Surfing and Masayoshi Son." *Financial Times*, 10 March.

13 Feiner, L. (2020). "SoftBank values WeWork at $2.9 billion, down from $47 billion a year ago." CNBC, 18 May.

14 Reuters (2019). "SoftBank CEO Son says his judgment on WeWork was poor in many ways." 6 November.

15 The VC Factory. "I don't look for companies. I look for Founders." Masayoshi Son.

16 Cited in Robson, D. (2022). *The Expectation Effect: How Your Mindset Can Transform Your Life.* Canongate Books. p. 147.

17 Joseph, S. (2011). "Is Shell Shock the Same as PTSD?" *Psychology Today*, 20 November.

18 BBC Newsbeat (2019). "Simples, whatevs and Jedi added to Oxford English Dictionary." 15 October.

19 Motoring Reporter (2022). "New advert clarifies pronunciation of Hyundai name." 28 December.

20 Stewart-Allen, A. & Denslow, L. (2019). *Working with Americans: How to Build Profitable Business Relationships*. Routledge.

21 Naimushin, B. (2021). "Hiroshima, Mokusatsu and Alleged Mistranslations." *English Studies at NBU*, 7(1): 87–96.

22 Bazerman, M., Loewenstein G. & Moore, D. (2002). "Why Good Accountants Do Bad Audits." *Harvard Business Review*, November.

23 Mak, T. (2017). "Inside the CIA's Sadistic Dungeon." *The Daily Beast*, 12 July.

24 Ross, B. & Esposito, R. (2005). "CIA's Harsh Interrogation Techniques Described: Sources Say Agency's Tactics Lead to Questionable Confessions, Sometimes to Death." ABC News, 18 November.

25 Liptak, A. (2007). "Suspected Leader of 9/11 Is Said to Confess." *New York Times*, 15 March.

26 Megaw, N. (2023). "Investors use AI to glean the truth behind executives soothing words." *Financial Times*, 14 November.

27 Brown, G. & Peterson, R. S. (2022). *Disaster in the Boardroom*. Springer Books.

28 Long, C. (2022). "5 of the biggest product recalls." Yahoo Finance, 14 March.

29 Hall, J. R. (2016). "Review Essay: Tim Stoen, Peoples Temple, the Concerned Relatives, and Jonestown." 22 September, jonestown.sdsu.edu/?page_id=67307

Chapter 4: Power-Based Traps

1 The Asset (2020). "We Must Do Away with Pawnshop Mentality." The Asset.com, 13 November.

2 Yang, J. (2023) "Jack Ma Cedes Control of Fintech Giant Ant Group." *Wall Street Journal*, 7 January.

3 Gardner, J. W. (1993). *On Leadership*. New York Free Press.

4 McGee, S. (2016). "Wells Fargo's Toxic Culture Reveals Big Banks' Eight Deadly Sins." *The Guardian*, 22 September.

5   Henry, M. (2018). "Attorney General Shapiro Announces $575 Million 50-State Settlement with Wells Fargo Bank for Opening Unauthorized Accounts and Charging Consumers for Unnecessary Auto Insurance, Mortgage Fees." 28 December.

6   Prentice, C. & Lang, H. (2022). "Wells Fargo to pay $3.7 billion for illegal conduct that harmed customers." *Reuters*, 20 December.

7   SwissInfo (2016). "Documentary sheds light on Zurich CFO suicide." www.swissinfo.ch/eng/business/pierre-wauthier_documentary-sheds-light-on-zurich-cfo-suicide/42558070

8   Hofling, C., Brotzman, E., Dalrymple, S., Graves, N. & Pierce, C. M. (1966). An experimental study in nurse-physician relationships. *The Journal of Nervous and Mental Disease*, 143(2), 171–180.

9   Zimbardo, P. (2011). "The Lucifer Effect." *The Encyclopedia of Peace Psychology*.

10 Talbert, M. & Wolfendale, J. (2018). *War Crimes: Causes, Excuses, and Blame*. Oxford University Press.

11 Osiel, M. (2002). *Obeying Orders: Atrocity, War Crimes, and the Law of War*. Routledge.

12 Glenza, J. (2015). "Abuse of Teen Inmate at Rikers Island Prison Caught on Surveillance Cameras." *The Guardian*, 24 April.

13 Grant, A. (2021). *Think Again: The Power of Knowing What You Don't Know*. Penguin.

14 O'Connor, S. (2021). *Rememberings*. Houghton Mifflin.

15 Pew Research (1998.) "Popular Policies and Unpopular Press Lift Clinton Ratings." 6 February.

16 Preslaw (1981). Extracts, Complaint Filed by the Presley Estate Against Colonel Tom Parker.

17 Simpson, P. (2022). "The truth behind the mismanagement of Elvis." *Management Today*, 24 August.

18 Tetlock, P. (2005). *Expert Political Judgment: How Good Is It? How Can We Know?* (pp. 1-31). Princeton University Press.

19 Feller, E. (2019). "Why do doctors overprescribe antibiotics?" *Rhode Island Medical Journal*, 102(1), 9–10.

20 Kiser, R., Asher, M. & McShane, B. (2008). Let's Not Make a Deal: An Empirical Study of Decision Making in Unsuccessful Settlement Negotiations. *Journal of Empirical Legal Studies*, 551.

21 O'Neil, M. (2023). "Beware of Wealth Managers Quoting Data." *Financial Times*, 17 August.

22 Banai, I., Banai, B. & Bovan, K. (2017). Vocal characteristics of presidential candidates can predict the outcome of actual elections. *Evolution and Human Behaviour*, 38(3), 309–314.

23 Tigue, C., Borak, D., O'Connor, J., Schandl, C. & Feinberg, D. (2012). Voice pitch influences voting behavior. *Evolution and Human Behaviour*, 33(3), 210–216.

24 Tiedens, L. (2001). Anger and advancement versus sadness and subjugation: the effect of negative emotion expressions on social status conferral. *Journal of Personality and Social Psychology*, 80(1), 86.

25 Gavett, G. (2013). "What It's Like to Work for Jeff Bezos (Hint: He'll Probably Call You Stupid)." *Harvard Business Review*, October.

26 Grind, K. & Sayre. K. (2022). "The Rise and Fall of the Management Visionary Behind Zappos." *Wall Street Journal*, 12 March.

27 Iwata, E. (1988). "NationsBank struck with brutal, military precision." *SFGate*, 25 October.

28 Brooks, R., Jaffe, G. & Brannigan, M. (1988). "Merger Has Rocky Start, With Bicoastal Friction." *Wall Street Journal*, 23 October.

29 Clifford, C. (2019). "Mark Zuckerberg: If I didn't have complete control of Facebook, I would have been fired." CNBC, 3 October. www.cnbc.com/2019/10/03/zuckerberg-if-i-didnt-have-control-of-facebook-i-wouldve-been-fired.html

30 Honig, E. (2023). *Untouchable: How Powerful People Get Away with It*. Harper Publishing.

31 Pfeffer, J. (2022). *7 Rules of Power: Surprising – But True – Advice on How to Get Things Done and Advance Your Career*. BenBella Books.

32 Eliason, M. & Storrie, D. (2009). Does job loss shorten life? *Journal of Human Resources*, 44(2), 277–302.

33 McEnroe, J. & Kaplan, J. (2002). *You Cannot Be Serious*. Penguin.

34 Pfeffer, J. (2010). *Power: Why Some People Have It—And Others Don't*. Harper Collins.

35 Wigglesworth, R. (2021). "The Ten Trillion-Dollar Man: How Larry Fink Became King of Wall St." *Financial Times*, 17 October.

36 Bloomberg (2023). "Larry Fink says ESG narrative has become ugly, personal." *Pensions and Investments*, 17 January.

37 Williamson, C. (2019). "BlackRock's BGI acquisition 10 years ago fuels rapid growth." *Pensions and Investments*, 11 June.

38 Ibid.

39 Javetski, B. (2012). "Leading in the 21st century: An interview with Larry Fink." McKinsey, 1 September.

40 Housel, M. (2020). *The Psychology of Money: Timeless Lessons on Wealth, Greed, and Happiness*. Harriman House Limited.

41 Address to Queens University, 25th Anniversary of the Good Friday Agreement, April 2023.

42 Ellick, A. B., Kessel, J. M. & Kristof, N. (2023). "In This Story, George W. Bush Is the Hero." *New York Times*, 21 March.

Chapter 5: Ego-Based Traps

1 Katte, S. (2022). "Texas to probe FTX endorsements by Tom Brady, Stephen Curry and other celebs." *Coin Telegraph*, December.

2 Osipovich, A. (2022). "FTX Founder Sam Bankman-Fried Says He Can't Account for Billions Sent to Alameda." *Wall Street Journal*, 3 December.

3 Kahneman, D. (2011). *Thinking, Fast and Slow*. Macmillan.

4 Snyder, B. (2010). "Tony Hayward's Greatest Hits." *Fortune*, June 10.

5 Krauss, C. (2010). "Oil Spill's Blow to BP's Image May Eclipse Costs." *New York Times*, 29 April.

6 Lakhani, N. (2020). "'We've Been Abandoned': A Decade Later, Deepwater Horizon Still Haunts Mexico." *The Guardian*, 19 April.

7 Collinson, D. (2020). "Donald Trump, Boris Johnson and the dangers of excessive positivity." *Medium*, 5 October.

8 Kahneman, D. (2011). *Thinking, Fast and Slow*. Macmillan.

9 Jacobson, J., Dobbs-Marsh, J., Liberman, V. & Minson, J. A. (2011). Predicting civil jury verdicts: How attorneys use (and misuse) a second opinion. *Journal of Empirical Legal Studies*, 8, 99–119.

10 Evans, B. (2021). "10 Reasons Why Salesforce Buying Slack Is the Deal of the Decade." 30 August, accelerationeconomy.com/cloud/10-reasons-why-salesforce-buying-slack-is-the-deal-of-the-decade/

11 Gara, A. & Aliaj, O. (2023). "Carl Icahn Admits Mistake With Bearish Bet That Cost $9bn." *Financial Times*, 18 May.

12 Oprah (2011). "What Oprah Knows for Sure About Trusting Her Intuition," Oprah.com Magazine, August 11 Issue. https://www.oprah.com/spirit/oprah-on-trusting-her-intuition-oprahs-advice-on-trusting-your-gut

13 Quote from Playboy interview (1980). quotepark.com/quotes/1408293-john-lennon-part-of-me-suspects-that-im-a-loser-and-the-other/

14 Haney, W. V. (1979). *Communication and Interpersonal Relations*. Irwin, Homewood, IL.

15 Accenture (2015). "Accenture Research Finds Listening More Difficult in Today's Digital Workplace." 26 February.

16 PGA Tour Vault (2008). "Rocco Mediate reflects on 2008 U.S. Open playoff with Tiger Woods." www.pgatour.com/video/features/6329565841112/rocco-mediate-reflects-on-2008-u.s-open-playoff-with-tiger-woods

17 Ben-David, I., Graham, J. R. & Harvey, C. R. (2013). Managerial miscalibration. *The Quarterly Journal of Economics*, 128(4), 1547–1584.

18 Hirshleifer, D. A., Myers, J. N., Myers, L. A. & Teoh, S. H. (2008). Do individual investors cause post-earnings announcement drift? Direct evidence from personal trades. *The Accounting Review*, 83(6), 1521–1550.

19 Schrand, C. M. & Zechman, S. L. (2012). Executive overconfidence and the slippery slope to financial misreporting. *Journal of Accounting and Economics*, 53(1–2), 311–329.

20 Barber, B. M. & Odean, T. (2001). Boys will be boys: Gender, overconfidence, and common stock investment. *The Quarterly Journal of Economics*, 116(1), 261–292.

21 Malmendier, U. & Tate, G. (2008). Who makes acquisitions? CEO overconfidence and the market's reaction. *Journal of Financial Economics*, 89(1), 20–43.

22 Brown, J., Muldowney, K. & Effron, L. (2017). "What OJ Simpson juror thinks of Simpson now, two decades after criminal trial." ABCNews, 20 July.

23 McFarland, J. (2001). "Laidlaw was a victim of CEO's overambition." *The Globe and Mail*, 30 June.

24 Bowers, S. & Treanor, J. (2011). "RBS 'gamble' on ABN Amro Deal: FSA." *The Guardian*, 12 December.

25 Wilson, H. & Aldrick, P. (2011). "RBS Investigation: Chapter 2 – The ABN Amro Takeover." *The Telegraph*, 11 December.

26 Sunderland, R. (2007). "Barclays Boss: RBS Overpaid for ABN Amro." *The Guardian*, 7 October.

27 UK Parliament Publications (2009). "Banking Crisis: dealing with the failure of the UK banks – Treasury." publications.parliament.uk/pa/cm200809/cmselect/cmtreasy/416/416weo1.htm

28 Graham, J. R., Harvey, C. R. & Puri, M. (2015). Capital allocation and delegation of decision-making authority within firms. *Journal of Financial Economics*, 115(3), 449–470.

29 Newton, E. (1990). "The rocky road from actions to intentions." Stanford University ProQuest.

30 Rozenblit, L. & Keil, F. (2002). The misunderstood limits of folk science: An illusion of explanatory depth. *Cognitive Science*, 26(5), 521–562.

31 PA (2022). "Boris Becker sentenced to two and a half years in jail after conviction in bankruptcy case." *Sky Sports*, 30 April.

32 Reuters (2011). "Steve Jobs refused cancer treatment too long – biographer." 21 October.

33 Ibid.

34 Turley, G. (1996). "25 Years After Veronica Guerin." EUSTORY History Campus, historycampus.org/2020/25-years-after-veronica-guerin-drug-addiction-in-ireland/

35 Collins, L. (2016). "Graham Turley: 'To Have Been Veronica's Husband Was a Great Privilege'." *The Independent*, 1 May.

36 Vanity Fair (2020). "'Ghislaine, Is That You?': Inside Ghislaine Maxwell's Life on the Lam." July.

37 Benoit, D. & Safdar, K. (2023). "JPMorgan Sues Former Executive Jes Staley Over Jeffrey Epstein Ties." *Wall Street Journal*, 9 March.

38 BBC News (2021). "Jamal Khashoggi: All You Need to Know About Saudi Journalist's Death." 24 February.

39 Nicholson, C. (2014). "Q&A: Why 40% of us think we're in the top 5%." ZDNet, 4 April, www.zdnet.com/article/qa-why-40-of-us-think-were-in-the-top-5/

40 PwC (2020). "Revealing leaders' blind spots." Strategy & Business, PwC publication, Autumn 2020, Issue 100, www.strategy-business.com/article/Revealing-leaders-blind-spots

41 Deloitte Insights (2022). "The C-suite's role in well-being." 22 June.

42 Morris, E. (2010). The Anosognosic's Dilemma: Something's Wrong but You'll Never Know What It Is (Part 1)." *New York Times*, 20 June.

43 Munger, K. & Harris, S. J. (1989). Effects of an observer on handwashing in a public restroom. *Perceptual and Motor Skills*, 69(3–1), 733–734.

44 Ariel, B., Sutherland, A., Henstock, D., Young, J., Drover, P., Sykes, J., Megicks, S. & Henderson, R. (2016). Report: Increases in police use of force in the presence of body-worn cameras are driven by officer discretion: A protocol-based subgroup analysis of ten randomized experiments. *Journal of Experimental Criminology*, 12, 453–463.

45 Ariel, B., Sutherland, A., Henstock, D., Young, J., Drover, P., Sykes, J., Megicks, S. & Henderson, R. (2017). "Contagious accountability" a global multisite randomized controlled trial on the effect of police body-worn cameras on citizens' complaints against the police. *Criminal Justice and Behaviour*, 44(2), 293–316.

46 Cohen, B. (2022). "The NASA Engineer Who Made the James Webb Space Telescope Work." *Wall Street Journal*, 8 July.

Chapter 6: Risk-Based Traps

1 Brueck, H. & Collman, A (2022). "Dead bodies litter Mount Everest because it's so dangerous and expensive to get them down." *Insider*, 24 December.

2 Gigerenzer, G. (2015). *Risk Savvy: How to Make Good Decisions*. Penguin.

3 Collins, M. (2001). *Carrying the Fire: An Astronaut's Journey*. Rowman & Littlefield.

4 Yerushalmy, J. & Kassam, A. (2023). "Titanic Submersible: Documents Reveal Multiple Concerns Raised Over Safety of Vessel." *The Guardian*, 21 June.

5 Sky News (2023). "Titanic sub implosion latest: New mission to debris site 'under way'; passengers had 'concerns' before trip; messages sent by Titanic sub chief revealed." 23 June.

6   Taub, B. (2023). "The Titan Submersible Was 'an accident waiting to happen'." *The New Yorker*, 1 July.

7   Oxfam International (2022). "Pandemic creates new billionaire every 30 hours now million people could fall." 23 May.

8   Davis, M. (2022). "The Impact of 9/11 on Business." Investopedia, 24 August.

9   Gigerenzer, G. (2015). *Risk Savvy: How to Make Good Decisions.* Penguin.

10 Russo, J. & Schoemaker, P. (1992). Managing overconfidence. *Sloan Management Review*, 33(2), 7–17.

11 Gigerenzer, G. (2004). Dread risk, September 11, and fatal traffic accidents. *Psychological Science*, 15(4), 286–287.

12 DW (2021). "Kremlin critic Alexei Navalny sentenced to prison." dw.com, *Law and Justice*, 2 February.

13 BBC News (2017). "Benazir Bhutto assassination: How Pakistan covered up killing." 27 September.

14 Miller, P (2022). www.linkedin.com/feed/update/urn:li:activity:6968879123012177920/

15 Schad, T. (2021). "Kobe Bryant crash caused by pilot's poor decision-making, disorientation, NTSB says." *USA Today*, 2 September.

16 Collins, M. (2001). *Carrying the Fire: An Astronaut's Journey*. Rowman & Littlefield.

17 Associated Press (2017). "Caesars releases casino losses of Celine Dion's husband, Rene Angelil." *Tahoe Daily Tribune*, 1 February.

18 Kahneman, D. & Tversky, A. (2013). Prospect theory: An analysis of decision under risk. In *Handbook of the Fundamentals of Financial Decision Making: Part I* (pp. 99–127) World Scientific Publishing, Hackensack, NJ.

19 Gächter, S., Johnson, E. J. & Herrmann, A. (2022). Individual-level loss aversion in riskless and risky choices. *Theory and Decision*, 92(3–4), 599–624.

20 Duhigg, C. (2022). "How Venture Capitalists Are Deforming Capitalism." *The New Yorker*, 23 November.

21 Plan Radar (2019). "5 Ways to boost construction productivity." 18 October.

22 de Barros Teixeira, A., Koller, T. & Lovallo, D. (2019). "Bias Busters: Knowing when to kill a project." McKinsey Quarterly, 18 July.

23 Krakauer, J. (2016). "When You Reach the Summit of Everest, You Are Only Halfway There." *Medium*, 24 May.

24 Voss, C. (2016). *Never Split the Difference: Negotiating as If Your Life Depended on It*. Random House.

25 Enough, B. & Mussweiler, T. (2001). Sentencing under uncertainty: Anchoring effects in the Courtroom. *Journal of Applied Social Psychology*, 31(7), 1535–1551.

26 Poundstone, W. (2010). *Priceless: The Myth of Fair Value (and How to Take Advantage of It)*. Hill & Wang.

27 Galinsky, A. D., Ku, G. & Mussweiler, T. (2009). To start low or to start high? The case of auctions versus negotiations. *Current Directions in Psychological Science*, 18(6), 357–361.

28 Karnitschnig, M. & Eder, F. (2015). "Why Merkel changed her mind." Politico, 15 September.

29 Aon (2021). "Aon and Willis Towers Watson Mutually Agree to Terminate Combination Agreement." 26 July.

30 Blinder, A. (2023). "PGA Tour and LIV Golf Agree to Alliance, Ending Golf's Bitter Fight." *New York Times*, 6 June.

31 Schulberg, J., twitter.com/jessicaschulb/status/1335265711581614080/photo/1

32 Reinl, J. (2023). "California's doctor-assisted deaths surged 63% to 853 last year." *Daily Mail*, 15 August.

33 Petrou, M. (2010). "Chilean miners: Voices from the underground." Macleans, 5 October, macleans.ca/news/world/voices-from-the-underground/

34 McLaren, S. (2019). "A Top FBI Negotiator Shares 5 Tactics for Getting the Outcome You Want." www.linkedin.com/business/talent/blog/talent-connect/negotiation-tactics-to-get-ahead-from-former-fbi-negotiator-chris-voss, 24 October.

35 Rowell, G. (1997). "Climbing to Disaster." *Wall Street Journal*, 29 May.

Chapter 7: Identity-Based Traps

1 Worrall, S. (2016). "Buzz Aldrin Hates Being Called the Second Man on the Moon." *National Geographic*, 18 April.

2 Whitehouse, D. (2019). "Apollo 11: The Fight for The First Footprint on The Moon." *The Guardian*, 25 May.

3 Collins, M. (2001). *Carrying the Fire: An Astronaut's Journey*. Rowman & Littlefield.

4 Aldrin, B. & Abraham, K. (2010). *Magnificent Desolation: The Long Journey Home from The Moon*. Three Rivers Press (CA).

5 Medvec, V. H., Madey, S. F. & Gilovich, T. (1995). When less is more: counterfactual thinking and satisfaction among Olympic medallists. *Journal of Personality and Social Psychology*, 69(4), 603–10.

6 Matsumoto, D. & Willingham, B. (2006). The thrill of victory and the agony of defeat: spontaneous expressions of medal winners of the 2004 Athens Olympic Games. *Journal of Personality and Social Psychology*, 91(3), 568–81

7 Medvec, V. H., Madey, S. F. & Gilovich, T. (1995). When less is more: counterfactual thinking and satisfaction among Olympic medalists. *Journal of Personality and Social Psychology*, 69(4), 603–10.

8 Veblen, T. (2005). *Conspicuous Consumption* (Vol. 38). Penguin UK.

9 Rhimes, S. (2022). "Inventing Anna." A Netflix Series. www.netflix.com/ie/title/81008305

10 Bazerman, M. H. & Tenbrunsel, A. E. (2012). *Blind Spots: Why We Fail to Do What's Right and What to Do About It*. Princeton University Press.

11 Arcidiacono, P., Kinsler, J. & Ransom, T. (2022). Legacy and athlete preferences at Harvard. *Journal of Labor Economics*, 40(1), 133–156.

12 Walsh, N. (2022). "How to Overcome Indecision." TEDx, www.youtube.com/watch?v=xLSAkVxPOko

13 Whipp, G. (2020). "Reese Witherspoon's phone stopped ringing. Now she's making the calls." *Los Angeles Times*, 9 June.

14 Varol, O. (2023). *Awaken Your Genius: Escape Conformity, Ignite Creativity, and Become Extraordinary*. PublicAffairs.

15 Briquelet, K. (2013). "'Harry Potter' author JK Rowling admits she's the scribe behind critically acclaimed detective novel 'Cuckoo's Calling'." *New York Post*, 14 July.

16 Aldrin, B. & Abraham, K. (2010). *Magnificent Desolation: The Long Journey Home from The Moon*. Three Rivers Press (CA).

17 Malone-Kircher, M. (2016). "James Dyson on 5,126 Vacuums That Didn't Work—and the One That Finally Did." *New York Magazine*, 22 November.

18 Connolly, R. (2017). *Being Elvis: A Lonely Life*. Liveright Publishing.

19 Martin, A. (2016). "Priscilla Presley: I lost myself during marriage to Elvis." UPI Entertainment News, 18 November.

20 Mayoras, D. & Mayoras, A. (2019). "Lisa Marie Presley & The Rise and Fall of the Elvis Estate." *Forbes*, 27 March.

21 Posner, G. & Ware, J. (1986). *Mengele, The Complete Story*. Cooper Square Press, New York

22 Ibid.

23 Bossert, W. (1985). Central Television London interview, HBO's "The Search for Mengele," August.

24 Ibid.

25 Martin, S. & Marks, J. (2019). *Messengers: Who We Listen To, Who We Don't, and Why*. Random House.

26 Kogut, T. & Ritov, I. (2007). "One of us": Outstanding willingness to help save a single identified compatriot. *Organizational Behavior and Human Decision Processes*, 104(2), 150–157.

27 Centers for Disease Control and Prevention. "The Untreated Syphilis Study at Tuskegee Timeline." www.cdc.gov/tuskegee/timeline.htm

28 Somers, M. (2019). "Your acquired hires are leaving. Here's why." *MIT Sloan Review*, 8 January.

29 Baker & MacKenzie (2014). "People matters. Accounting for culture in mergers and acquisitions."

30 Innocence Project Network (2022). "Freed & Exonerated Women Speak Out." 4 October, www.youtube.com/watch?v=ioDTadqj22g

31 Obama, B. (2020). *A Promised Land*. Penguin, New York.

32 en.wikipedia.org/wiki/List_of_nicknames_used_by_Donald_Trump

33 Gross, T. (2018). "Muhammad Ali Biography Reveals a Flawed Rebel Who Loved Attention." NPR, 21 September.

34 Goh, Z. K. (2021). "Vera Wang talks about her Olympics ambitions." Olympic Channel, 19 April.

35 UNDP (2020). "Innovative ringtone messages positively impact knowledge, perceptions and behaviours related to COVID-19 in Pakistan." 24 July, www.undp.org/pakistan/blog/innovative-ringtone-messages-positively-impacts-knowledge-perceptions-and-behaviours-related-covid-19-pakistan

36 Bond, R. M., Fariss, C. J., Jones, J. J., Kramer, A. D. I., Marlow, C., Settle, J. E. & Fowler, J. H. (2013). A 61-million-person experiment in social influence and political mobilization. *NIH Public Access Author Manuscript*, 489(7415), 3–9.

37 BBC Archive. "1980: Change of Direction: Buzz Aldrin on depression." www.facebook.com/watch/?v=630964334647868

38 Bernard Mannes Baruch. en.wikiquote.org/wiki/Bernard_Baruch

Chapter 8: Memory-Based Traps

1 Whittingham, R. B. (2004). *The Blame Machine: Why Human Error Causes Accidents*. Oxford: Elsevier Butterworth-Heinemann.

2 LA Times Archives (1987). "Judge Blames 'Sloppiness' in Ferry Wreck." *Los Angeles Times*, 24 July.

3 The Maritime Executive (2017). "Remembering the Herald of Free Enterprise." 6 March.

4 Department of Transport (1987). mv Herald of Free Enterprise, Crown report. assets.publishing.service.gov.uk/media/54c1704ce5274a15b6000025/FormalInvestigation_HeraldofFreeEnterprise-MSA1894.pdf

5 RTE (2021). Colm Tóibín: On Memory's Shore – inside the new documentary.

6 Ebbinghaus, H. (1885). "Memory: A Contribution to Experimental Psychology." Teachers College, Columbia University, New York.

7 Aftermath (2022). "2021 Accidental Gun Death Statistics in the US." February, www.aftermath.com/content/accidental-shooting-deaths-statistics/

8 Lagasse, J. (2016). "Damages from left-behind surgical tools top billions as systems seek end to gruesome errors." *Healthcare Finance*, 6 May.

9 Hales, B. M. & Pronovost, P. J. (2006). The checklist—a tool for error management and performance improvement. *Journal of Critical Care*, 21(3), 231–235.

10 Lieber, M. (2018). "Surgical sponges left inside woman for at least 6 years." CNN.

11 Runciman, W., Kluger, M. T., Morris, R. W., Paix, A., Watterson, L. & Webb, R. (2005). Crisis management during anaesthesia: development of an anaesthetic crisis management manual. *BMJ Quality & Safety*, 14(3), e1.

12 de Vries, E. N., Hollmann, M. W., Smorenburg, S. M., Gouma, D. J., Boermeester, M. A. & STS Task Force, the Netherlands Association of Anaesthesiologists, and the Dutch Society of Surgery. (2010). Development and validation of the Surgical Patient Safety System (SURPASS) checklist. *Quality and Safety in Health Care*, 19(6), e36.

13 Kirabo, J. C. & Schneider, H. S. (2015). Checklists and Worker Behavior: A Field Experiment. *American Economic Journal: Applied Economics*, 7(4): 136–68.

14 McKie, R. (2009). "How Michael Collins Became the Forgotten Astronaut of Apollo 11." *The Guardian*, 19 July.

15 Hoare, C. (2020). "'I Have Some Regrets' Michael Collins' Candid Moon Landing Confession 50 Years on Revealed." *The Express*, 9 May.

16 Wood, T. (2020). Original documentary series, "Ted Bundy: Falling for a Killer," Amazon Reviews.

17 Daniel, K. (2017). *Thinking, Fast and Slow*. Penguin.

18 Amar, M., Ariely, D., Bar-Hillel, M., Carmon, Z. & Ofir, C. (2011). Brand names act like marketing placebos. The Hebrew University of Jerusalem. Center for the Study of Rationality. Discussion Paper, 566, 1–8.

19 Loftus, E. F. (2005). Planting misinformation in the human mind: A 30-year investigation of the malleability of memory. *Learning & memory*, 12(4), 361–366.

20 Loftus, E. F. & Pickrell, J. E. (1995). The formation of false memories. *Psychiatric Annals*, 25(12), 720–725.

21 Loftus, E. F. (2005). Planting misinformation in the human mind: A 30-year investigation of the malleability of memory. *Learning & Memory*, 12(4), 361–366.

22 East Kent Mercury Reporter (2017). "Zeebrugge ferry disaster: Seaman blamed for causing tragedy." 6 March. www.kentonline.co.uk/dover/news/seaman-haunted-by-ferry-disaster-121619/

23 Ibid.

24 Associate Press (2009). "Garrido's Odd Behaviour on Berkeley Campus Would Unravel Dugard Case." *Reno Gazette Journal*, 29 August.

25 Echterhoff, G., Hirst, W. & Hussy, W. (2005). How eye-witnesses

resist misinformation: Social post- warnings and the monitoring of memory characteristics. *Memory & Cognition*, 33(5), 770–782.

26 Hirst, W., Phelps, E. A., Buckner, R. L., Budson, A. E., Cuc, A., Gabrieli, J. D., Johnson, M. K., Lustig, C., Lyle, K. B., Mather, M. & Meksin, R. (2009). Long-term memory for the terrorist attack of September 11: flashbulb memories, event memories, and the factors that influence their retention. *Journal of Experimental Psychology: General*, 138(2), 161.

27 Byfield, C. (2022). "Sir Alex Ferguson's Five Most Frightening Hairdryer Treatments: 'Tears In My Eyes'." *The Daily Express*, 1 January.

28 Twitter, twitter.com/SkySportsPL/status/1584947713975750657

29 Gibbs, S. & Hanrahan, J. (2018). "How Life Was Different In 1970s Australia." *Daily Mail Australia*, 20 December.

30 Ebbinghaus, H. (1885). "Memory: A Contribution to Experimental Psychology." Teachers College, Columbia University, New York.

31 Asch, S. (1946). Forming impressions of personality. *Journal of Abnormal and Social Psychology*. 41(3), 258–290.

32 Strack, F., Martin, L. & Schwarz, N. (1988). Priming and communication: Social determinants of information use in judgments of life satisfaction. *European Journal of Social Psychology*, October–November, 18(5), 429–42.

33 Zajonc, R. B. & Rajecki, D. W. (1969). Exposure and affect: A field experiment. *Psychonomic Science*, 17(4), 216–217.

34 Pennycook, G., Cannon, T. D. & Rand, D. G. (2018). Prior exposure increases perceived accuracy of fake news. *Journal of Experimental Psychology: General*, 147(12), 1865.

35 Pennycook, G., McPhetres, J., Zhang, Y., Lu, J. G. & Rand, D. G. (2020). Fighting COVID-19 misinformation on social media: Experimental evidence for a scalable accuracy-nudge intervention. *Psychological Science*, 31(7), 770–780.

36 Jacques, J. (2013). "Your Memory: More Powerful Than You Realize!" *Philadelphia, The Trumpet*, January.

37 Associated Press (2004). "NASA studying 'Rain Man's' brain." NBC News, 8 November.

38 Dresler, M., Shirer, W. R., Konrad, B. N., Müller, N. C., Wagner, I.

C., Fernández, G., Czisch, M. & Greicius, M. D. (2017). Mnemonic training reshapes brain networks to support superior memory. *Neuron*, 93(5), 1227–1235.

39 Pennycook, G. & Rand, D. G. (2022). Nudging social media toward accuracy. *The ANNALS of the American Academy of Political and Social Science*, 700(1), 152–164.

Chapter 9: Ethics-Based Traps

1 Steig, C. (2019). "What Exactly Was the Theranos Edison Machine Supposed to Do?" Refinery 29, 12 March.

2 Leuty, R. (2018). "'Ultimately, Elizabeth made the decisions': A look inside Theranos's ineffective board." www.Bizjournals.com, 8 August.

3 McKay, R. (2015). "Former peanut company CEO sentenced to 28 years for salmonella outbreak." *Reuters*, 22 September.

4 Sifferlin, A. (2015). "When Tainted Peanuts Could Mean Life in Prison." *TIME*, 17 September.

5 McGreal, C. (2022). "McKinsey Denies Illegally Hiding Work for Opioid-Maker Purdue Pharma While Advising FDA." *The Guardian*, 27 April.

6 Jordan, D. (2019). "Is This America's Most Hated Family?." BBC News, 22 March.

7 Hoffman, J. (2022). "CVS and Walgreens Near $10 Billion Deal to Settle Opioid Cases." *New York Times*, 2 November.

8 Forsythe, M. & Bogdanich, W. (2021). "McKinsey Settles for Nearly $600 Million Over Role in Opioid Crisis." *New York Times*, 3 February.

9 Bogdanich, W. & Forsythe, M. (2020). McKinsey Issues a Rare Apology for Its Role in OxyContin Sales." *New York Times*, 8 December.

10 Dash, M. (2012). "Colonel Parker Managed Elvis' Career, but Was He a Killer on the Lam?" *Smithsonian Magazine*, 24 February.

11 Comey, J. (2018). *A Higher Loyalty: Truth, Lies, and Leadership*. Pan Macmillan.

12 PBS Frontline (2000). "Jefferson's Blood, Is It True?" www.pbs.org/wgbh/pages/frontline/shows/jefferson/true/

13 Vohs, K. D. (2015). Money priming can change people's thoughts,

feelings, motivations, and behaviours: An update on 10 years of experiments. *Journal of Experimental Psychology: General,* 144(4), e86.

14 Stothard, M. (2016). "Jérôme Kerviel's SocGen Damages Slashed to €1m." *Financial Times,* 23 September.

15 AA.com (2022). "149 medals revoked due to doping violations in Olympic history." www.aa.com.tr/en/sports/149-medals-revoked-due-to-doping-violations-in-olympic-history/2503085

16 Majendie, M. (2015). "Doping Scandal: Russian Athletes Suspended after IAAF and Sebastian Coe Get Tough." *The Independent,* 13 November.

17 Phillips, M. (2016). "Athletics: Coe lauds 'landmark changes'." Yahoo Sports, 11 August.

18 Bamberger, M. & Yaeger, D. (1997). Over the edge. *Sports Illustrated,* 14, 62–70.

19 Associated Press (2017). "Nazi doctor Josef Mengele's Bones used in Brazil Forensic Medicine Courses." *The Guardian,* 11 January.

20 Zhong, C.-B., Liljenquist, K. & Cain, D. M. (2009). Moral self-regulation: Licensing and compensation. In D. De Cremer (Ed.), *Psychological Perspectives on Ethical Behavior and Decision Making* (p. 75–89). Information Age Publishing, Inc.

21 Monin, B. & Miller, D.T. (2001). Moral credentials and the expression of prejudice. *Journal of Personality and Social Psychology,* 81(1), 33.

22 IMDb (2021). "Savile: Portrait of a Predator." Documentary, www.imdb.com/title/tt15581190/

23 Kassirer, S., Jordan, J. J. & Kouchaki, M. (2023). Giving-by-proxy triggers subsequent charitable behavior. *Journal of Experimental Social Psychology,* 105, 104438.

24 Bazerman, M. H. & Tenbrunsel, A. E. (2012). *Blind Spots: Why We Fail to Do What's Right and What to Do About It.* Princeton University Press.

25 Viewpoints unplugged (2019). "What is Ethical Fading?" November, viewpointsunplugged.com/2019/11/26/what-is-ethical-fading/

26 Global Prison Trends (2023), www.penalreform.org

27 Benner, K. & Dewan, S. (2019). "Alabama's Gruesome Prisons: Report Finds Rape and Murder at All Hours." *New York Times,* 3 April.

28 Tenbrunsel, A. E. & Messick, D. M. (2004). Ethical fading: The role of self-deception in unethical behavior. *Social Justice Research*, 17, 223–236.

29 CBS News (2011). "Sandusky on horsing around in the shower: 'That was just me'." www.cbsnews.com/news/sandusky-on-horsing-around-in-the-shower-that-was-just-me, 5 December.

30 Yad Vashem, "Oskar and Emilie Schindler." www.yadvashem.org/righteous/stories/schindler.html

31 Brockell, G. (2021). "'A Japanese Schindler': The remarkable diplomat who saved thousands of Jews during WWII." *Washington Post*, 27 January.

32 Awad, E., Dsouza, S., Kim, R., Schulz, J., Henrich, J., Shariff, A., Bonnefon, J-F. & Rahwan, I. (2018). The moral machine experiment. *Nature*, 563(7729), 59–64.

Chapter 10: Time-Based Traps

1 ASN Accident Description (2011). Aviation Safety Network, May 11.

2 BBC News (2019). "Grenfell Tower: What Happened." 29 October.

3 Mortimer, J. (2020). "Grenfell Tower Inquiry: The 6 key findings for anyone who hasn't followed the investigation." MyLondon, 14 June.

4 Knapton, S. & Dixon, H. (2017). "Eight Failures That Left People of Grenfell Tower at Mercy of the Inferno." *The Telegraph*, 16 June.

5 Gladwell, M. (2006). *Blink: The Power of Thinking Without Thinking*. Penguin.

6 Mischel, W. & Ebbesen, E. (1970). Attention in delay of gratification. *Journal of Personality and Social Psychology*, 16(2), 329.

7 Whitmer, M. " Factory Workers and Asbestos." www.asbestos.com/occupations/factory-workers

8 Watts, H. G. (2009). The consequences for children of explosive remnants of war: land mines, unexploded ordnance, improvised explosive devices, and cluster bombs. *Journal of Paediatric Rehabilitation Medicine*, 2(3), 217–227.

9 Taylor, H. (2022). "Kwasi Kwarteng says he and Liz Truss 'got carried away' writing mini-budget and 'blew it'." *The Irish Times*, 10 December.

10 Shendruk, A. (2021). "As the US Supreme Court revisits Roe v. Wade, let's revisit its history of overturned rulings." *Quartz*, 4 December.

11 Forest History Society. "Mann Gulch Fire, 1949." foresthistory.org/research-explore/us-forest-service-history/policy-and-law/fire-u-s-forest-service/famous-fires/mann-gulch-fire-1949/

12 Nobel, C. (2016). "Bernie Madoff Explains Himself." Harvard Business School, Working Knowledge, 24 October.

13 Dixit, P. (2023). "'Buying Netflix at $4 billion would've been better instead of...': Former Yahoo CEO Marissa Mayer." *Business Today*, 8 May, https://www.businesstoday.in/technology/news/story/buying-netflix-at-4-billion-wouldve-been-better-instead-of-former-yahoo-ceo-marissa-mayer-380349-2023-05-07

14 Mellers, B. A. & McGraw, A. P. (2001). Anticipated emotions as guides to choice. *Current Directions in Psychological Science*, 10(6), 210–214.

15 The Beatles (2000). *The Beatles Anthology*. Chronicle Books, San Francisco.

16 Salthouse, T. A. (1994). The aging of working memory. *Neuropsychology*, 8(4), 535.

17 Financial Conduct Authority (2017). "The Ageing Population: Ageing Mind. Literature Review Report." Commissioned to the Big Window Consulting.

18 Campbell, R. (1969). *Seneca: Letters from a Stoic*. Penguin.

19 Woodzicka, J. & LaFrance, M. (2001). Real versus imagined gender harassment. *Journal of Social Issues*, 57(1), 15–30.

20 Kahneman, D., Sibony, O. & Sunstein, C. R. (2021). *Noise: A Flaw in Human Judgment*. Hachette UK.

21 Grimstad, S. & Jørgensen, M. (2007). Inconsistency of expert judgment-based estimates of software development effort. *Journal of Systems and Software*, 80(11), 1770–1777.

22 Einhorn, H. J. (1974). Expert judgment: Some necessary conditions and an example. *Journal of Applied Psychology*, 59(5), 562–571.

23 Rowe, M. B. (1986). Wait time: Slowing down may be a way of speeding up! *Journal of Teacher Education*, 37(1), 43–50.

24 Cited in Robson, D. (2019). *The Intelligence Trap: Revolutionise Your Thinking and Make Wiser Decisions*. Hachette UK.

25 Charles Schwab (2020). "Judge the Judges: With Guests Daniel Kahneman, James Hutchinson & G.M. Pucilowski." Choiceology with Katy Milkman, 15 March.

26 Agnew, P. (2023). "Mr Beast: How to Capture the Attention of Billions." NudgePodcast.com, 1 January.

Chapter 11: Emotion-Based Traps

1 Rinek, J. & Strong, M. (2018). *In the Name of the Children: An FBI Agent's Relentless Pursuit of the Nation's Worst Predators*. BenBella Books.

2 Ibid.

3 Indursky, M. (2012). "In Search of Happiness." *Huffington Post*, 3 July.

4 Lerner, J. S., Li, Y., Valdesolo, P. & Kassam, K. S. (2015). Emotion and decision making. *Annual Review of Psychology*, 66, 799–823.

5 Herbert, I. (2020). "The day Kevin Keegan QUIT in the loos." *The Daily Mail*, 6 October.

6 Loewenstein, G., Nagin, D. & Paternoster, R. (1997). The effect of sexual arousal on expectations of sexual forcefulness. *Journal of Research in Crime and Delinquency*, 34(4), 443–473.

7 UN Women (2019). "UN Women Statement: Confronting femicide—the reality of intimate partner violence." 13 November.

8 Mail Foreign Service (2020). "The 60-year-old feud that got the boot: Adidas and Puma finally bury the hatchet." *The Daily Mail*, 18 September.

9 Schwar, H. (2018). "Puma and Adidas' rivalry has divided a small German town for 70 years — here's what it looks like now." *Insider*, 1 October.

10 Talaska, C. A., Fiske, S. T. & Chaiken, S. (2008). Legitimating racial discrimination: Emotions, not beliefs, best predict discrimination in a meta-analysis. *Social Justice Research*, 21(3), 263–296.

11 Botti, S. (2004). The psychological pleasure and pain of choosing: when people prefer choosing at the cost of subsequent outcome satisfaction. *Journal of Personality and Social Psychology*, 87(3), 312.

12 Simonson, I. (1992). The influence of anticipating regret and responsibility on purchase decisions. *Journal of Consumer Research*, 19(1), 105–118.

13 P&J Investments (2013). "Blackstone's Schwarzman regrets selling BlackRock in 1994." 30 September.

14 Schwarzman, S. (2019). "Why There are No Brave Old People in Finance." *Forbes*, 16 September.

15 Mehrotra. K. (2022). "Where Are Cary and Steven Stayner's Parents Now?" *The Cinemaholic*, April.

16 Steiner, S. (2012). "Top Five Regrets of The Dying." *The Guardian*, 1 February.

17 Brainy Quotes. www.brainyquote.com/authors/neil-armstrong-quotes

18 Vedantam, S. (2020). "The Influence You Have: Why We Fail To See Our Power Over Others." Hidden Brain, 24 February, www.npr.org/transcripts/807758704

19 Ethan Allen HR Services (2018). "Revenge in the Workplace: Top 10 Ways Employees Get Back at Each Other," Employee Relations, 18 May.

20 Kolhatkar, S. (2023). "Inside Sam Bankman-Fried's Family Bubble." *The New Yorker*, 25 September.

21 Gielan, M. (2016). "You Can Deliver Bad News to Your Team Without Crushing Them." *Harvard Business Review*, 21 March.

22 Karlsson, N., Seppi, D. & Loewenstein, G. (2005). The 'ostrich effect': Selective attention to information about investments (Working Paper Series). Social Science Research Network.

23 Aversa, J. (2005). "Alan Greenspan Enjoys Rock Star Renown." *Houston Chronicle*, 5 March.

24 Stewart, H. (2005). "After Greenspan, the Deluge?" *The Guardian*, 30 October.

25 Pierce, A (2002). "The Queen Asks Why No One Saw the Credit Crunch Coming." *The Guardian*, 5 November.

26 Sky News (2012). "Queen Asks Bank Bosses About Financial Crisis." 13 December. news.sky.com/story/queen-asks-bank-bosses-about-financial-crisis-10460821

27 Huet. E. (2022). "There Are Now 1,000 Unicorn Startups Worth $1 Billion or More." *Bloomberg Law*, Feb 9.

28 Sharot, T. (2017). *The Influential Mind: What the Brain Reveals About Our Power to Change Others*. Henri Holt and Co.

29 Sutherland, R. (2019). *Alchemy: The Surprising Power of Ideas That Don't Make Sense*. Random House.

30 According to usaforafrica.org.

31 Ferdinand, D. (2005). "Interview: Deirdre Fernand meets Claire Bertschinger." *The Times*, 3 July.

32 Carucci, J. (2020). "35 years after Live Aid, Bob Geldof assesses personal toll." *Washington Post*, 10 July.

Chapter 12: Relationship-Based Traps

1 "Post Office and Horizon – Compensation: interim report." House of Commons, 8 February 2022, committees.parliament.uk/publications/8879/documents/95841/default

2 Hetherington, M., Anderson, A., Norton, G. & Newson, L. (2006). Situational effects on meal intake: A comparison of eating alone and eating with others. *Physiology & Behavior*, 88(4–5), 498–505.

3 De Castro, J. M. (2000). Eating behavior: lessons from the real world of humans. *Nutrition*, 16(10), 800–813.

4 Shimizu, M., Johnson, K. & Wansink, B. (2014). In good company. The effect of an eating companion's appearance on food intake. *Appetite*, 83, 263–268.

5 Wansink, B. & Van Ittersum, K. (2012). Fast food restaurant lighting and music can reduce calorie intake and increase satisfaction. *Psychological Reports*, 111(1), 228–232.

6 Nevill, A. M., Balmer, N. J. & Williams, A. M. (2002). The influence of crowd noise and experience upon refereeing decisions in football. *Psychology of Sport and Exercise*, 3(4), 261–272.

7 Mitchell, J. P., Banaji, M. R. & MacRae, C. N. (2005). The link between social cognition and self-referential thought in the medial prefrontal cortex. *Journal of Cognitive Neuroscience*, 17(8), 1306–1315.

8 White, J. B., Langer, E. J., Yariv, L. et al. (2006). Frequent Social Comparisons and Destructive Emotions and Behaviors: The Dark Side of Social Comparisons. *Journal of Adult Development*, 13, 36–44.

9 Kuhn, P., Kooreman, P., Soetevent, A. & Kapteyn, A. (2011). The effects of lottery prizes on winners and their neighbors: Evidence from the Dutch postcode lottery. *American Economic Review*, 101(5), 2226–2247.

10 Surowiecki, J. (2005). *The Wisdom of Crowds*. Anchor.

11 Nadeau, R., Cloutier, E. & Guay, J. H. (1993). New evidence about the existence of a bandwagon effect in the opinion formation process. *International Political Science Review*, 14(2), 203–213.

12 Kiss, Á. & Simonovits, G. (2013). Identifying the bandwagon effect in two-round elections. *Public Choice*. 160(3–4), 327–344.

13 Baggs, M. (2019). "Fyre Festival: Inside the World's Biggest Festival Flop." BBC Newsbeat, 18 January.

14 Huddleston, T. (2019). "Fyre Festival: How 25-year-old scammed investors out of $26 million." CNBC Make It, 18 August.

15 Mackay, C. (1841). *Extraordinary Popular Delusions and the Madness of Crowds*, The Tulipomania, Chapter 3.

16 Moehring, C. (2021). "Season 3, Episode 2: Eugene Soltes, Harvard Professor With an Inside Look to the Mind of White Collar Criminals." University of Arkansas, Walton College, 28 January, walton.uark.edu/business-integrity/blog/eugene-soltes.php

17 Higginbotham, A. (2002). "Doctor Feelgood." *The Guardian*, 11 August.

18 Hodge, N. (2020). "KPMG faces $306m negligence claim over Carillion audit." *Compliance Week*, 13 May.

19 Timmins, B. (2022). "Bain consultancy banned from government work over 'misconduct'." BBC News, 3 August, www.bbc.com/news/business-62408116

20 Waters, N. L. & Hans, V. P. (2009). A jury of one: Opinion formation, conformity, and dissent on juries. *Journal of Empirical Legal Studies*, 6(3), 513–540.

21 Kuran, T. (1997). *Private Truths, Public Lies: The Social Consequences of Preference Falsification*. Harvard University Press.

22 Associated Press (2023). "Months after Adidas cut ties with Kanye West, Yeezy shoes are back on sale." NBC News, 31 May.

23 Irish Independent (2018). "Coca-Cola launches 'Designated Driver' campaign to help save lives on Irish roads this Christmas." 5 December.

Chapter 13: Story-Based Traps

1 Power, S. (2001). "Bystanders to Genocide." *The Atlantic*, September Issue.

2 Vedantam, S. (2020). "Romeo & Juliet In Rwanda: How a Soap

Opera Sought to Change a Nation." Hidden Brain, 13 July, www. npr.org/transcripts/890539487

3 Staub, E., Pearlman, L. A., Gubin, A. & Hagengimana, A. (2005). Healing, reconciliation, forgiving and the prevention of violence after genocide or mass killing: An intervention and its experimental evaluation in Rwanda. *Journal of Social and Clinical Psychology*, 24, 297–334.

4 Vedantam, S. (2020). "Romeo & Juliet In Rwanda: How a Soap Opera Sought to Change a Nation." Hidden Brain, 13 July, www. npr.org/transcripts/890539487

5 Shead, S. (2021). "Elon Musk's tweets are moving markets — and some investors are worried." CNBC.com, 29 January.

6 Martin, S. & Marks, J. (2019). *Messengers: Who We Listen To, Who We Don't, and Why*. Random House.

7 Durantini, M. R., Albarracin, D., Mitchell, A. L., Earl, A. N. & Gillette, J. C. (2006). Conceptualizing the influence of social agents of behavior change: A meta-analysis of the effectiveness of HIV-prevention interventionists for different groups. *Psychological Bulletin*, 132(2), 212.

8 Karlan, D. & Appel, J. (2011). *More Than Good Intentions*. Dutton, New York.

9 Morisky, D. E., Nguyen, C., Ang, A. & Tiglao, T. V. (2005). HIV/AIDS prevention among the male population: results of a peer education program for taxicab and tricycle drivers in the Philippines. *Health Education & Behavior*, 32(1), 57–68.

10 Hartford, T. (2016). "The Dubious Power of Power Poses." *Financial Times*, 10 June.

11 Landy, D. & Sigall, H. (1974). Beauty is talent: Task evaluation as a function of the performer's physical attractiveness. *Journal of Personality and Social Psychology*, 29(3), 299.

12 Manavis, S. (2021). "How the internet dehumanised Chris Whitty." *The New Statesman*, 29 June.

13 Lee, S., Pitesa, M., Pillutla, M. & Thau, S. (2015). When beauty helps and when it hurts: An organizational context model of attractiveness discrimination in selection decisions. *Organizational Behavior and Human Decision Processes*, 128, 15–28.

14 Shahani, C., Dipboye, R. L. & Gehrlein, T. M. (1993). Attractiveness bias in the interview: Exploring the boundaries of an effect. *Basic and Applied Social Psychology*, 14(3), 317–328.

15 Duhigg, C. (2020). "How Venture Capitalists are Deforming Capitalism." *The New Yorker*, 23 November.

16 Staunton, C. (2019). "Wicked, shockingly evil and despicably vile… so why are we so fascinated by serial killers?" *The Journal*, 2 February.

17 Antonakis, J. & Dalgas, O. (2009). Predicting elections: Child's play! *Science*, 323(5918), 1183–1183.

18 Etcoff, N. (2011). *Survival of the Prettiest: The Science of Beauty*. Anchor.

19 Moreland, R. L. & Beach, S. R. (1992). Exposure effects in the classroom: The development of affinity among students. *Journal of Experimental Social Psychology*, 28(3), 255–276.

20 Stewart, J. E. (1985). Appearance and punishment: The attraction-leniency effect in the courtroom. *The Journal of Social Psychology*, 125(3), 373–378.

21 Thornton, J. I. (1996). A Review of Hung Jury: The Diary of a Menendez Juror. *Journal of Forensic Sciences*, 41(5), 899–899.

22 Goldstein, N. J., Cialdini, R. B. & Griskevicius, V. (2011). The influence of social norms on compliance: The role of context and strength of norm. *Social Influence*, 6(4), 215–226.

23 Forrest, A. (2018). "Jair Bolsonaro: the worst quotes from Brazil's far-right presidential frontrunner." *Independent*, 8 October.

24 Brenner, M. (1997). "American Nightmare: The Ballad of Richard Jewell." *Vanity Fair*, February.

25 Ibid.

26 Postman, L. J. & Allport, G. W. (1965). *The Psychology of Rumour*. Russell & Russell, New York.

27 Told to Daily News in 2016.

28 Duhigg, C. (2020). "How Venture Capitalists are Deforming Capitalism." *The New Yorker*, 23 November.

29 Tinsley, C., Dillon. R. & Madsen, P. (2011). How to Avoid Catastrophe. *Harvard Business Review*, April.

30 Rahim, S. (2016). "The People vs OJ Simpson: to win the argument, tell a story." Prospect, 18 April.

31 Cantrell, L. (2020). "Where Are They Now: The OJ Simpson Trial." *Town & Country*, 3 October.

Chapter 14: Hearing What Matters: SONIC Strategies

1   Sutherland, R. (2019). *Alchemy: The Surprising Power of Ideas That Don't Make Sense*. Random House.

2   Cummings, J. (2023). "Sometimes silence says a lot." Center for Effective School Operations, 26 April, www.theceso.com

3   Koriat, A., Lichtenstein, S. & Fischhoff, B. (1980). Reasons for confidence. *Journal of Experimental Psychology: Human Learning and Memory*, 6(2), 107.

4   Markman, K. D., Gavanski, I., Sherman, S. J., & McMullen, M. N. (1993). The mental simulation of better and worse possible worlds. *Journal of Experimental Social Psychology*, 29, 87–109.

5   Altpeter, T., Luckhardt, K., Lewis, J., Harken, A. & Polk Jr, H. (2007). Expanded surgical time out: a key to real-time data collection and quality improvement. *Journal of the American College of Surgeons*, 204(4), 527–532.

6   Haynes, A. B., Weiser, T. G., Berry, W. R., Lipsitz, S. R., Breizat, A. H., Dellinger, E. P., Gawande, A. A. et al. (2009). A surgical safety checklist to reduce morbidity and mortality in a global population. *New England Journal of Medicine*, 360(5), 491–499.

7   Lee, J. Y., Donkers, J., Jarodzka, H., Sellenraad, G. & van Merriënboer, J. (2020). Different effects of pausing on cognitive load in a medical simulation game. *Computers in Human Behavior*, 106385.

8   Gabaix, X. (2019). Behavioural inattention. In *Handbook of Behavioural Economics: Applications and Foundations 1* (Vol. 2, pp. 261–343). North-Holland.

9   Harvard Business Review Analytic Services (2019). "The CEO's Innovation Playbook."

10 Gallup (2006). "Too Many Interruptions at Work?" Interview with Gloria Mark, *Business Journal*, June 8.

11 Asprey, D. (2021). "7 Ways to Influence People – Robert Cialdini, Ph.D." Interview #821, Bulletproof Radio, May, www.daveasprey.com

12 Bazerman, M. H. & Neale, M. A. (1982). Improving negotiation

effectiveness under final offer arbitration: The role of selection and training. *Journal of Applied Psychology*, 67(5), 543.

13 Heath, C. & Heath, D. (2013). *Decisive: How to Make Better Choices in Life and Work*. Random House.

14 Ibid.

15 Colvile, R. (2017). *The Great Acceleration: How the World Is Getting Faster, Faster*. Bloomsbury Publishing.

16 Thaler, R. H. & Sunstein, C. R. (2009). *Nudge: Improving Decisions About Health, Wealth, and Happiness*. Penguin.

17 Palmer, M. (2022). "NUDGES and Choice Architecture: Introducing Nobel-Winning Concepts." Interview with Cass Sunstein, The Brainy Business Podcast #35.

18 Grant, A. (2021). *Think Again: The Power of Knowing What You Don't Know*. Penguin.

19 Safran, J. D. (2011). Theodor Reik's listening with the third ear and the role of self-analysis in contemporary psychoanalytic thinking. *The Psychoanalytic Review*, 98(2), 205–216.

20 Munger, C. "My mental models' checklist." www.mymentalmodels. info/Mental-Models-Checklist.pdf

21 Clear, J. (2018). *Atomic Habits: An Easy & Proven Way to Build Good Habits & Break Bad Ones*. Penguin.

22 Milkman, K. (2021). *How to Change: The Science of Getting from Where You Are to Where You Want to Be*. Penguin.

23 Gollwitzer, P. M. & Sheeran, P. (2006). Implementation intentions and goal achievement: A meta-analysis of effects and processes. *Advances in Experimental Social Psychology*, 38, 69–119.

24 Greenwald, A. G., Carnot, C. G., Beach, R. & Young, B. (1987). Increasing voting behaviour by asking people if they expect to vote. *Journal of Applied Psychology*, 72(2), 315.

25 Nickerson, D. W. & Rogers, T. (2016). Do you have a voting plan? Implementation intention, voter turnout, and organic plan making. *Psychological Science*, 21(2), 194–199.

26 Rogers, T., Milkman, K. L., John, L. K. & Norton, M. I. (2015). Beyond good intentions: Prompting people to make plans improves follow-through on important tasks. *Behavioral Science & Policy*, 1(2), 33–41.

27 Goldstein, N. J., Martin, S. J. & Cialdini, R. (2008). Yes! *50 Scientifically Proven Ways to Be Persuasive*. Simon and Schuster.

28 Robson, D. (2023). *The Expectation Effect: How Your Mindset Can Transform Your Life*. Canongate.

Chapter 15: In Tune: The Decision Ninja

1 Innocence Network (2022). "Freed and Exonerated Women Speak Out." 4 October, www.youtube.com/watch?v=i0DTadqj22g

2 McEnroe, J. (2023). Stanford Commencement Speech, www.youtube.com/watch?v=wzhsT3ojyz0

INDEX

ABOUT THE AUTHOR

NUALA WALSH IS an award-winning business consultant, behavioural scientist and non-executive director.

Recognised among the Top 100 Most Influential Women in Finance, her 30-year distinguished investments career includes executive positions at BlackRock, Merrill Lynch and Standard Life Aberdeen where she served as chief marketing officer and, notably, architected the first global Ryder Cup sponsorship deal in its 100-year history. She began her career with PA Consulting Group, spending a year in Africa on an assignment for the World Bank.

Today, as MindEquity CEO, she consults with Fortune 500 firms, commercial brands, human rights organisations and sports associations, advising on matters of strategy, reputation, culture and behaviour change.

Nuala holds numerous advisory and board appointments. Formerly vice-chair of UN Women (UK), she serves as an independent non-executive director at the British & Irish Lions and Basketball Ireland.

A founding director of the Global Association of Applied Behavioural Scientists, she is president of the Harvard Club of Ireland, council member at The Football Association, chair of the Innocence Project London, gender advisor at World

Athletics and Ethics Committee member at the Chartered Institute of Securities and Investments.

Reaching millions through a popular TEDx talk on Overcoming Indecision, she writes regularly for top-tier media outlets such as *Forbes, Psychology Today, Inc.* and the *Harvard Business Review.* Her insights also feature in the *Financial Times, Fox Business,* the *Telegraph, Benchmark Asia* and on BBC World Service.

Nuala is a visiting lecturer on business, criminology, finance and decision science programmes at leading institutions that include INSEAD, the Harvard Kennedy School, the University of Greenwich and the London School of Economics and Political Science where she earned a first-class master's degree in behavioural science. She also holds a first-class master's in business studies from University College Dublin, a degree in philosophy from Trinity College Dublin, and is trained in forensic psychology.